Glen Allen, Va 23060

JUN 0 1 2012

Travel and Dislocation in Contemporary American Fiction

Routledge Transnational Perspectives on American Literature

EDITED BY SUSAN CASTILLO, *King's College London*

1 **New Woman Hybridities**
New Woman Hybridities
Edited by Ann Heilmann and Margaret Beetham

2 **Don DeLillo**
The Possibility of Fiction
Peter Boxall

3 **Toni Morrison's *Beloved***
Origins
Justine Tally

4 **Fictions of the Black Atlantic in American Foundational Literature**
Gesa Mackenthun

5 **Mexican American Literature**
The Politics of Identity
Elizabeth Jacobs

6 **Native American Literature**
Towards a Spatialized Reading
Helen May Dennis

7 **Transnationalism and American Literature**
Literary Translation 1773–1892
Colleen Glenney Boggs

8 **The Quest for Epic in Contemporary American Fiction**
John Updike, Philip Roth and Don DeLillo
Catherine Morley

9 **The Literary Quest for an American National Character**
Finn Pollard

10 **Asian American Fiction, History and Life Writing**
International Encounters
Helena Grice

11 **Remapping Citizenship and the Nation in African-American Literature**
Stephen Knadler

12 **The Western Landscape in Cormac McCarthy and Wallace Stegner**
Myths of the Frontier
Megan Riley McGilchrist

13 **The Construction of Irish Identity in American Literature**
Christopher Dowdt

14 **Cities, Borders and Spaces in Intercultural American Literature and Film**
Ana Mª Manzanas and Jesús Benito

15 **American Utopia and Social Engineering in Literature, Social Thought, and Political History**
Peter Swirski

16 **Transnationalism and American Serial Fiction**
Edited by Patricia Okker

17 **Nature, Class, and New Deal Literature**
The Country Poor in the Great Depression
Stephen Fender

18 Travel And Dislocation in Contemporary American Fiction
Aliki Varvogli

Travel and Dislocation in Contemporary American Fiction

Aliki Varvogli

Taylor & Francis Group
NEW YORK LONDON

First published 2012
by Routledge
711 Third Avenue, New York, NY 10017

Simultaneously published in the UK
by Routledge
2 Park Square, Milton Park, Abingdon, Oxon OX14 4RN

Routledge is an imprint of the Taylor & Francis Group, an informa business

© 2012 Taylor & Francis

The right of Aliki Varvogli to be identified as author of this work has been asserted by her in accordance with sections 77 and 78 of the Copyright, Designs and Patents Act 1988

Typeset in Sabon by IBT Global.
Printed and bound in the United States of America on acid-free paper by IBT Global.

All rights reserved. No part of this book may be reprinted or reproduced or utilised in any form or by any electronic, mechanical, or other means, now known or hereafter invented, including photocopying and recording, or in any information storage or retrieval system, without permission in writing from the publishers.

Trademark Notice: Product or corporate names may be trademarks or registered trademarks, and are used only for identification and explanation without intent to infringe.

Library of Congress Cataloging-in-Publication Data
A catalog record has been requested for this book.

ISBN13: 978-0-415-99582-5 (hbk)
ISBN13: 978-0-203-80247-2 (ebk)

To the memory of Allan Lloyd Smith

Contents

Acknowledgments xi
Introduction xiii

PART I
Africa and the Limits of Fiction 1

1   Philip Caputo, *Acts Of Faith*; Dave Eggers, *What Is the What*   10

2   Norman Rush, *Mortals*; Russell Banks, *The Darling*   30

PART II
Travel and Globalization 47

3   Amy Tan, *Saving Fish from Drowning*; Garrison Keillor, *Pilgrims*   55

4   Jonathan Safran Foer, *Everything Is Illuminated*; Dave Eggers, *You Shall Know Our Velocity*   74

PART III
Dislocation and/at Home 91

5   Chang-rae Lee, *A Gesture Life*; Ethan Canin, *Carry Me Across the Water*   96

6   Dinaw Mengestu, *How To Read The Air*; Jhumpa Lahiri, *The Namesake*   117

Notes 139
Bibliography 141
Index 147

Acknowledgements

Over the years, I have attended a number of conferences, officially to present work in progress, but really to meet and talk with a bunch of very clever and very passionate people. My understanding of American literature has been greatly enriched and energized through conversations with Bill Boelhower, Dorothea Fischer-Hornung, Wai Chee Dimock, Ian Bell, Judie Newman, Alan Rice, David Brauner, Catherine Morley and a host of other scholars who, like me, enjoy our annual pilgrimages. I wouldn't normally thank anyone who recommended that I read a 700-odd-page novel, but thanks go to Tony Hutchison who put me on to Norman Rush's *Mortals*. Susan Castillo deserves special mention for being an exemplary scholar whose generous support and genuine warmth are an inspiration.

The idea for this book came, rather appropriately, during a car journey with my husband, Chris Gair, who over the years has listened patiently to my ideas and helped to knock them into shape. He has a knack for asking difficult questions, but I'm grateful to him for asking them. It was he who reminded me of the passage in *Pudd'nhead Wilson* that I use in Chapter 3, and though he remains suspicious of any author who has not been dead for at least fifty years, he has done his best to share my enthusiasm for new writing.

An earlier version of Chapter 4 was published in *Atlantic Studies*, and I would like to thank Taylor and Francis for permission to re-use that material. I would also like to thank my editor at Routledge, Liz Levine, whose patience and encouragement sustained me as completion of this project drew nearer.

The female scholar needs a room of her own, but sometimes she needs a good childcare provider as well. The one person without whom this book would not have been completed is Mrs Renée Hepburn. I wouldn't have been able to shut my study door if it wasn't for the knowledge that she makes my daughter Anna happy, and for that I am truly grateful.

Introduction

Judging the best of young American novelists for *Granta* magazine in 2007, Meaghan O' Rourke remarked:

> I was struck by the degree to which American writers are looking outward ... There's a sense now that to be an American fiction writer is to deal with America in the world—and the world in America. If in the past American fiction dealt with the rest of the globe by trying hard to assimilate it, today it deals with it by going outward towards it. (Jack)

This book offers a critical study and analysis of American novels that 'go outward' both literally and metaphorically. It discusses a range of contemporary novels, published around the first decade of the twenty-first century, whose protagonists go abroad, or who carry within them a sense of being abroad. The study concentrates on narratives that take place mainly away from the geographical borders of the US, and also suggests that the ones set on US soil are shaped by spatial relationships that cross geographical boundaries. The fictional characters discussed here include soldiers, immigrants, refugees, missionaries, tourists, heritage travellers, fugitives from the law, aid workers and aspiring philanthropists. What do these characters reveal about what it means to be American at the beginning of the twenty-first century? And what do these novels tell us about the place of America in the world, and about the nature of American literature itself? These are some of the broader themes and questions that this study explores. By discussing a range of well-known and less familiar contemporary novels I am hoping to show how American literature both reflects and helps to shape a new, changing world where older ideological frameworks and aesthetic approaches are proving inadequate as means of inquiry and analysis.

'It is not exactly clear where America might be located' asserts Geoff Ward in *The Writing of America* (11). He goes on to note that even though our understanding of where America is may still be largely shaped by the contours of the map, this no longer tallies with the experience of globalization and the ways in which America makes its presence felt around the world. If we are no longer certain we know where America is, it follows that we need to question the existence of a national literature as well. 'What exactly is "American Literature"?' asks Wai Chi Dimock. 'Is it a sovereign domain ... or is it less autonomous than that?' (1). The argument she puts forth in *Shades of the Planet: American Literature as World Literature* suggests that even if the notion of the 'sovereign domain' had any validity to begin with, it no longer does. This may seem obvious to many scholars of American literature past and present, but it is less obvious in the world's wider understanding of American literature and American culture. The meanings of nation and national literature are changing rapidly as globalization spreads and technology abolishes geographical demarcations. In this new, post-national world, we need to find new ways of understanding American literature, and at the same time we need to understand how these changes have altered the course of the American novel.

As globalization continues to Americanize the rest of the world, stories about American insularity remain as popular as ever: far too many Americans don't have passports; US politicians can hardly tell Iran from Iraq, or North Korea from its Southern neighbour; the news is almost exclusively domestic and national, unless it involves countries the US is waging war against. Views such as these must have been on Horace Engdahl's mind in 2008 when he declared American literature parochial. Engdahl spoke in his capacity as permanent secretary of the Nobel Prize jury, and noted that even though there is 'powerful literature in all big cultures,' 'you can't get away from the fact that Europe still is the centre of the literary world ... not the United States'. 'The US is too isolated,' he claimed, 'too insular' (Goldenberg). Perhaps unsurprisingly, this did not go down well in literary circles on either side of the Atlantic. Among the many critical voices speaking in support of American literature was that of Giles Foden, who noted the two-way traffic that defines American literature: the immigrants that energize the literature just as they energize the country, and the contributions that American authors have made to the development of international movements such as detective fiction and Modernist poetry. Concluding with a few examples taken from contemporary literature, Foden pointed out that any reader who suspects that American literature is indeed insular 'only has to look at *What Is the What*, a recent novel about a Sudanese refugee by Dave Eggers, to know that's not the way things are going.' Dave Eggers is the only novelist I discuss in two separate sections of this study because the range of his engagement with the world is only matched by the range of his commitment to the exploration of new aesthetic possibilities. He not only tells stories about other people and other places, he also uses and invents different genres and techniques to achieve that.

Engdahl's complaint may have been ill-advised in the face of so much evidence against it, but it also contained echoes of a much older one. Back in the 1820s, the Reverend Sydney Smith noted that during the 'thirty or forty years of their independence, they [Americans] have done absolutely nothing for the Sciences, for the Arts, for Literature, or even for the statesman-like studies of Politics or Political Economy.' In order to prove his point, he asked a series of rhetorical questions. The most memorable among them, of course, was this: 'In the four quarters of the globe, who reads an American book?' (36–7). The question of America's contribution to the world in terms of culture and science has probably been answered by now, but questions about American literature are still being asked at the beginning of the twenty-first century. Increasingly, though, what is being called into question is not the prestige or standing of American letters in the literary world, but rather its very Americanness. Engdahl's argument relied on an outmoded perception of national literature, and it seemed a little quaint to hear him speak of 'the centre of the literary world' when so much thinking of the past few decades has shifted the focus from the centre to the periphery, or more generally has questioned and eroded the very concept of a centre. The nature of the new questions being asked of American literature was captured by Liesl Schillinger who, writing in *The New York Times*, wondered: '[W]hat does it mean to write an "American" book, if you don't need an American address to do it?' She went on to consider novelists with multiple national allegiances, and concluded that 'the connection between passport and pen' was no longer to be assumed unproblematically.

The relations between 'passport and pen' are questioned and tested to the limits by the authors this study examines. By offering a snapshot of American literature at the beginning of the twenty-first century, I am hoping also to demonstrate the extent to which our understanding of the *American* in American literature has evolved. With that in mind, the words 'travel' and 'dislocation' have been selected not only because they are so central to the American story and to American literary history, but also because they are relatively neutral, descriptive terms. Underneath those umbrella terms we find a host of often competing ideas, concepts and paradigms that attempt to describe, define, or even predict the movements of people and ideas, and this is therefore a good place to consider their various uses and misuses.

Travel and dislocation are two concepts that have always been central to the American story. With the exception of Native Americans who have experience only of dislocation, all others have at some point known both dislocation and travel. Whether they came to the country willingly as immigrants or unwillingly as slaves, their journeys have shaped, and continue to redefine, the US today. What is different at the beginning of the twenty-first century, though, is the rapid change brought about by technological progress, and by global politics and economic policies after the end of World War II. Globalization means to a large extent the Americanization of the world, but the term also describes a process of moving freely across borders that are no longer tied to geographical locations. When it became clear that passports and postal addresses were no longer adequate criteria for defining American nationality, various theories of the postnational, the transatlantic, the circumatlantic or the cisatlantic sought to reposition the United States of America so it would be perceived not as a land mass containing its various peoples, but as a concept that both shapes and is shaped by its interactions with the rest of the world. Though many of these terms are in conflict with one another, Heidi Slettedahl Macpherson astutely points out that the very nature of what these theories attempt to describe and explain demands a sense of fluidity and open-endedness. She argues that 'the sense that the transatlantic offers *unfinished*, continuously evolving cultural encounters is paramount for our understanding of the journey' (14, emphasis in the original). She goes on to note that the various terms and theories used in discussions of the movement of people, such as 'exile, expatriate, refugee or immigrant' are unstable (14). This point is illustrated amply in the work of Caren Kaplan. Kaplan offers one of the most thorough and helpful accounts of the competing theories of immigration, exile, diaspora and expatriation. She notes how during the course of the twentieth century 'increasing numbers of people have become disengaged or dislocated from national, regional, and ethnic locations or identities,' and notes that 'the reasons for our movement, and the terms of our participation in this dynamic must be historically and politically accounted for' (101–2). She goes on to demonstrate that historical and political approaches of dislocation inevitably offer a range of competing accounts. Some overemphasize differences while others risk sacrificing specificity through an emphasis on similarities; some are too rigid, others too loose. Many of these, she suggests, risk losing sight of the bigger picture, of a world where 'new subjectivities' produce 'new relationships to space as well as time' (142). Literature is one the best places to look if we want an insight into these new subjectivities, and the novels I have selected here are both indicative of those new subjectivities and participants in their creation. Moreover, the novel's capacity to create microcosms and offer concrete manifestations of abstract notions further allows us to appreciate the fluidity of these competing terms. Through its emphasis on subjectivity and interiority, the novel can show that to be an exile or an expatriate may mean different things to different individuals. Through its ability to tell the stories of generations over time, the novel can also chart the processes by which one category turns into another: the expatriate may one day stop missing home, and the émigré may one day understand that she is after all an immigrant.

The way I use the terms 'travel' and 'dislocation' in this study occasionally involves some overlap. As a rule, though, I take travel to be one of the important manifestations of dislocation. In other words, travel is one of the main processes by which one becomes dislocated, but it is not the only one. Trauma and memory, family ties and family rifts can also dislocate individuals, and it is this more general sense of the term that I wanted to preserve. Another important sense in which dislocation does not have to involve either travel or the memory or imprint of travel stems from Fredric Jameson's theories of postmodernity's preoccupation with spatial categories. Alison Russell takes her cue from Jameson's assertion that postmodernism is dominated by categories of space rather than time, and she argues that 'his commentary on the spatial disorientation of postmodern society certainly captures the sense of dislocation created by our global network of electronic communications and multinational corporations' (14). Russell goes on to declare an interest in 'texts that offer new ways of mapping and reconceiving the space of the world' (23), and that is a good description of the books I am interested in too.

If it is a condition of postmodernity that we are all permanently dislocated on some level, then travel becomes a useful image, shorthand or symbol for those more abstract ways in which we have been dislodged in place. Alasdair Pettinger notes that it has become 'something of a cliché to assert that some travelling figure such as the migrant or the tourist is simply a more visible, dramatic embodiment of a universal condition' (xi). Pettinger finds that idea useful to the extent that it helps to abolish clear-cut distinctions between natives and foreigners, but he also warns of its possible dangers. If we lump together 'refugees, conscripts, au pairs, holiday-makers, diplomats and visiting professors,' we risk losing important distinctions between 'forms of displacement' (xi). Pettinger recommends that we remain 'alert to certain similarities without losing sight of the differences' (xi), and this is an important distinction that I have borne in mind throughout this study.

The novels I discuss all attempt to negotiate a space where identity in the late twentieth and early twenty-first century can be not only understood but actively constructed and reconfigured. The books analysed in this study are of course not unique in this endeavour, but they have in common a number of tropes that are deployed in the exploration of personal and national identity. The most prominent tropes are Africa, international travel and the American home. Those three categories have shaped and guided my literary analysis, and I am hoping to show that, in addition to being key concepts that unlock the texts in question, they are also categories that help us to approach and evaluate American fiction at the beginning of the twenty-first century.

The suggestion that Africa is a trope is of course a contentious one. 'Africa' is a contested, much debated term, and it is beyond the scope of this study to survey the various competing theories or to suggest new ones. My interest in Africa as a trope means that the four novels I discuss in Part I are set in Africa and are about Africa, yet at the same time they are American novels about American concerns. The various ways in which the four authors imagine, represent and conceptualize Africa represent a departure from the more familiar uses of the continent in American fiction in two important senses. Firstly, these books are written by white authors, but they represent a break from the earlier American tradition that saw the white author employ Africa as a backdrop for or symbol of the white protagonist's existential crisis. Secondly, they are books written by white authors who understand that the story of what it means to be American cannot ignore the legacy of slavery. Despite the many critical advances in our understanding of the cultural contributions of African Americans to

American culture, there is still a sense that these achievements took place alongside the mainstream developments in American culture. These books show that this is not the case. The interaction between Africa and America is pertinent not only to the lives and stories of African Americans, and the story of the transatlantic slave trade is one of relevance not only to the descendants of the African slaves. This inclusion of Africa into the mainstream, I suggest, is one of the ways in which American literature goes outwards and in so doing also takes a look at itself.

I started writing the chapter on Africa while visiting the US, staying in New Haven, CT. One of my strongest recollections is of two contrasting images: young white men, presumably Yale students, walking downtown in their 'Remember Darfur' T-shirts, mingling among a crowd of African Americans who bore the visible signs of severe poverty and deprivation. This contrast reveals a lot about the ways in which Americans today relate to Africa: for those with the resources to know and care about the world outside the US's geographical borders, Africa often stands for war, famine and suffering. For those who are described as African American, Africa refers not so much to a geo-political contemporary presence as to their distant ancestry and America's shameful past as a slave-holding nation. If Africa holds an ambivalent place in the American imagination, it certainly does so in the literary imagination as well. A number of important studies have moved African traditions, and the African American contribution to the nation's cultural development, from the margins to the centre, and yet contemporary Africa still occupies an unusual place in American literature. For African American writers, it is a place that belongs to the past; a place of ancestry and descent, a place to which traditions may be traced so that a narrative of cultural continuity may be constructed. In addition to being a depository for cultural capital, Africa is also a place of departure: much contemporary literature (aided and encouraged by Gayle Jones, Toni Morrison and Paul Gilroy) has concentrated on the middle passage, the journey *out* of Africa. Africa, then, is a place that remains largely unimagined and under-represented. For white authors, Africa is often what it was for Joseph Conrad, according to Chinua Achebe: a backdrop to an individual's existential crisis or psychological deterioration. This is the Africa of Saul Bellow's *Henderson the Rain King*, and of Hemingway's 'The Snows of Kilimanjaro'. In more recent decades, Africa has had a strong media presence relating to a series of catastrophes (and, thankfully, one triumph too: Nelson Mandela's release from prison in 1990): the Famine in Ethiopia that prompted the release of 'Do they know it's Christmas' in 1984, re-released in 2004 to aid Sudanese refugees in Darfur, and the Al Qaeda-led bombings of US embassies in Tanzania and Kenya in 1998. Authors have revisited the past, imagined the slave trade and the middle passage. They have looked at expressions of African American culture, and sought its roots in Africa. But what of contemporary Africa? What of the Africa seen in the news, and the one not seen? Several books published in the early twenty-first century have sought to represent, narrate and perhaps make sense of places in contemporary Africa, and in order to do so their authors have adopted a series of notable strategies that will be examined here.

Since Paul Gilroy introduced the paradigm of the 'Black Atlantic,' several theorists and critics have sought to understand the relations between self and world in terms of a dynamic, ongoing transaction. Arjun Appadurai participates in the debate around modernity instigated by Gilroy and identifies media and migration as the two major and interconnected factors that have a 'joint effect on the work of the imagination as a constitutive feature of modern subjectivity' (3). He sees the expansion of electronic media as facilitators for 'the construction of imagined selves and imagined worlds,' while noting that technological advances in electronic media have also altered profoundly the way we understand and experience migration. 'The story of mass migrations,' he writes, 'is hardly a new feature of human history. But when it is juxtaposed with the rapid flow of mass-mediated images, scripts, and sensations, we have a new order of instability in the production of modern subjectivities' (4). That instability, in turn, is closely related not only to mass migration, but also to the many aspects of modern travel.

Perhaps no one has done more to shape and redefine the idea of travel and its significance in assessments of modernity than James Clifford. His *Routes* began with the 'assumption of movement, arguing that travels and contacts are crucial sites for an unfinished modernity,' and he defined his general topic as 'a view of human location as constituted by displacement as much as by stasis' (2). Travel, he noted, 'emerged as an increasingly complex range of experiences: practices of crossing and interaction that troubled the localism of many common assumptions about culture' (3). Clifford is American educated and American based, but the argument in the book was not specific to his country. Nevertheless, America can be said to embody and exemplify in amplified terms the importance of travel in the production of culture, and the involvement of travel in conceptions of localism. James Clifford went on to note that

> [d]welling was understood to be the local ground of collective life, travel a supplement: roots always precede routes. But what would happen, I began to ask, if travel were untethered, seen as a complex and pervasive spectrum of human experiences? Practices of displacement might emerge as *constitutive* of cultural meanings rather than as their simple transfer or extension. (3, emphasis in the original)

America has always relied on the rhetoric of home in order to constitute itself, and home implies stasis and dwelling. What Clifford's theory allows us to do is to uncover the routes that go into the making of a seemingly stable nation/home. Judith Hamera and Alfred Bendixen have built on Clifford's theories in order to suggest that 'travel and the construction of

American identity are intimately linked' (1). In assessing the importance of travel in constructions but also in articulations of American identities, they identify various 'personae' that 'produced "Americanness" through assertion or negation,' including 'the expat,' 'the tourist,' 'the pious pilgrim,' 'the good-natured American gentleman,' the sailor 'who goes native only to flee to literally save his skin' and 'the adventurer' (6). Though most of these categories relate to work produced in previous centuries, it is surprising how many of them could still be used to describe the novels this study deals with. Through the deployment of the figure of the traveller in his or her several guises or permutations, these books undermine older conceptions of Americanness and propose new ones that are better suited to the complexities of our times.

Liselotte Glage also notes that dislocation 'is not such a recent experience after all;' travel and migration have been taking place over the centuries, she writes, in the form of '[q]uest, pilgrimage, journey of discovery or exploration, merchant adventure, grand tour, globetrotting, or simply travelling,' all of which she considers 'dislocating movements' (x). She goes on to contrast such instances of dislocation with migration, which is seen as teleological and as implying 'a process of no return' (x). The study of American literature within these parameters is complex because more than most countries, the US has been shaped both by the teleological journey of migration and by all the other dislocating movements. In the case of migration, the US has been almost exclusively on the receiving end, whereas the other forms of mobility have worked both ways. What my analysis suggests is that ultimately those various forms of movement are intricately linked; they have always been, perhaps, but the extent of their relations has been widened through the phenomena that characterize late twentieth and early twentyfirst-century life: new media and technologies, and global capitalism.

Given the emphasis on travel and movement, it may seem surprising that the third part of this study concentrates on the idea of home. The ways in which we speak of home link the domestic space to national space, and emphasize ideas of stasis, of dwelling, of abiding, of staying put. America excels at this kind of rhetoric and imagery, from Abraham Lincoln's 'house divided' speech to the enduring image of the 1950s suburban home as a defence against the perils of the Cold War. Yet, as the Part III title is meant to suggest, home is not as stable as we imagine it to be. Clifford understood that when he realized the significance of travel: 'when travel ... becomes a kind of norm', he argued, 'dwelling demands explication. Why, with what degrees of freedom, do people stay home?' (5). More provocatively, he went on to argue that domestic space can also be defined by movement and not stasis: 'a location ... is an itinerary rather than a bounded site—a series of encounters and translations' (11). The home is therefore a complex trope that contains its opposite and confounds our expectations. I have used it as a means of understanding the significance of travel and dislocation in American literature because I believe it to be as crucial as that of the transatlantic journey to and from Africa, or modern travel in its various manifestations. Rosemary Marangoly George notes that 'the concept of home (and of home-country) has been re-rooted and re-routed in fiction' through the course of the last century, but that above all it is postcolonial literature that has generated a 'reassessment of our understanding of belonging' (1). This sense of belonging is imagined through the trope of the home in the novels I examine, and it is contested through the telling of the stories of the people who live in these homes. These people are not for the most part postcolonial subjects, but many of them and their creators write from the periphery, not the mainstream. By offering a view of the 'ethnic' American home, these books interrogate America itself as 'home.' The very term 'home-country,' suggests Marangoly George, 'expresses a complex yoking of ideological apparatuses considered necessary for the existence of subjects: the notion of belonging, of having a home, and a place of one's own' (2). It is these issues that my discussion of the trope of home involves, bringing together the representation of built structures with the representation of the ideologies of national belonging. The context of globalization is also relevant here because, as Judie Newman has argued, 'globalisation affects the reader's perception of "home"—nation, family, affiliations—in complex ways' (2).

In many ways, perceptions and conceptualizations of the tropes of Africa, travel and the American home have all been affected by the events of 9/11 and its aftermath. When I started work on this project, I assumed that 9/11 would in fact be the defining factor and the most meaningful context in which to view my chosen novels. However, a decade after the event, it is becoming a little easier to place 9/11 itself in the wider context of the rapid changes that globalization brought about in the late twentieth- and early twenty-first centuries. The earliest of the novels I discuss was published in 1999; the most recent near the end of 2010. The ones published in the first couple of years after 2001 qualify as 'post 9/11' in the literal sense, but it is likely that they were conceived and written before the event itself. All the books' preoccupation with travel and dislocation needs to be considered in a wider context, but one that relates to 9/11. I am referring to the context that helps us to understand how new technologies facilitated the flow of capital, ideas and bombs, as well as altering the place of the United States on the world map, and its relations to other countries. Perhaps historians will not choose September 11, 2001 as the beginning of the new century for America, and for its friends and its foes. By going back a few years, we can begin to assess the ways in which people were able to communicate more quickly and effectively than ever before; the ways in which previously privileged information was now available to the masses, and the ways in which networks and action groups could connect and spread with unprecedented ease. Perhaps the future historian will select 1996 or 1997 as the watershed year. 1996 saw the launch of Hotmail; a year later, it was acquired by Microsoft and gave the world access to a free email account. 1997 was also the year that the Google domain name was registered, with the company being incorporated a year later. Skype brought us free phone calls via the internet in 2003, and Facebook launched a year later. In 2005, the world shrank a little more when Google maps arrived, altering our spatial visualizations and creating new relations between the individual at home and the vastness of the world outside. In February 2011, the media reported that an Egyptian man had named his newborn daughter Facebook, in honour of the medium that facilitated the uprising that toppled an unpopular ruler. What all of these examples show is that the world is better connected than ever before, and that movement has been freed from its association with travel through physical space. The ease with which new technologies are being incorporated into our daily lives means that the conception of the world as a dynamic place, always on the move, is now stronger than ever. How this will affect the novel's unique ability to engage with subjectivity remains to be seen, but the novels I discuss here do offer us a glimpse into what it means to have a sense of self, and a sense of an American self, in a changed and changing world. It is a world dominated by the conflicting experiences of being able, on the one hand, to transfer money or speak to a person at the other end of the world in seconds, and on the other hand having to form long lines at airports and border crossings in order to prove our claims of legitimacy. The characters in these novels travel on planes, trains, cars and tourist coaches. It may take them just minutes to research, plan and pay for their journeys, but the ways in which travel alters their sense of self and their place in the world takes much longer to work out. Travel and dislocation are terms that aid our understanding of the dynamic models of nation and ethnicity, but they are also terms that help us to redefine the nature and parameters of American literature: they describe thematic preoccupations as much as they describe claims to authorial national identities.

* *

Part I of this study, 'Africa and the Limits of Fiction,' is a concurrent investigation into two issues: it offers an analysis of novels set in Africa, and it seeks to understand why writing about Africa has produced different modes of writing. More specifically, all of the books under consideration here stretch, challenge and redefine the limits of fiction in various ways. They are based on real events, and some of them contain historical figures who interact with fictional characters. Caputo and Eggers borrow from non-fiction genres such as reportage and memoir, and Eggers recasts autobiography as fiction. The novels by Banks and Rush are built around an awareness of their literariness. Banks opts for an unreliable narrator whose telling of the story actively questions not only memory and selfhood, but also narrative construction itself. Rush writes in the type of third person closely indebted to literary modernist experiments with interiority, and he punctuates the narrative with literary allusions and references that create a rich and complex intertextual web.

Caputo's novel deals with American humanitarian aid in Sudan. Although it is a work of fiction, the writing is 'unliterary' and aspires rather to the clarity and precision of the reportage. The blending of fiction and non-fiction becomes an important feature of novels that deal directly with contemporary, unfolding events, which have yet to be concluded, and which we cannot yet assess from a safe critical distance. Reviewing the book in *The New York Times*, Michiko Kakutani predicted that 'it will be to the era of the Iraq war what Graham Greene's *The Quiet American* became to the Vietnam era,' thus emphasizing that the context for this novel is not only America's involvement in Africa, but also its military incursions in Iraq and Afghanistan. The novel contains a large cast of American characters who between them encompass different aspects of the American abroad, from the unscrupulous profiteers familiar from Joseph Heller's work, to the tolerant, assimilationist missionaries whose lives are changed more radically than the lives of those they encounter.

Eggers's novel tells the story of Sudanese refugee Valentino Achak Deng who walked from Sudan to Ethiopia and then Kenya, before making his way to the US where he now lives. Deng told his story to Eggers, who re-wrote it as fiction, a move that was described as 'a startling act of literary ventriloquism' (Kakutani 2006). This, then, is not a novel about an American abroad, but rather a book by an American novelist who speaks in the voice of, and at the same time fictionalizes, the African odyssey of a Sudanese refugee. As I shall be arguing, though, the experience of turning the African story into an American novel is also one that turns the African subject into an American authorial figure. Deng, I argue, becomes American by telling the story of travel and dislocation in Africa, and by contrasting it with his status as a legal refugee in the US. The book highlights the complexity of fictionalizing a life: the story is true, it has been told by Valentino to Eggers, and Eggers has turned it into a book. Only Eggers's name appears on the cover, and the book is classed as fiction. By telling a black African's story of suffering and eventual triumph against the odds, Eggers is reviving the old slave narrative mode. The dislocated person is Deng, both in Africa and in the US, but also Eggers, who 'dislocates' his American authorial voice by lending it to another man with a story to tell.

Russell Banks's *The Darling* is set in Liberia in the 1980s and 1990s, as well as in post-9/11 America. Its fictional protagonist, pursued by the FBI for her involvement in the Weather Underground, interacts with real historical figures who have shaped Liberia's present, such as Samuel Doe and Charles Taylor. However, unlike the books by Caputo and Eggers that seek to distance themselves from the traditional techniques and tropes of the fictional novel, this one is much more literary in its use of anachrony, unreliable narration and symbolism. Above all, though, this is a novel that confirms Banks's commitment to explore the story of race in the US, which he considers to be the most important aspect of US history of the past 200 years. The African setting, in other words, is used not so much to turn the spotlight on forgotten places in other continents, but rather to emphasize the fact that US history cannot be understood without a consideration of America's involvement in the world. Where Banks's novel insists that the personal is the political, Norman Rush's takes on the appearance of the political to speak mainly of the personal. It tells the story of a CIA operative in Botswana, but focuses mainly on his marital problems and personal crises. It is notable, though, that Rush is perhaps unique in being an American novelist whose books are always set in Africa, and this leads to an examination of our understanding of 'national writing.' Botswana, moreover, has no particular link with the US; it is certainly not related in the way Liberia is, and it is free of associations with civil war, famine, or any of the other catastrophes that put African countries on the news.

Part II, 'Travel and Globalization,' examines novels that seemingly deal with uncomplicated, conventional instances of travel: they all involve American citizens who travel to other countries for short periods of time and then return to the US. However, travel is rarely uncomplicated. The travels are life-defining and life-changing for the fictional protagonists, and the experience of travel is central rather than incidental to the plots. Moreover, not all of the characters can be described simply as tourists. We can discern distinct categories such as the pilgrimage, heritage tourism, dark tourism or the grand tour, all of which bring about a sense of conflict or crisis in the subject's perception of the self, and their place in the world. Amy Tan reverses the logic of Orientalism by sending her Chinese American narrator and her group of tourists from mixed ethnic backgrounds to China and Burma. China is not only the narrator's land of ancestry; it is also a place that the narrator herself has mythologized heavily, and one that leads several of the characters to re-examine their understanding of ethnicity and nationality. China and Burma are countries that impose restrictions on the individual and repress democracy in ways the American tourists find upsetting, thus raising questions about the ethics of travel. The book, which is funny and light-hearted for the most part, uses its humour to ask important questions about how ethnicity can shift and be redefined through travel, and about the extent to which globalization has liberated or further imprisoned the oppressed and powerless. Garrison Keillor's comic novel shares with Tan's the use of humour to explore serious and complex issues. By transporting his regional tales of small-town America to Italy, Keillor explores what happens when the local meets the global. At the same time, by taking Italy as his setting, and using Henry James as his main intertextual frame of reference, Keillor inserts his novel into a long literary tradition in America that has used Italy as a backdrop, and that has examined collisions between the old and new worlds.

The novels by Eggers and Foer tell stories of young males in search of identity, of history and of their place in the world. Their journeys are both real and metaphorical, and the lessons they learn subvert their, and our, expectations. Both books note the sameness that globalization has brought to the world, but they also attempt to speak up for the value of the local and the particular. They do it in very different ways, but they emphasize issues of connectedness; Eggers's does it primarily on the thematic level, whereas Foer's achieves it through the structure of the epistolary novel that it uses. Though the protagonists of both novels make important connections and develop ties with the people they meet abroad, neither book offers a naïve vision of globalization bringing strangers together so they can bond over a frappuccino. The nature of the journey that each of the two main characters undertakes is such that it underscores the inequality and dissymmetry between the US and the countries they visit, while in both novels the travellers are seen by those they visit as potential sources of exploration and income. The characters in these two books would probably have to tick the box that indicates pleasure as the main purpose of their trip, but the reality is much more complex and a lot darker than that.

Part III, 'Dislocation and/at Home,' moves away from narratives of Americans abroad, and from stories of travel outside the US. It considers instead dislocation as a way of understanding the cultural dissonance felt by those who come to the US and make it their home. That word, home, is used throughout this section to link domestic space with national space, and to link the idea of stasis with the idea of movement. Using the tropes of travel and dislocation helps us to understand their supposed opposites as well: home and belonging, which at the beginning of the twenty-first century were hijacked and nostalgically evoked by neo-cons and supporters of US military intervention. Two of the novels discussed here deal with 'model' American citizens whose beautiful homes are the outward markers of success and assimilation. Both houses, though, contain dark secrets and shameful, painful memories, and more to the point these memories relate to deeds performed during the Second World War. The returning soldier's suppression of trauma is figuratively represented here through the notion of the exterior, and more specifically the façade of the suburban home. Canin's novel is a fine observation of an American family; it focuses on a man in his seventies and his relationship with his son. What emerges as its real theme, though, is this man's attempt to come to grips with his past, before he became a typical American grandfather. Originally a Jew from Germany, he escapes to the US and later fights in WWII. At the heart of this novel is his desire for reconciliation and atonement following the killing of a Japanese soldier. My approach to this novel suggests that the immigrant is twice shaped by dislocation: in addition to the familiar trip of the European Jew who finds sanctuary in the US, the ethnic subject is here also seen as American aggressor. His identity is shaped by three journeys: one as persecuted victim, one as US soldier abroad, and one as post-war penitent. Guilt and penance are also at the heart of *A Gesture Life*, which tells the story of a seemingly well assimilated Japanese American man. The secrets of his identity and his guilt have to do with his own hidden Korean ancestry, and his treatment of a Korean comfort woman during the war.

Like Canin's book, Lee's suggests that the story of the ethnic subject in the US should not only be told through a linear narrative that takes the subject from country of origin to country of destination. The seemingly well-established immigrants that Lee and Canin write about have unfinished business in their past lives, and they need to return, either literally or figuratively, to the site of an earlier trauma. The journey to and from the site of the trauma is not shown as an isolated incident, either thematically or structurally. In thematic terms, both novels explore how the traumatic journey affects the subject's sense of belonging at home. On the structural level, both novels narrate the scene of the trauma out of sequence, and interspersed with more recent events. In this way, they show that to be home, and to feel at home in the American house, is not to have reached the end of the journey.

The novels by Mengestu and Lahiri that conclude this study bring together many of the themes and ideas I have been exploring, and they may also be indicative of new directions in American literature. Natalie Friedman discerns a whole new trend of immigrant writing that reflects the profound changes that have taken place at the end of the twentieth century, and that have altered our understanding of immigration to the US:

> This difference between the immigrant generation and its children is important in understanding how the immigrant novel has changed. Lahiri is part of a vanguard of young, contemporary ethnic American writers whose novels, short fiction, and memoirs suggest that assimilation—cleaving to the hope of an "American Dream"—is no longer at the heart of the immigrant story. Instead of shedding the trappings of the home culture and throwing himself headlong into the work of Americanizing, the protagonist of the contemporary immigrant novel—whether an immigrant or a child born to immigrants—is more concerned with his or her dual identity as it manifests itself in America and in the shrinking global community. (112)

Some of the identities Lahiri and Mengestu explore are not even double; they are multiple. The protagonist's wife in *The Namesake* is an Indian who has moved to the US after her parents' original emigration to England. As an embodiment of historical circumstances, she represents not only the past (which has shaped her parents' movements from home to home), but also the future. Fully acknowledging her multiple allegiances, she is comfortable in that multiplicity. After her marriage, she does not change her name because she does not want to be hyphenated. The literal hyphen, though, is not the same as the metaphorical one. Moushumi may not want two Bengali names, but she appears to have no problem being hyphenated as Indian-American, especially since that description also needs to take into account her stay not only in London as a little girl, but also in Paris as a young adult. Her husband, meanwhile, spends most of his life resenting his first name, conferred upon him by his Bengali parents, but he ends the novel by embracing its legacy. As the perfectly assimilated American son finally decides symbolically to 'return' to his Indian home, his immigrant mother sells the family house and opts for a nomadic lifestyle. These intergenerational transformations and subversions point again to a sense of multiplicity that cannot be contained or explained using the familiar models of the immigrant story. Meanwhile, Mengestu also places multiplicity at the heart of his novel. His protagonist narrator is the American child of Ethiopian immigrants, but the novel exploring his character involves more than duality. By telling two stories, that of his faltering career and marriage, and that of his immigrant parents' road trip across America, Jonas Woldemariam stresses the numerous strands that have gone into making him an American of sorts. By jeopardising his career and his marital home, Jonas reverses the story of success of the typical immigrant at the same time that he seeks to understand what it was like for his parents to 'discover' America as immigrants on the road.

The novels discussed in this volume do not merely describe or reflect American identities at home or abroad. They help actively to shape and deepen understanding of the construction of those identities, and they reaffirm the role of literature as America's conscience and chief negotiator. The world, as I argue in Chapter 4, changes more rapidly than we can adjust mentally and ideologically, and fiction can help us to process those changes. We need to reconceptualize and create new notions of nationhood, of self and belonging, of travelling and emigrating, of home and abroad. These books explore the rich possibilities of self-determination and the limits imposed by ideologies of the nation state, while also showing that the meaning of America itself shifts and evolves with the progress of globalization. Explaining the methodology and rationale that informed *Fictions of Globalization*, James Annesley wrote that his study set out to 'read the debates around globalization . . . in terms that open up the analysis of recent American fiction.' However, he went on to note that the relationship works two ways; just as the debates can inform the analysis of literary texts, so the literary texts themselves can help us 'develop critical perspectives upon the understandings and positions that inform those same debates' (10). It is this sense of a two-way traffic that also informs the approach to my chosen novels. The terms travel and dislocation are conceptual categories that help me to analyse the books I have selected, but it is hoped that, in turn, that analysis will add further texture and nuance to our understanding of these categories.

Part I
Africa and the Limits of Fiction

How and why do white American authors write about Africa? These are the two main questions this part of the study addresses. The responses outlined here show two opposing approaches to the representation of Africa, with two of the authors opting for a style that aspires to the relative objectivity of non-fiction, while the other two aim for a high literary style. Philip Caputo and Dave Eggers have gone for a documentary style that blurs the line between fact and fiction. Caputo is best known as a foreign correspondent, writing in a genre that is not free of ambiguity, but relies on the assumption of a more or less unproblematic relationship to reality. *Acts of Faith* is a novel based on the real situation in Sudan, but inhabited by fictional characters. However, the style and organization of the book aspire to the objectivity of the documentary. Eggers has 'ghost written' a Sudanese refugee's story of escape to the US, but the complex relationship between author and subject raises a number of questions about generic boundaries, vexing notions of authorship, fiction and autobiography. *Mortals* and *The Darling* are both set in African countries; the former exclusively in Botswana, the latter partly in Liberia as well as briefly in Ghana. The two authors are unusual in American letters, each for different though not unrelated reasons: Rush has only written novels set in Africa, while Banks, unusually for a white author, considers race to be the defining narrative of the United States. In addition to *The Darling* with its Liberian setting, he has also written *Cloudsplitter*, a novel concerning abolitionist John Brown, and narrated by his son. Rush's and Banks's engagement with Africa has few similarities with previous literary endeavours in American letters. Though neither can fully escape cliché or stereotyping, they depict their chosen countries in ways that do not eliminate the human factor, to echo Achebe (8), nor do they merely provide an exotic background for an essentially Euro-American story. Despite their many and obvious differences, what these books have in common is the fact that they use their African settings in order to interrogate notions of belonging, home, and the nation-state more generally, and the effects of America's foreign policies not only on these countries, but also on the US itself. In other words, these are not novels that simply tell us how America has shaped African politics;

they also tell us how US involvement abroad cannot be separated from issues closer to home.

The African countries that my selected novelists deal with have been shaped by US foreign policy in varying degrees, and some in ways that are much more direct and obvious than others. The conflict in Sudan, for example, can be traced back to the days of joint British and Egyptian rule. Sudan gained its independence in 1956, but its former rulers did little to help resolve the tension arising from the North/South divide. More than half a century later, Sudan's problems can no longer be understood in the context of its colonial past alone, and the various conflicts within the country are of course far too complex to outline here. What is of interest, though, is the US's attitude to Sudan. Officially designated a state sponsor of terrorism by the State Department in 1993, Sudan has recently become 'a strong partner in the war on terror' ('Council on Foreign Relations'). In 2004, Secretary of State Colin Powell drew attention to the conflict in Darfur, using careful language to reveal but also mask the Bush administration's views: 'Call it a civil war. Call it ethnic cleansing. Call it genocide. Call it "none of the above,"' Powell told the Senate Foreign Relations Committee. 'The reality is the same: There are people in Darfur who desperately need the help of the international community' (Grzyb 36–7). Sudan is an oil-rich country, and therefore its relationship to the US is driven by material as well as ethical considerations. The ambivalent and changing attitudes towards Darfur and civil war in Sudan, and the campaigning of high-profile celebrities such as George Clooney and Mia Farrow have sustained media interest, and prompted the London *Times* correspondent Rob Crilly to call his book on the subject *Saving Darfur, Everyone's Favourite African War*. In sharp contrast with Sudan, Liberia is hardly ever in the news. Ellen Johnson-Sirleaf's election to the presidency in 2005 drew considerable attention, but on the whole the country has remained obscure in the western media. Even the trial of Charles Taylor did little to shine light on this small, much-suffering country, since he was being tried for crimes committed in neighbouring Sierra Leone. And yet Liberia occupies a unique place in the story of US relations with African countries. Established as a homeland for freed American slaves, it soon became a two-tier society, where those returning slaves replicated the patterns of dominance and oppression they were accustomed to, and assumed superiority over the natives they displaced in order to build their imagined African homeland. Given the complex ironies and the rich opportunities Liberia can afford the American novelist interested in exploring African American ideologies and representations, it is surprising that Liberia does not feature more prominently in American letters. Finally, Botswana, setting of Norman Rush's epic spy novel, occupies an entirely different place in the western imagination, though it is admittedly a very small place. Botswana, which gained its independence from the British in 1966, is one of Africa's great success stories. With the exception of AIDS, which remains its largest problem, it is a stable democracy with an expanding economy. It rarely makes the news and is not associated with any of the great humanitarian catastrophes of the twentieth century, and its profile in the Anglophone world has been raised significantly with the publication of the gentle, cosy tales of Alexander McCall Smith and his *No. 1 Ladies' Detective Agency* series.

The image of happy Africa that we find in Scottish McCall Smith's stories is largely absent from American literature, which is likely to concentrate on the more familiar images of suffering, war and slavery. In addition to happy Africa and suffering Africa there is also symbolic Africa, and it is the latter that dominates the white literary imagination in America. How does an American author around the beginning of the twenty-first century write about Africa? These questions may of course be answered in as many ways as there are countries in Africa, but the four books discussed here in Part I have been selected not only for the critical interest they arouse but also because they can be shown to be representative of wider trends in American writing. The words 'Africa' and 'America' are themselves inaccurate, problematic, and more often than not chosen for the sake of convenience. Nevertheless, they do help to highlight precisely the role that language plays in both constructing and obscuring identities, and above all they point up the arbitrariness of much of the discourse surrounding race, ethnicity and nationality. This can be seen more clearly if one uses the example of two countries: the USA and Sudan, subject of two of the books under discussion. The CIA Factbook, which is reasonably reliable at the same time that it betrays the US's imperialist tendencies, describes the makeup of the two countries as follows: USA ethnic groups are 79.96 per cent white, 12.85 per cent black, 4.43 per cent Asian, 0.97 per cent Amerindian and Alaska native, 0.18 per cent native Hawaiian and other Pacific islander, 1.61 per cent are two or more races (July 2007 estimate). A note further clarifies that 'a separate listing for Hispanic is not included because the US Census Bureau considers Hispanic to mean persons of Spanish/Hispanic/Latino origin including those of Mexican, Cuban, Puerto Rican, Dominican Republic, Spanish, and Central or South American origin living in the US who may be of any race or ethnic group (white, black, Asian, etc.); about 15.1 per cent of the total US population is Hispanic.' Sudan, meanwhile, is 52 per cent black, 39 per cent Arab, 6 per cent Beja, 2 per cent foreigners and 1 per cent other. It is obvious that the meaning of 'black', for example, is different in each case, while the designations of 'foreigner' and 'other' seem more like gifts to the humanities scholar than meaningful categories to describe groups of people.

What this attempt to name and classify racial or ethnic groups demonstrates is that language can be used to create meaningless entities and artificial distinctions, and that the pseudo-science of the nineteenth century that first proposed these categories has left a lasting legacy that seems hard to shift. One need only compare the CIA's description of Sudan with an earlier attempt to impose the meaning and order of language onto an African landscape. In his *Journey Without Maps* (1936), Graham Greene set out to explore Liberia and did, in fact, consult not one but two maps of the country. One was produced by the British, and it contained dotted lines to indicate where rivers might be, and names for villages that Greene never found, probably because they did not exist. The second map was produced, tellingly, by the United States War Department, and it was completely different: it depicted a big, empty space with the words 'Cannibals' written across it. 'It has no use for dotted lines and confessions of ignorance,' writes Greene.

> [I]t is so inaccurate that it would be useless, perhaps even dangerous, to follow it, though there is something Elizabethan in its imagination. 'Dense Forest'; 'Cannibals'; rivers which don't exist, at any rate anywhere near where they are put; one expects to find Eldorado, two-headed men and fabulous beasts represented in little pictures in the Gola Forest. (46)

The British and American maps, which are also not unlike Charlie Marlow's childhood maps, tell us a lot about the ways in which the Euro-American imagination has constructed Africa, and even though today's maps are more sophisticated and accurate, the gap between imagination and reality remains a large one. Maps have long been sites were westerners project their fears and desires of the 'other,' but they are also visual representations of the ideology of the nation-state: they represent visually the idea that a demarcated geographical space contains a race, a people, a nation. Reality often evolves more quickly than our conceptions of it, and at the beginning of the twenty-first century it is not just the shifting borders in numerous countries that render maps quickly obsolete; it is also the ease with which ideas, capital and people flow, communicate and travel across real and virtual space that challenges the usefulness of the map.

Such notions are relevant in the study of *Acts of Faith* and *What Is the What*. Both novels open with maps of Sudan, and to examine them side-by-side is to begin to understand some of the complexities and challenges involved in the representation of contested space in Africa, and of imagined space in books. First of all, the shape of the country itself provides a lesson in geopolitics: most of the northern border with Egypt, and some of the western border with Libya and Chad is drawn in straight horizontal and vertical lines: the lines that speak of negotiation, compromise, and international treaties portioning out space. The rest of the country's outline is jagged and irregular, indicating the natural borders of geographical space. Eggers's map is crude and lacking in detail: it only contains place names relevant to the story, and it only represents two of Sudan's neighbours: Ethiopia and Kenya, places of refuge for the Lost Boys. Caputo's map depicts all the neighbouring countries, it gives more place names, and more crucially it gives some idea of the country's internal divisions: where Eggers's map has Northern and Southern Sudan (the main warring parties), and a place called Darfur, Caputo's further clarifies the areas of Northern, Western and Southern Darfur. Finally, by the time this book goes into print, Sudan may well be split into two separate countries, and the map therefore redrawn one more time.

In addition to their interest in maps and borders, the books I examine here use other tropes of space to engage with Africa, and in so doing they tell us a lot about American conceptions of 'the dark continent.' Caputo represents a series of temporary dwellings where his aid workers attempt to combine the small comforts of domestic space with the demands of the humanitarian mission. The natural environment is not depicted as particularly hostile, with the threat coming from militiamen and not animals, disease or hostile terrain. Deng's narrative in Eggers's book juxtaposes the image of the American home with that of the African bush. Because the narrative begins with Deng's apartment being broken into, and Deng being tied up by his assailants, the narrative actually begins by questioning our assumptions regarding safe and dangerous spaces. Norman Rush depicts a modern Botswana and describes cinemas, shopping malls and gated communities for privileged foreigners, but as the plot unfolds his protagonist leaves behind the relative safety of built-up Africa and confronts his arch-enemy in the Kalahari desert, away from the city and the confidence that brings him. In addition, Rush uses the trope of Hell throughout his narrative. Although he does not make a simplistic or obvious connection between Africa and Hell, the inclusion of such discourse in the novel cannot easily be separated from the African setting. Russell Banks uses the narrative structure of his novel to distance himself from and question the moral values of his deeply flawed white American protagonist and narrator; her views of a grotesque Africa are not his own, and the juxtaposition of the jungle with the all-female American farm at the beginning of the novel invite a consideration of space: of black and white, safe and perilous spaces, and gendered spaces.

In all four novels, Africa is represented as a site of war. Caputo's and Eggers's books deal with real wars, while Rush and Banks both pit white Americans against black Africans, and engage in various forms of confrontation. Rush more explicitly and Banks by implication associate their African characters with the grotesque and the devilish. However, none of these books perpetuates the image or myth of Africa so familiar from books like *Heart of Darkness*. The spaces and sites of conflict are not symbolic landscapes, or representations of mental dispositions; at least not exclusively. The authors depict real countries, victims of political machinations. These are countries that are not lawless and chaotic; they are governed and misgoverned, and also aided and betrayed by the US and other 'protectors'. The historical and political specificity of these books, coupled with the imaginative use of Africa as backdrop for conflict effectively ensure that these are texts that make a dual use of Africa, seeing it as real and symbolic at the same time. The various ways in which the authors combine the two uses of Africa depend a lot, as I shall be demonstrating, on their chosen genres and narrative strategies.

The novels by Rush and Banks can be described fairly unproblematically as literary novels, while the other two stretch and redefine the limits of fiction. Caputo's and Eggers's books deal with war in Sudan, and in many ways they can both be described as narratives of trauma. Robert Eaglestone has explored the ways in which African trauma has been represented and has shaped western narratives. Reading Gil Courtemanche's *A Sunday at the Pool in Kigali* (2003), Paul Rusesabagina's *An Ordinary Man* (2006), Uzodinma Iweala's *Beasts of No Nation* (2005), Dave Eggers's *What Is the What* (2006), and Ismael Beah's *A Long Way Gone* (2007), Eaglestone concludes that a 'harsh critic' might easily accuse them of offering 'a voyeuristic opportunity or of colonizing atrocity. It is true that they criticize the West . . . [but] these critiques are located in an English-speaking, Western-facing context that reduces the force of the critique' (84). The books discussed in Part I are all certainly 'Western-facing,' but there lies their strength: they are not only Western-facing in their representations of African traumas, but also in their scrutiny of Western—and more specifically American—identities and narrative forms. Eaglestone describes the books he analyses as 'forms of engaged literature that seek to influence, explain, and educate' (84); this is true of the books I discuss too, but the point that needs to be stressed is that they do not only explain what goes on in Sudan, Botswana or Liberia. They illuminate the role of the US as world policeman, philanthropist, liberator and colonizer, and they suggest that our understanding of American identity cannot, and should not, be separated from a consideration of the US's role on the world stage.

Caputo and Eggers deal with unfolding realities and unfinished wars, and their engagement with the contemporary to some extent shapes their chosen forms. Eaglestone usefully compares narratives of African trauma to holocaust narratives, but for the comparison to be meaningful, the African trauma narratives need to belong to a past that is deemed 'closed,' concluded in a meaningful way. This is not the case with the war in Sudan depicted in Caputo's novel, and it is not true in Eggers's novel in the sense that Valentino Deng does start a new life in the US but is also able to return to the scene of trauma where the strife he left behind is still present. Both authors have developed narrative strategies that enable them to engage with unfolding events, and that help them to overcome the problem of writing with little or no hindsight. Caputo has chosen to tell his story as fiction, and he has made some important choices: his novel contains a large cast of characters and does not have a single identifiable protagonist of the kind we normally expect in a white American novel. Moreover, the stories are told in a straightforward chronological order that lends the book the feel of a soap opera but serves the more important function of highlighting the lack of closure or distance from the events depicted. The novel's last chapter is narrated in the present tense, thereby emphasizing the fact that there is no looking back, no re-assessment of lives lived and mistakes made. Eggers similarly ends with no resolution, summing-up or sense of closure. This is inevitable given that the book tells the real story of a young man's adventures, but given that Eggers and Deng have decided to fictionalize what is effectively a ghost-written autobiography, the decision to imitate life rather than fiction by eluding narrative closure is instructive.

Chapter 2 scrutinizes two literary novels that participate in but also subvert the literary tradition of white imaginative engagement with Africa. These novels emphasize their literariness through allusion, intertextuality, elaborate narrative strategies, self-reflexiveness and unreliable narration, thus placing themselves at the other end of the spectrum from the reality-based, documentary-style fictions of Caputo and Eggers. Norman Rush has a Milton scholar as his protagonist, and the novel contains several allusions to the work of James Joyce and Gustave Flaubert. Though the book tells a spy story and contains mystery and suspense, it is also a text that places great emphasis on interiority and aligns itself with the modernist tradition of literary fiction. In his review of the novel, James Wood notes that

> *Mortals* is many things, and does many things beautifully, but its central achievement has to be the fidelity with which it represents consciousness, the way in which it tracks the mind's own language. This concern with the insides of our minds makes Rush almost an original in contemporary American writing.

Wood argues that Rush's engagement with interiority owes a debt to Joseph Conrad. According to Wood, Conrad has had little influence on American authors, but Rush is the exception to the norm. He sees the 'Conradian alienation principle' being masterfully employed, and applauds Rush's adaptation of Conrad's action sequences and plot structuring. Curiously, though, he has little to say about Conrad's depictions of Africa. He does note that 'knowledge is not simply exotic and informational, but something amassed as life is amassed, as a pile of experiences rather than a wad of facts,' which can be understood indirectly as praise for Rush's depiction of Botswana. He further refers to the setting as 'the fabric' rather than the 'backdrop' of Rush's fictions, and yet stops short of making a direct comparison between Rush and his literary ancestor in their attitudes to representations of Africa. Through this omission, Wood perhaps unwittingly illustrates the fact that the assumption that Africa serves as backdrop to a novel primarily interested in interiority is one that the western reader and critic cannot entirely shake.

Russell Banks is also interested in interiority, but he goes about exploring it in a different way. His novel is narrated by an unreliable narrator who revises, disguises, suppresses and reveals facts about her life in Liberia while all the time moving from past to present and back again. The disorienting effect of her narrative serves as an analogue for her own confused and conflicting feelings towards her African self, but it is not the actual Liberian setting that causes such disorientation. It is rather her attitudes to gender and sex relations, her white liberal guilt and her attempt to reconcile her various roles as wife, mother, political activist and animal carer that cause the confusion. Still, upon its publication the book received criticism for its depiction of Liberia. Mary Gordon, reviewing in *The New York Times*, noted that

> [t]he Liberia to which Hannah returns is a country destroyed by years of brutal fighting and a destruction of ordinary life; but even years earlier, before the fighting, it was, for Hannah, a nightmare place, where the cockroaches in her shower are described, brilliantly, as "brooch sized."

Gordon is right to point out that Liberia holds a different meaning for Hannah when she goes back, years after she thought she had left for good. Yet the confusing chronology of her narrative, and the clear sense of retrospection it imparts, make it harder for the reader to get a clear sense of the Liberia Hannah encounters before the civil war, when she is courted by the government minister who later becomes her husband, and the Liberia she sees after the bloodshed and destruction of the war, and her own children's gruesome involvement in bloody events. The novel's structure, then, can be said to collapse the different perceptions of Liberia and leave the reader with an image of suffering, abject Africa. As Gordon points out in her review, most characters in the book are 'moral wrecks. And so *The Darling* takes its place in the canon of books that offer us only despair in our understanding of the continent'. Gordon is right, but only up to a point. Leaving aside the fact that a story about Liberia could never actually tell us much about the whole continent of Africa, we can argue that the novel offers much more than despair, though there is certainly a lot of that. Crucially, the book does not simply tell a story of Africans killing one another; rather, it reminds us that Liberia is the daughter of American slavery, and that Liberia's problems in the twentieth and twenty-first centuries cannot be extricated from American foreign policy or American ideologies. Hannah is our guide and mediator, but she is also an unsympathetically drawn character. Banks is therefore placing a certain amount of distance between himself and his narrator, and his readers are hardly expected to espouse Hannah's world view. Her view of Liberia and its politics needn't be our own, just as her radical past in the Weather Underground, and the conviction that political change must come at any cost, needn't be a position we applaud.

As Kwame Anthony Appiah demonstrated with his study *In My Father's House*, Africa continues to be shaped by the Western gaze, following the 'ugly path' of 'ethnocentrism' (5). Yet Appiah himself received criticism for not engaging with contemporary African political realities. Perhaps the lesson to be drawn from this is that no single work, be it fiction or non-fiction, can adequately engage with the complexities of 'Africa' as it exists in western discourse. The four books discussed in Part I cannot escape the western gaze, but they are conscious of its existence rather than taking it for granted, and that is why they make a significant contribution to our understanding of the opening out of the American novelistic gaze: they not only scrutinize Africa; they also scrutinize the American gaze and the fascination Africa holds in American Letters.

1 Philip Caputo, *Acts Of Faith*; Dave Eggers, *What Is the What*

PHILIP CAPUTO, *ACTS OF FAITH*

Philip Caputo's *Acts of Faith* received favourable reviews upon its publication. Michiko Kakutani, not one prone to exaggeration, proclaimed it a 'devastating' novel that would be

> to the era of the Iraq war what Graham Greene's novel *The Quiet American* became to the Vietnam era: a parable about American excursions abroad and the dangers of missionary zeal, a Conradian tale about idealism run amok, capitalistic greed sold as paternalistic benevolence, ignorance disguised as compassion.

Returning to the Conradian connection later in her review, she also described the book as 'a modern day *Nostromo* that reverberates with echoes from today's headlines'. Indeed, the parallels with Greene and Conrad turned up elsewhere in criticism, creating a context that was instructive for two reasons: it placed the novel within a literary continuum that explores questions of morality and human consciousness against backgrounds that highlight western cruelty and hypocrisy, and it also placed the novel within a literary tradition that was decidedly non-American. In this sense, *Acts of Faith* can be understood as a book that participates in western literary traditions and also offers a wide international scope. It is an American novel best illuminated when seen through the lens of international fiction.

This novel, and Eggers's, is about aspects of the war in Sudan, and both writers face similar problems: how to write about an unfamiliar reality, and how or even why to use fiction to explain and illuminate complex realities. What they also have in common is they both have things to say about being American in the early twenty-first century. Caputo's book participates in (though it does not entirely belong to) a tradition exemplified by Graham Greene that uses writing about another country to point out one's country's shortcomings, and to offer criticism of where that country has lost its way. Eggers tells the story of a boy who survives war in Africa, but also survives hardship in America. It is a book about being an African Lost Boy, but also about becoming an American. The two novels featured in the next chapter are more traditional in the sense that they belong to recognizable genres (the literary novel), and in that ultimately they tell stories about one American individual and their domestic and personal crises seen in and illuminated by the context of world politics and America's role in Africa. The books in this chapter are different. Eggers's does have a single narrator/protagonist, but engages in a form of ventriloquism that complicates conceptions of the narrator as self and subject. Caputo's has a large cast of characters (listed in the beginning of the novel, thereby indicating there isn't a traditional main character) and also lacks the familiar markers of the literary novel.

Philip Caputo has said in interviews that he is an admirer of Graham Greene (Charlie Rose), and he considers Greene's 'intertwining of good and evil' to be his main point of influence. However, in addition to the moral ambiguities borrowed from Greene, Caputo's novel can also be usefully compared to Greene's writing in terms of generic hybridity. Douglas Kerr, for instance, describes *The Quiet American* as 'a text in which different modes of writing mix and jostle for supremacy—the epical story of war and the romance story of love, grimy *policier*, exotic orientalism, topical reportage . . . , existential fable, the monodrama of faith and unbelief' (95), and with some qualification this could equally serve as a fair description of *Acts of Faith*. Caputo's novel is indeed hard to pin down in generic terms. Though clearly a novel, a work of fiction, it has a sense of the factual about its articulation, a lack of artifice that worries generic boundaries, and produces a book that reads more like a non-fiction novel. The question that arises is how this generic blurring relates to the book's subject matter, and it is this question that I will attempt to answer before moving on to consider other aspects of the American experience abroad that the book engages with. *Acts of Faith* deals with events that are still ongoing. Indeed, Caputo thinks, pessimistically, that the war in Sudan may never end; as one of the characters in the book puts it, 'There is war in Sudan because there is war' (83). As I will also argue in the next chapter, the writer who engages in contemporary unfolding events faces a particular challenge: the lack of hindsight creates difficulties of judgment and interpretation, and these can manifest themselves in plot structure and resolution, but also in the choices a writer makes in relation to genre. Russell Banks, for example, opts for historiographic metafiction: he has fictional characters interacting with 'real' ones, thereby highlighting the difficult intersections of the real and the imagined. Dave Eggers tells a real story in a voice that is and is not his own, ordering events that did happen but probably not in the order presented in the text, and he employs these strategies because they are best suited to the telling of a traumatic and dramatic narrative. Philip Caputo creates wholly fictional characters but places them in circumstances closely modelled on real events. He also creates a sense of objectivity, a documentary-like effect through his use of omniscient narration. Such style of narration may appear old-fashioned, and it does introduce a certain element of didacticism into the novel, but it nevertheless serves the author well.

Every few years, American critics and commentators announce the death of the literary novel, citing the growing sales of non-fiction titles and the public appetite for a seemingly unmediated 'reality'. More specifically, it has been argued that the best writing on America's current wars and other operations abroad is indeed non-fictional (see Dyer, for example). However, it should be noted that major events take time to filter through the novelistic conscience. *Catch-22* and *Slaughterhouse-5* are examples of that, and they remind us that novels benefit from re-contextualisation in a way that non-fictional books rarely do. It may be that novels about 9/11 and its aftermath, and about the wars in Iraq and Afghanistan, will not make their mark for another decade or so. In the meantime, the novelist who is brave enough to handle the subject of current events needs to make choices relating to form and genre that will best enable them to engage with unfolding realities without the benefit of hindsight. If, as Kakutani implies, there are parallels to be drawn between the American presence in Sudan as depicted by Caputo and the American invasion of Iraq, the full significance of the analogy could not possibly have been clear to Caputo, and may only become available to the next generation of critics.

Although he has published several well-received novels, Philip Caputo is best known as a non-fiction writer. His *A Rumor of War* (1977), which recounts his service with the US Marines in Vietnam, is considered one of the most powerful examples of war writing, and has recently been discussed in new and illuminating ways by William Spanos in *American Exceptionalism in the Age of Globalization: The Specter of Vietnam*. Spanos discusses the discrepancies between the rhetoric of intervention in the name of freedom, and the reality of the 'genocidal conduct' (145) of the Vietnam war, arguing that the realities of that war have been disguised and suppressed by an 'imperialist exceptionalist discourse' (x) that has been greatly amplified since the 9/11 attacks, and which is no less than an attempt to rewrite American national identity, and assert the US's place as world policeman and ruler. Although *Acts of Faith* deals with the war in Sudan and is ostensibly far removed from the world depicted in *A Rumor of War*, it is in the context outlined by Spanos that the novel is best understood.

The war in Sudan has, needless to say, long and complicated causes, but it is fair to claim that the US has, directly, little to do with most of them. Sudan is a country dominated by a North–South divide. Granted independence from the British in 1956, the country was soon plunged into war. In simplistic terms, one can grasp the enmity between the Muslim North and the Christian or Animist south, but what is harder to comprehend is the bloody fighting and genocidal tendencies among ethnic groups in the south. For instance, attempting to outline the history of the conflict in *The New York Times* in 2009, Jeffrey Gettelman described the Bor Massacre of 1991 as 'a civil war within a civil war,' exemplifying in that phrase the failure of familiar words, such as 'civil war' to convey the geo-political complexities of the Sudan conflict. It is well beyond the scope of this study to examine the causes and continuing tensions of the war in Sudan, but more to the point this does not appear to be Caputo's aim either. The length of the novel, and its large cast of characters, do allow him to represent some complex and competing stories of that war, but, like all good war writing, the novel is not *about* this particular war. In imagining and representing the conflicting emotions, motivations and actions of his American missionaries and aid workers, Caputo examines American identities and questions the US's narrative of intervention and humanitarianism. In a sense, this book is the opposite of the non-fiction novel: where the latter tells of real lives and real events using fictional, novelistic techniques, this one contains fictional characters and made-up events that are presented with little in the way of symbolism, metaphor, leitmotif or other devices associated with the literary novel. Despite its perceived transparency, though, the book does convey a sense of moral complexity: as the story unfolds, and the reader over the course of 700 pages becomes acquainted with the characters, the lines between good and evil are blurred, and uncomfortable questions are asked about responsibility and complicity. These questions link the book's moral outlook to Conrad's, and illuminate Kakutani's observation that this is a *Nostromo* for our times. Caputo makes the Conrad connection explicit by taking one of his three epigraphs from *Nostromo*: 'It seemed to him that every conviction, as soon as it became effective, turned into that form of dementia the gods send upon those they wish to destroy'. The novel goes on to trace the destructive paths taken by well-meaning Americans, but, unlike *Heart of Darkness*, it does not depict a moral descent brought on by a dehumanized and brutalizing Africa; rather, it shows a gradual erosion, or perhaps an adjustment of morals that retains the moral questioning seen in *Nostromo* without laying the blame on Africa, as in *Heart of Darkness*.

Acts of Faith has a large cast of characters, but there are two Americans who stand out because of the transformation they undergo during the course of the novel: Douglas Braithwaite, a pilot and manager of KnightAir Services, and Quinette Hardin, a Christian missionary. Douglas is introduced through the eyes of Fitzhugh Martin, a multiracial Kenyan who in many ways represents the book's moral conscience:

> Straight away Fitzhugh knew he was an American. It wasn't the cowboy boots and Levi's that declared his nationality, nor the scrubbed, healthy complexion, as if he'd just stepped out of the shower after a game of pick-up baseball. It was the way he stood, chin cocked up, shoulders slouched just a little, projecting the relaxed belligerence of a citizen of the nation that ran the world. Fitzhugh imagined that a young Englishman would have struck a similar stance out in India a century ago, or a young Roman in the court of some vassal Gaul. (230)

The comparison with the English colonialist is instructive here: though the American is in Sudan ostensibly to offer humanitarian aid, his manner, and later his actions, do indeed suggest a sense of entitlement similar to that felt by the imperialists towards those they colonized. More to the point, by drawing the comparison between the American aid provider and the English colonialist of a century earlier, Caputo not only makes a point about the attitudes and motivation of relief workers, but also aligns his novel with a tradition of books that concern themselves with the fate of the colonizer under the influence of the 'strange,' 'exotic' land they have colonized. Douglas Braithwaite does indeed suffer a moral degradation as the novel progresses, but he is no Mr Kurtz. There is no suggestion of a deeper existential crisis precipitated by the otherness of Africa, or the horrors of an African war. Douglas Braithwaite does not suffer a mental breakdown, nor does he abandon his earlier beliefs. Instead, he is gradually eroded by greed and becomes increasingly victim to a moral relativism that allows him to pursue profit while arguing that he is helping those most in need.

An early episode depicts him as an innocent, idealistic American who has to make tough choices under difficult circumstances. He defends his decision to evacuate a group of people pursued by the Murahaleen, against the wishes of the pilot who suffers from dysentery, and whose plane Douglas practically hijacks in order to effect the rescue. In his defence, Douglas points out he was the first officer and therefore not in a position to 'hijack' the plane. More to the point, he stands by his decision even though the people he helped were incarcerated by immigration, then 'packed . . . off, back to where they'd come from' (68). The more experienced Tara Whitcomb tells him that he did 'the wrong thing for all the right reasons' (67), an assessment that turns out to be prophetic, and one that also introduces the moral ambiguities and uncertainties that all the aid workers will come to face. Douglas insists that 'sometimes people make things more complicated than they have to be so they don't have to get off their asses and take a stand. Sometimes neutrality is just another word for cowardice' (69). Tara, an Anglo-Kenyan who is sceptical of the American's complete faith in his moral clarity, agrees that his words 'sounded like one of those bumper stickers Americans are so fond of' (69). Douglas's words, however, do not simply reflect the easy pronouncements some US citizens are fond of. His rhetoric is reminiscent of the patriotic speeches of several US Presidents who have justified their excursions abroad, from Vietnam to Iraq and Afghanistan, using similar arguments that to take no action is worse than to take the action that one feels morally compelled, and morally justified in taking.

Near the end of the narrative, Fitzhugh uncovers the truth and realizes the extent of Douglas's corruption: in addition to providing guns to the SPLA under the guise of humanitarian aid, Douglas has also embezzled company funds and sabotaged another plane in order to prevent a CNN reporter from uncovering the truth about KnightAir. Ultimately, he is responsible for two planes crashing, killing all on board. When Fitzhugh confronts him, Douglas tries to buy his silence and shows no sign of remorse, and it is then that Fitzhugh comes to an important realization: 'Like most people, he'd always assumed the face of evil would look its part, monstrous, grotesque, theatrically ugly; but here it was before him, the face of a bird-watcher, blandly handsome, veiled in innocence' (647). This realization is typical of that rare thing: an American novel set in Africa that contains nothing of the theatrical, the monstrous or the grotesque. Not only Douglas, but all the other characters, African and Euro-American alike, are portrayed as ordinary, unremarkable people caught in extraordinary circumstances, and facing difficult choices ranging from self-preservation to personal gain. Douglas's moral disfigurement is explained in words that are highly reminiscent of Marlow's voice in *Heart of Darkness*: 'He had broken faith with the best that was in him and with the humanity he professed to serve. A malevolent voice had whispered a summons; he'd answered. Anyone who does not acknowledge the darkness in his nature will succumb to it' (648). The crucial difference, of course, is that Africa is not mentioned in the passage, nor is it implied as the agent that unleashes the 'darkness'. Rather, it is Douglas's desire for material wealth that is the main factor in his downfall, and if one were to take away the African setting and the particulars of the war in Sudan, as a fictional character Douglas would be comparable to the 1980s yuppies satirized and criticized in the film and literature of the time.

Alongside the story of Douglas's moral disintegration, the novel also tells the surprising and powerful story of the white American missionary Quinette Hardin. Quinette works for an organization that 'buys' Sudanese people taken into slavery, sets them free and teaches them about Christianity. Though there is no doubt that the operation is legitimate and well-meaning, the moral complications of this enterprise soon become apparent: CNN reporter Phyllis Rappaport wonders whether 'if this slave trade were left to—to—ah . . . market forces, it would just disappear,' further implying that the operation to free the slaves in fact encourages the practice of taking them into slavery in the first place. 'This is politics,' is the reply she gets. 'Economics has nothing to do with it' (152). These arguments are familiar in American discourse from the time when the US itself was debating the pros and cons of the abolition of slavery, and the novel makes a number of subtle parallels between these situations. These parallels serve as a reminder that the novel is not just about Sudan, or even about a particular war in Sudan: it is also about the US today, and about the ways in which humanitarian intervention is woven into the story that Americans tell themselves about their identity and their place in the world. On first seeing the Nile, Quinette recalls the first time she saw the Mississippi. The comparison ostensibly relates simply to the size of each river, but with its connotations of the American South, slavery and being 'sold down the river,' it is easy to see that Caputo is inviting comparisons between the seemingly barbaric practices in Sudan and the humanitarian benevolence of the US, whose wealth and prosperity are largely owed to slavery. On hearing the story of one of the captives who was branded on the face, Quinette 'backed away, trying to imagine what that felt like. A branding iron in your face. She wasn't ready for this' (151). Quinette attempts to be empathetic here because she tries to be a good Christian, but her unfamiliarity with the practice of branding may imply an ignorance of her own country's past: while learning something about Sudan, she fails to understand something about where she comes from. This is further emphasized when she sits down to share a meal with the freed captives and finds herself unable to eat:

> Quinette felt wrong just being here, a woman whose flesh was ignorant of rape and the lash and the circumciser's blade. How stupid she'd been to think she had touched the people with her impromptu sermon . . . The chasm between her and them was wider than the one between America and Africa, between black and white; they had suffered greatly, she had not. It troubled her to feel so separated from them, the women most of all. She stared at the thornbush beside her, barbed with spikes as long as her thumb. It beckoned her to throw herself into its bristling arms, to make herself bleed and hurt and bind herself to the Dinka women in a sisterhood of pain. (161)

At this point, this is no more than a semi-comical portrait of a well-meaning white American woman well out of her depth, a Christian who entertains thoughts of self-flagellation as a means of understanding and sharing someone else's pain. However, as the novel unfolds and Quinette undergoes a gradual and strangely plausible transformation, these words become proleptic of some of the changes that take place.

When she goes on to marry Michael Goraende, she insists on going through a painful initiation ritual, and goes against her husband's advice to acquire the tribal marking other women have tattooed on their bodies. The tribal marks on the white American's body link the images of the branding iron, the scars left by torturers, and the Christ-like suffering that she aspires to. In bringing these images together, Caputo makes complex points about Christian compassion, about female solidarity, and about the role of a formerly slave-holding country and liberator and saviour of Africa (and the rest of the world). Just as Douglas starts off as an enterprising American who wishes to put action and tangible results before moral questions, so Quinette starts off as a humble aid worker who goes rapidly from feeling like 'a true African adventurer' (134) to feeling out of her depth. After her marriage to Michael she becomes, in her creator's words, 'a minor-league lady Macbeth' (Charlie Rose), and her transformation is presaged in another early passage where she is listening to and transcribing the stories of the redeemed slaves. One of the women recounts her horrific ordeals, and concludes: '*I wish I was a man so I could carry a rifle. I would find Ahmed and kill him. I would kill his wife and all his children. I would massacre them all*' (159). Despite her Christian views, Quinette finds herself attracted to this woman's words:

There was a kind of beauty, an appealing purity in the woman's longing for retribution. It was even refreshing, after listening to the others recite the outrages they'd suffered with such forbearance. Quinette typed, *I would massacre them all*, and the crisp black letters seemed to leap from the glowing screen and enter her, feeling like a midwife's hands, drawing out her own incubated rage. (160)

Later on in the novel, Quinette will become used to war, death and retribution, and the moral complexities of killing and revenge will seriously compromise her professed Christian values. In addition to highlighting the genesis of Quinette's moral transformation, the passage quoted above is also important for the ways in which it highlights issues of writing and translation. The redeemed slave is telling the story, a local man, Manute, is translating, and Quinette is typing it up. However, Quinette is not merely transcribing the words that are being translated: Manute adds asides and explanations, which she is asked to put into parentheses. The passages quoted above are therefore more complicated than they first appear for the following reason: the first time we read the woman's account of her ordeal, her story is given in italics. The second time, her words are repeated, in italics, within a passage that describes Quinette's inner thoughts and feelings. The phrase 'I would massacre them all' therefore appears first in italics as part of a first-hand account that comes to the reader twice mediated, and then a second time in italics again but incorporated within the main narrative discourse, in a sentence from Quinette's point of view. This complex embedding of the woman's story of suffering has a two-fold effect. It highlights the nature of writing and the problems and challenges of telling other people's stories of trauma, and it illustrates visually on the page how Quinette 'takes in' the stories she hears, and goes from being an observer and transcriber to becoming part of the slaves' stories.

The issue of translation, which in this instance was both literal and metaphorical, is taken up again when Quinette meets her future husband, the SPLA Lieutenant Commander Michael Goraende. Michael correctly surmises that Quinette is American, and asks: 'So, Miss Hardin, what do you speak besides English?' 'Nothing. Unless you want to count two years of high school Spanish,' she replies. Michael retorts: 'I would be delighted to meet someday an American who speaks more than English. You Americans own the world now and you don't have to learn' (315). This exchange reverses the prevailing image of the colonial master exasperated by the colonial subject's inability or unwillingness to speak his language, and it also serves as an image of the novel itself: one that speaks American English, but seeks to understand and represent other realities. In a sense, Caputo does speak 'more than English' by writing a novel that takes his Americans out of their country and places them in the middle of an African conflict where they become complicit while remaining apart.

Quinette's early self-perception as an 'African adventurer' connects her character to a long tradition of Western writing that imagines Africa as a dangerous playground where fantasies of exploration and conquest are played out against a backdrop of non-human elements: hostile climate, jungle, dangerous animals, and sadly, of course, African people. In *Artificial Africas*, Ruth Mayer describes adventure fiction as the 'best point of departure for the exploration of artificial Africa' (25). She goes on to note that in the adventure genre

> geographical locations are also artificial realms, spaces of fantasy and speculation cast in the guise of the far-away, so that the all-too-familiar may be overcome. Here, the transgression into unknown territory—the jungle, the desert, the magic castle—is a purely vicarious journey, which permits the audience "to explore in fantasy the boundary between the permitted and the forbidden and to experience in a carefully controlled way the possibility of stepping across this boundary." (25)

Quinette's story can usefully be read against this backdrop of adventure fiction because it contains and transgresses several of the elements identified by Mayer; indeed, large sections of the entire novel derive some of their impact from the author's knowing participation in the genre. However, the spaces of fantasy and speculation become all too real for Quinette who lives out her fantasies and discovers that the reality of being an adventurer does not quite match the storybooks. When she writes to her family in the US to announce her marriage, she resents having to explain herself. 'Those dull people who had never done anything out of the ordinary and whose lives were set up to protect them from powerful emotions were incapable of understanding the ecstasy of great love' (460). It doesn't take long though for her great romantic affair to be radically re-contextualized when she discovers her husband practises polygamy, and it is this discovery that effects her transition from a dreamy adventurer to a pragmatic and later morally compromised wife.

The story of Quinette's transformation fits in with the author's undermining of the traditional African adventure story but at the same time, because Quinette is a Christian missionary, her story can also be illuminated when placed in a different literary context. The best known fictional depiction of American missionaries in Africa is Barbara Kingsolver's *The Poisonwood Bible* (1998), and even though that novel is set in a different time period and a different African country, some of its larger points about American ideologies and the work of missionaries are comparable to the issues raised by Caputo through Quinette's story. In one of the most perceptive analyses of the novel, Kimberley Koza has argued that

> Kingsolver's exploration of the interrelationship between the personal and the political is shaped in part by the feminist insight that relationships within the family mirror, and are in large part constructed by, power relationships within the larger society. . . . The Price family is

clearly an example of the personal as political because the family structure replicates the power structure of colonialism. (285)

Susan Strehle has added strength to Koza's reading by linking the politics of the American home with the politics of American exceptionalism, and demonstrating how patriarch Nathan's grip on his wife and daughters is inseparable from his belief in his civilizing mission in the Congo. 'He serves as a negative portrait,' she writes, 'not of the Christian missionary or the masculine head of household, but rather of the American exceptionalist convinced of his own righteousness' (419). She goes on to distinguish American imperialism from earlier European colonizing missions in Africa by noting that the former champions 'freedom and democracy, disavowing outright profits, claiming benevolence, and asserting that American righteousness makes American acts right' (416). As I argued earlier, *Acts of Faith* also depicts American characters convinced of their own righteousness, and like Kingsolver, Caputo is interested in notions of home, homeland and the intersections between private lives and public politics. His portrait of Quinette, though, is much more nuanced and troubling than that of Nathan in *The Poisonwood Bible*. Quinette 'goes native' by marrying Goraende and having tribal marks inscribed on her body. By becoming the wife of a powerful leader, she relinquishes the authority afforded to her by her nationality and assumes an inferior position determined by her gender: being female in this case trumps being an American.

In her subordinate role, Quinette also begins to absorb the ideology of her new master. After witnessing an execution by firing squad ordered by Goraende, she feels '[f]loating free of her body,' and in this state of heightened awareness she sees a face, her own, that does not look familiar: 'She had become someone else she did not recognize; yet she felt that she could get to know this stranger and make friends with her' (565). As the story unfolds, not only does she make friends with her new morally compromised self, she soon stops noticing that this is a compromise in the first place. When Goraende blames himself for the death of Tara Whitcomb, Quinette argues it was done for survival: 'Do you think Christ doesn't understand that? Of course he does, and he forgives . . . The only thing that's unforgivable is to think you can't be forgiven' (615). Quinette's bumper-sticker philosophy exemplifies the triumph of rhetoric and ideology over morality. Her justification of her husband's actions, and also of her own when she betrays another woman, do not stem from her having 'gone native' and abandoned her American Christian beliefs. It is rather those very beliefs that lead to her moral blindness, because she has transplanted them from her comfortable American background to a context in which they are no longer fit for purpose. The irony is that she, the once compassionate missionary, cannot see that. The novel explicitly links Quinette's moral compromise with that of Douglas Braithwaite. Though the latter lacks the former's religious conviction, he is driven by the same kind of ideology. In a passage that recalls the *Nostromo* epigraph, Fitzhugh Martin realizes that Douglas was able to hide not only his appetites and ambitions but also 'the derangement wrought by his faith in the rightness of his actions' (648), a phrase that resonates with readers who are familiar with British and American justifications for the wars in Iraq and Afghanistan.

Fitzhugh Martin is a key character in the novel's complex engagement with ethical questions. The story ends with his point of view and his pronouncements on those whose American idealism has proved most false. It is significant that the moral centre of the novel belongs to a non-American because this way the author can acknowledge the limitations of his own American viewpoint, but also point to a frame of reference outside the American one. The novel ends with no sense of the triumph of good over evil, and no punishment or redemption. Fitzhugh alone represents hope and an alternative to the bleak outlook of the other characters and their actions. He is the only one to emerge almost intact after nearly 700 pages of adventure, war, moral compromise and destruction, and he is the one who defies categorization. In addition to being neither black nor white, neither African nor non-African, he also marries an older woman and adopts two AIDS orphans with her, thus undermining another cherished myth, that of the perfect American family. Fitzhugh concludes that Quinette had asked Africa 'to redeem her from the bonds of the commonplace and give her an extraordinary life. It had, but now it was extracting the price. It was keeping her' (669). One wonders whether this might not also be an apt way to describe a very different type of adventure story: that of 'Lost Boy' Valentino Achak Deng, who walked across Sudan to Ethiopia and ended up bound and gagged on his American living room floor at the beginning of *What Is the What*.

DAVE EGGERS, *WHAT IS THE WHAT*

When Wesley Dare's sabotaged plane crashed and his partner Mary died, Dare tried to bury her body and then, injured, awaited his own death. Soon, however, he was roused from his semi-unconscious state by a tug at his foot, and found himself surrounded by a dozen boys led by Matthew Deng. Deng explained that the boys were walking to a camp in Kenya, a place called Kakuma, 'where we will be fed and sleep in houses . . . Tell me, mister, how far is it to Kenya?' (606). Kenya being at least two hundred kilometres away, Dare thought these sickly, tired boys would never make it, but marvelled at their optimism and determination:

> This kid had tramped a thousand miles on an artificial leg, he'd led a band of orphaned boys on a march that would have turned U.S. Marines into a mob of blubbering babies, he'd killed a lion, and for what? To get to an overcrowded refugee camp . . . To go through so

much for so little required either complete stupidity or a powerful belief that the future would somehow be better. That any African, even a kid, could have faith in the future baffled him. (607)

It is, perhaps, this faith in the future that sustained Valentino Achak Deng on his journey to Kakuma, and which finally took him to a new life in the US. Though the story that Eggers tells is an African one, it also partakes of that great American narrative of self-preservation, self-invention, and unfailing faith in a future in which one's hard work and sacrifices will be rewarded. Though the story is one of an African nightmare, it is also a story of the American Dream with its attendant joys as well as its attendant sorrows and disappointments.

Among the several editorial decisions that have turned a real, lived experience into a fictional one, perhaps the most striking one is the setting at the beginning of the novel. The story starts with Valentino Achak Deng in his American home, where he is the victim of burglary, then beaten and tied up. A large part of the narrative that follows is ostensibly addressed to the boy who is left to guard him until his burglar parents can return to claim the loot. The striking opening sequence emphasizes the role that notions of 'home' play in this book as it interrogates belonging, crossing boundaries, following routes and putting down roots. In *Acts of Faith*, home was more notable for its absence. Most of the action that did not take place outdoors unfolded in company offices, on the rescue planes, or on makeshift and often unsafe accommodation. The absence of the traditional house as home highlighted in that novel the transient nature of the American characters' commitment to Sudan. Neither immigrants, nor expats, these temporary workers made a moral and financial commitment to a country they would never call 'home'. Eggers explores the various meanings of 'home' for Deng by juxtaposing the perilous African journey with perils of a different kind within the American house. The journey of the 'Lost Boys' was meant to be one from danger to safety, but the truth has turned out to be much more complicated.

Deng is not only burgled in his own home; he is burgled by an African American who calls him 'Africa' and treats him with the same racist attitude he must have endured as an American citizen himself. Deng notes with some surprise this lack of allegiance, but tries to be sympathetic. Addressing himself to the boy guarding him, he says '[p]erhaps you, too, are a child of war' (57), thereby implying that the peace and safety of the American nation is disrupted by its racial and class inequalities. After the robbers finally leave, Deng kicks on his door, hoping that a neighbour or passerby might hear him and come to his aid. Unsurprisingly, no one turns up. 'Is the noise of the world so cacophonous that mine cannot be heard?' (162) he asks in despair. However, the image of the victim, still bound and gagged, kicking the front door, can also be reversed and viewed from outside: the narrator acknowledges that he doesn't know his neighbours well. The ones living in the apartment below his are 'decent people,' but he's only ever spoken to them once (139). He knows that they are evangelical Christians, and he is now struck by the irony of the fact that they are not able to save him. 'Christian neighbors below, where are you tonight? Are you home? Would you hear me if I called?' (139). With this despairing address, he is not just pleading with his neighbours, of course. He is also expressing the fear that he has been silenced and rendered invisible, and that those 'at home' in America will not come to his aid. It is impossible to tell whether in real life Deng did have evangelical Christians for neighbours, but it is the kind of symmetrical irony that one imagines must be made up: that whereas evangelical Christians will travel to Africa to 'save' others, they are not able to help the African living just one story above. As he continues to knock and kick, he also becomes aware of the ways he might be perceived by those invisible neighbours: not as a desperate soul in need of salvation, but as a peril to steer clear of. Who would come to investigate the noise made by their African neighbour? 'It is unexpected. You have no ears for someone like me,' he concludes (142).

By introducing the inside/outside perspective of the desperate narrator and his indifferent neighbours, Eggers underscores several important preoccupations in his novel. Deng remains bound and gagged in his American home for all of Book I, which takes up 230 of the book's 535 pages. During his protracted captivity, deprived of safety in his own home, Deng tells the story of his early life in Sudan, and narrates many of the perils he has encountered. The stark juxtaposition of the bound victim, his African American assailants, and the African story he recounts all serve to unsettle the categories of home, safety and adventure. The flashbacks tell of events that go way beyond the experience or understanding of most ordinary Americans, and the strangeness and 'exoticism' of his tale seem at odds with the ordinary setting of an apartment block in Atlanta. Yet as we shall also see in Part III of this study, American literature often relies on the assumption that unspeakable or unimaginable tales of 'other' people and 'other' places can indeed be found within the supposed safety of the American home. As Deng feels the physical pain of the assault, he also feels a strange kind of nostalgia:

> In my life I have been struck in many different ways but never with the barrel of a gun . . . I have been starved, I have been beaten with sticks, with rods, with brooms and stones and spears. I have ridden five miles on a truckbed loaded with corpses . . . And yet at this moment, as I am strewn across the couch and my hand is wet with blood, I find myself missing all of Africa. (7)

By inverting our ordinary understanding of security and danger, escape from a traumatic past and nostalgia for a lost childhood, Deng does not seek to diminish his gratitude for the safety he has been granted, but rather to point out that ideas and preconceptions about home and abroad, about safe havens and dangerous places, are all fluid constructs whose meaning shifts and changes. The Western imagination has for too long relied on the idea of Africa as a large, dangerous playground where western fears and desires are projected, and the jarring realization that one might miss being beaten with stones and spears or being chased by lions introduces a perspective that highlights the potency of the inverted gaze. Deng is well aware of the powers of cultural stereotyping. Eager to give his African American assailants the benefit of the doubt, he notes that '[i]t is a terrible thing, the assumptions that Africans develop about African-Americans. We watch American films and we come to this country assuming that African-Americans are drug dealers and bank robbers' (19). There is, of course, no reason to doubt the sincerity of the sentiment, but in places like this one, the reader becomes aware of the novel's unorthodox authorship: is the Sudanese 'Lost Boy' entirely responsible for this forgiving perception of African Americans, or is this realization the result of a dialogue with the white liberal author of the novel? Whichever way we choose to answer that question, the conclusion to be drawn, as I will be arguing further on, is that the narrator becomes American in the act of re-telling his story and in the act of having it re-told through the authorial voice of Dave Eggers.

The preoccupation with homes and places of safety continues to find expression in Deng's tale. When he and the other boys cross the Gilo River, a tributary of the Nile, they arrive in Ethiopia, which in their imagination has been elevated to a place of safety and rest. The place they reach, however, does not match up to their imagination:

> I looked at the land. It looked exactly like the other side of the river, the side that was Sudan, the side we left. There were no homes. There were no medical facilities. No food. No water for drinking . . . This was not the Ethiopia we had walked for . . . We are not in Ethiopia, I thought. This is not the place. (227)

To readers old enough to remember the 1980s, Ethiopia is a country tragically associated with the famine of 1984–5. The shocking images of starving, dying children came to define late-twentieth century perceptions not only of that particular country, but of the whole continent. To read of this place of suffering now imagined as a place of refuge is to experience another jarring reversal of perceptions and expectations. It is also interesting that Deng finds the other side of the river identical to the one he left behind. Beneath the childish disappointment of a promised land that fails to live up to one's fantasies lies the serious point that geographical boundaries cannot create clear-cut distinctions between 'here' and 'there,' war and peace, danger and safety. If borders are not meaningful markers of nationality and belonging, then displacement is internalized. 'This is not the place' is a phrase that we suspect our narrator has said to himself more than once.

The novel ends with the narrator longing to return home: 'I should be home. It seems wrong that I am not home . . . For years I have vowed to return home,' he writes (534). However, he goes on to note that his father does not want him to return until he has rebuilt his business and until their compound 'was again as it was when I came into the world' (534). In other words, the place imagined as 'home' does not really exist anymore. The dream of returning to a place once it has been restored to what it was when one was born is an expression of nostalgia, and therefore a longing for and an allegiance to an imaginary home. To go home, in this case, would mean to return to the past and undo the suffering, but Deng knows this is not possible. Further, his education and his life experience in the US have already remade him in ways that are bound to render a return home problematic: he can only return as an outsider, having come of age elsewhere and been made famous by an American book. Meanwhile, on another fictional level, as a character/narrator in a big American book officially credited to an American author, he is also 'home' already in his book.

The authorship question at the heart of this novel links the idea of home as a place of safety and belonging with the idea of telling one's story and thereby creating a stable self and inserting oneself in a national tradition. Deng tells a story of fleeing Africa and settling in America, but the very act of telling also effects his transformation from African to American. Near the end of the narrative of his life, Valentino Achak Deng recounts the events leading up to his departure from Kakuma, a camp for displaced persons, to a new life in the US: 'The first step in leaving Kakuma was the writing of our autobiographies . . . [W]e knew that our stories had to be well told, that we needed to remember all that we had seen and done; no deprivation was insignificant' (485). Even with such firm instructions, Deng found the writing a struggle: 'It was the first time I told my story, and it was very difficult to know what was relevant and what was not' (485). The first draft Valentino produced was only a page long. His friend Achor Achor encouraged him to include several episodes on their perilous journey, but Deng still thought the task impossible: 'How could I put everything down on paper?,' he wondered. 'No matter what, the majority of life would be left out of this story' (485). This was perhaps his first lesson on the challenges of autobiographical writing, but nevertheless he made a second attempt. He spent weeks re-working his narrative, and with some help and encouragement he was able to produce a longer, nine-page account of his astonishing life. The paperback edition of his American-authored life runs to 535 pages, and the transformation of the one-page account to the 535-page version is one that says a lot about how discourse is implicated in the acts of self-perception, memory and identity formation. It also says a lot about the primacy of the American self, as illustrated in another episode that takes place at Kakuma. After handing in his short 'autobiography,' Valentino undergoes another highly symbolic procedure: 'When I turned it in,' he recounts, 'the UN took a passport picture of me to attach to my file' (486). He then goes on to note that this was the first individual picture of himself he had ever seen: 'I had been in group pictures before, my head a blur in a crowd, but this new picture, of only me, staring straight ahead, was a revelation. I stared at this photo for hours and held the folder close for days, debating with myself whether or not this picture, these words, were truly me' (486). It is thus in two acts of self-representation that Deng becomes aware of the creation of identity, and the significance of these two events is not lost on the reader who has followed this man's journey and his transformation from 'Lost Boy' to narrator, spokesperson and campaigner for his people. The extent to which he has also become American is debatable, but the episodes of writing the self and seeing one's self represented in a picture are tropes familiar from several works of African American writing.

Despite the peculiarity surrounding its authorship, and despite its actual subject matter, *What Is the What* is a book that fits easily into US literary history. The articulation of the long, fictional, 'American' self owes as much to Walt Whitman's bold construction and celebration of himself as it does to Frederick Douglass's narrative of a life that moved from bondage to freedom, from darkness to enlightenment. *What Is the What* partakes of the two traditions. The transformation of the nine-page account into a fat, internationally acclaimed book can be read as representative of the emerging American self: the more Deng tells us, the more he writes himself into American literary history. His story is an African one, but the telling is American, containing at its core the essential values of individualism, self-expression, re-invention and faith in the future. Near the beginning of the twentieth century, Mary Antin told in *The Promised Land* her story of becoming American, and the telling also *made* her American. About a century later, Deng also tells a story that is typical and unique at the same time, celebrating the achievement of the individual, but also telling a story that represents other, untold ones. At the same time, the incident recounted of the narrator seeing himself alone in a picture for the first time holds a double significance in its American context: the emergence of selfhood is an oft-explored and much celebrated theme in American letters, but the act of seeing oneself represented for the first time also carries racial overtones. More specifically, it is reminiscent of the DuBoisian concept of double-consciousness, and of the revelatory moment in the lives of many African American subjects, when their blackness and otherness becomes real to them when perceived from the outside.

What Is the What has another strong link with classic American literature. In addition to its charting and articulation of an emergent black/American self, the novel inserts itself into an American literary tradition by borrowing and redeploying some of the tropes and techniques of the slave narrative. The full title of the work is *What Is the What: The Autobiography of Valentino Achak Deng*, but the book is designated a novel, and Dave Eggers is credited as its sole author. This confusing layering of authors and genres is not too far removed from the slave narrative's strategies, though there are important differences alongside the obvious similarities. The novel opens with a preface by Valentino Achak Deng who asserts that '*What Is the What* is the soulful account of my life ... The book is historically accurate, and the world I have known is not different from the one depicted within these pages' (xiii–xiv). This assertion inverts the hierarchy of the slave narrative, where the stamp of authenticity was placed on the book's preface by a white person who could also vouch for the slave's honesty and integrity. Whereas in Douglass's *Narrative* William Lloyd Garrison thought it necessary to remind his readers that the testimony of Mr Douglass was 'sustained by a cloud of witnesses, whose veracity is unimpeachable' (1998) with Wendell Phillips further stressing the author's 'truth, candor, and sincerity' (1999), Deng here describes his collaboration with Eggers as a partnership of equals, and exclaims 'thank God Dave and I met and certainly became good friends' (xiv). The story that Deng tells through the agency of the white author has similarities with the slave narrative in that it is a story of overcoming the odds, of hardship and great suffering followed by deliverance. However, the opening sequence with the African American burglar immediately challenges the teleological narrative, and indicates that the end of Deng's journey did not involve security and stability. At the same time, the burglary sequence allows the narrative levels to be re-organized in a way that playfully subverts the hierarchies of the slave narrative. With authorship attributed to a white person, the book announces that though this is an African story, it is one fashioned for the white market. Following the success and critical acclaim of *A Heartbreaking Work of Staggering Genius*, many readers would have bought this as another Eggers book. Yet when the narrative voice of Deng starts telling Michael, the young boy guarding him in his apartment, of his early adventures in Sudan, he repositions the narrative's audience. By having an African American narratee to whom the African attempts to appeal, and whom he hopes to educate, the book acknowledges its African gaze, and seeks a common bond, to be found in the two young men's geographical origins.

American authors often tell stories of immigration and stories of origins. As Werner Sollors has argued, these stories have the function of creating 'peoplehood' (259); they act as foundation myths for a country that was built on various acts of displacement and dislocation. The journey from Africa to the US is the story of the transportation of slaves rather than a story of migration, while the journey from the US to Africa, whether in the geographical or the aesthetic and imagined realm, is often a search for origins and heritage. Though journeys of origin are by no means unique to African Americans (we will see in Part II an example of a Jewish American heritage journey), what gives the journey to Africa more resonance is the common perception that a return to Africa is also a return to origins not only for African Americans but for all mankind. Africa has throughout the nineteenth and twentieth centuries been represented as 'primeval,' and the journey to Africa almost inevitably contains reference to the idea of a return to the past: not a concrete historical reality (such as the descendants of slaves looking for signs of their ancestors), but the past as the origin of the human race. The spread of media and globalization may have helped to dispel that image of Africa to some extent, but it is surprising how much of it is still with us. V.S. Naipaul's *The Masque of Africa*, for instance, published in 2010, aims to reach 'far back to the beginning of things' by examining African magic, witchcraft and native belief. As Robert Harris perceptively put it in his review for the *Sunday Times*, that is 'like trying to write about modern Britain in terms of pre-Roman Druids and newspaper astrologers.'

What Is the What is notable for breaking with familiar and established ways of conceptualizing African journeys. Much of the strangeness and 'exoticism' of Deng's long walk with the Lost Boys is taken away by the familiarity of Deng's American surroundings, while his compassionate and thoughtful narrative voice also normalizes for the western audience this strange, almost incredible tale. In addition, despite the stories of war, hunger and hardship during the African journey, Deng also presents a modern image of Africa. He is amused to discover that though arranged marriages still exist, Sudanese prospective brides can now use the internet to look at pictures of their proposed husbands before making a commitment. He further tells stories of relatives back in Kakuma wanting the familiar commodities of modern America: sneakers, watches, iPods and Levi's (246–7). Despite its several attempts to 'normalize' the exotic journey, Deng's tale also replicates older patterns by tapping into the hunger for stories of peril, adventure and survival. The narrator warns his readers from the outset that his own story 'includes enough embellishments' (21) that he cannot criticize other Lost Boys for exaggerating their plight, and including in their accounts what their audiences expect:

> Didn't we all eat the hides of hyenas and goats to keep our bellies full? Didn't we all drink our own urine? This last part, of course, is apocryphal, absolutely not true for the vast majority of us, but it impresses people . . . the tales of the Lost Boys have become remarkably similar over the years . . . sponsors and newspaper reporters and the like expect the stories to have certain elements, and the Lost Boys have been consistent in their willingness to oblige. Survivors tell the stories the sympathetic want, and that means making them as shocking as possible. (21)

Deng thereby places his story within a recognizable 'genre' while also signalling the superiority of his account, which must be more authentic because it does not contain all of the sensations associated with the journey of the Lost Boys.

Further evidence of Deng's and Eggers's 'knowing' reconstruction of the tale can be found in one of the hospital scenes. Finally rescued by his flatmate, Deng goes to the hospital, where he is treated with indifference and left to wait. In the hospital waiting room, he sees a magazine article on Darfur, illustrated with the picture of a woman 'with cracked lips and yellow eyes

... at once despairing and defiant' (249). As a narrative device, the magazine article affords him the opportunity to tell some of the back story of American involvement in the Darfur region, which he imagines delivering as a lesson for the African American receptionist, Julian. He tells Julian of George Bush Sr.'s interest in Sudan because of its oil deposits, and he hopes to bring the story home by convincing Julian that the plight of the Sudanese is not unrelated to the story of American prosperity. Needless to say, as with the narrative addressed to Michael, none of this is actually spoken. Deng knows that his story works best as the story of an 'other,' taking place away from the US, and unrelated to it. Further proof of that is found in the anticlimactic scene of the police officer's arrival. Deng is disappointed that his case does not produce the indignation he had himself felt, and the police seem uninterested in such a trivial crime, which they classify as a 'complaint'. 'We refugees are celebrated one day, helped and lifted up, and then utterly ignored by all when we prove to be a nuisance' (239). In this self-reflexive passage, he tacitly acknowledges the sensationalism of his own narrative, and realizes that the interesting part is simply the African journey. For most American readers, this needs to be a traditional narrative of hardship and obstacles overcome, with the arrival to the US representing the happy resolution and the end of his suffering and adventures. By starting the narrative with the burglary, Eggers/Deng draws attention to the ways in which this book deviates from that expected norm: this is not a story of 'happily ever after,' of escape from the hell of African war to the h(e)aven of US prosperity.

The theme of escape is made prominent through its doubling: the story of the Lost Boy escaping persecution in Africa is coupled with the adventure of the refugee in America captured in his own apartment. Though the two stories have no equivalence in terms of the suffering endured by the individual, they bring to the fore the idea of dislocation and the ways in which it permeates the whole text. Deng is displaced by war and in simple terms, the book is a story of dislocation because it recounts his long journey from Marial Bai to Kakuma and on to the United States. It is also a story of dislocation in that it shows him struggling to find a place for himself in his new American home. In addition to struggling with the enormity of his trauma, he has to deal with racism and discrimination, but the hopeful positive tone of his story suggests that he is embracing the American narrative of success, of looking forward to the future rather than dwelling on the past, of making and remaking the self in the pursuit of freedom and happiness. Final proof of Deng's transformation from Sudanese Lost Boy to American, of sorts, can be found in the book's title. Deng's father told him the story of God offering the Dinka the gift of cattle, which would bring them 'milk and meat and prosperity' (62). However, he also gave them the chance to turn down the cattle and accept the What instead. The catch was that he would not tell them what the What was, and so the Dinka wisely chose the cattle and prospered. Near the end of the book, Deng recounts the events of his last few days in Kakuma. He is able to make contact with his father back in Marial Bai, and wonders whether he should abandon his plans to go to the US and return home instead. His father encourages him to get on the plane to the US, but Deng tries to raise an objection: 'But what if I never see you again? I said . . . But father, what–' 'Yes, the What,' replies his father. 'This is it. Go' (513). In this modern version of the story, then, Deng is encouraged to launch himself into the unknown; America is the What that he has to choose over the predictable life back in Sudan. In one final twist of fate that no novelist would have dared invent for fear of ridicule, Deng boards a plane to the US on September 11, 2001. After a long wait on board, his flight is cancelled and he is transferred to an airport hotel where he watches the twin towers collapse on TV. 'Who is the enemy? I asked a Kenyan porter. He shrugged. No one knew who had done this' (525). Who is the enemy, and what is the what, are the two questions that perhaps best encapsulate this book's complex involvement with notions of dislocation and belonging, danger and safety, home and exile.

2 Norman Rush, *Mortals*; Russell Banks, *The Darling*

NORMAN RUSH, *MORTALS*

The books discussed in the previous chapter sought in many ways to blur the line between fact and fiction, and they did this by employing techniques more familiar from non-fiction narratives. Unlike them, Norman Rush's *Mortals* and Russell Banks's *The Darling* emphasize their literariness and foreground their artificiality. Paradoxically, the effect may be similar to that produced by Caputo and Eggers, in that these strategies question the relationship between lived experience and representation, but the means of enquiry are markedly different.

Mortals is a novel of epic aspirations that relies heavily on literary allusion, while *The Darling* primarily uses unreliable narration to interrogate both its construction and the articulation of the power structures it criticizes. However, what the two novels have in common is their use of the main theme of a disintegrating marriage against an African backdrop; this forms the main thrust of their narratives, but also relates to the wider points they are making about the new world order that has emerged since the collapse of the Soviet Union and the end of the Cold War. Both novels engage with the condition of dislocation because they focus on ways of being American in the world that do not involve the more traditional models of inquiry, namely immigration and the middle passage. Rush's Ray Finch is a CIA spy, and because his real reasons for being in Botswana have to remain hidden, he occupies an uneasy position: he is neither traveller, nor expatriate, nor exile. His job denotes his allegiance to the US, so he is perhaps best understood as a temporary worker with lasting bonds tying him to his host country. Hannah Musgrave starts out as a fugitive from justice: she ends up in Liberia because she is fleeing the FBI, and she is fleeing the FBI because of her involvement in the Weather Underground movement. As a radical activist, then, Hannah is very American in her devotion to her country's founding principles, and un-American in her embrace of terrorist tactics to fight the government. Once in Liberia, though, she gets married and has children; in establishing herself as part of a Liberian family unit, she becomes Liberian, though she is later able to shake that identity off and re-invent herself as American once more. We are more used to thinking about slavery, the middle passage, and the contributions of African Americans to American culture, but the novels I discuss here reveal another aspect of the US's engagement with Africa. Africa does, of course, have a long presence in white American literature, but it is an Africa of the white mind rather than an actual continent. These novels are different. The African countries that provide their setting are realistically depicted places populated by realistically depicted people; more to the point, these African countries are seen to be shaped (and deformed) by western intervention, past and present. The authors I am looking at use their African settings not in order to explore a western individual's existential crisis, but rather in order to interrogate what it means to be American in the world today. At the same time, these novels also offer adequate, detailed representations of their African settings. Though it could be argued that to allow our fictional views of Africa to be shaped by white American authors is just another form of cultural imperialism, it is nevertheless true that these authors bring hidden aspects of their settings to a wide readership, and do so in a way that shows cultural sensitivity and an awareness of the debates surrounding the various processes of the 'othering' of Africa. Norman Rush's *Mortals* is perhaps the book that best illustrates this point. As I will be arguing, despite being set entirely in Botswana, this is primarily a book that examines what it means to be American today, but it does that in a way that does not push the actual setting to the background; it does not render it picturesque, nor does it use it metaphorically. Instead, the Botswana setting allows Rush to explore how American identities shift and evolve as the US interacts with the world, showing ultimately that US foreign policy does not only shape the rest of the world, but also changes, in subtler ways, the stories Americans tell themselves about who they are.

Norman Rush is an author who tests the criteria by which we define nationality in literature. Born and raised in the US, he lives in New York, and writes in American English. However, his novels to date are set in Botswana, a place which is not a second home, nor a place of exile or expatriation: he worked there on a Peace Corps project for a mere five years. Moreover, Botswana is not tied to the US in the way that, for example, Liberia is: it was a British colony that gained its independence in 1966, and in its relative stability and prosperity it offers few of the sensations associated with traditional Western views of African nations (usually involving war, famine, tribal conflict and AIDS). The book itself is perhaps best described as a literary spy novel. It is set in Botswana in 1989, and it tells the story of white American CIA agent Ray Finch, married to the beautiful Iris. Iris has an affair with a charismatic black doctor, Davis Morel, whom Ray is investigating as part of his work. In addition to the spy plot, the novel is also the portrait of a disintegrating marriage and an ensuing crisis of masculinity. Despite its echoes of Hemingway, this is different because the African setting is not an external manifestation of inner crises. The

Botswana setting helps the author to re-assess the changing dynamics of the post Cold War era, and the complex power struggles the book depicts on a personal as well as an international level suggest that a sense of what it means to be white, American, and male are categories that are not fixed.

Running at 712 pages of dense text, *Mortals* also encompasses themes of religion, the power and dangerous appeal of ideologues, and the delights of literary contemplation. Ray Finch is a Milton scholar, and throughout the narrative the reader has access to Finch's views on his beloved poet. In choosing to make his character an expert on an English poet, Rush has passed up an opportunity to relate his character to his country of origin, but on the other hand the Milton context underscores several of the novel's themes and tropes. Chief among them are national allegiance and the idea of the fall, with Finch and his wife losing their 'prelapsarian' bliss through the agency of the 'devil' Morel. As I shall be arguing, this schema does not really do justice to the book's complexity: though the Milton references, along with several explicit references to Morel as the devil, certainly invite this type of reading, the novel finally resists and rejects such polarities. Alongside the idea of the marriage as 'paradise lost,' the book develops the notion of the African setting as Hell. The word hell is repeated with alarming regularity throughout the narrative, but the book finally distances itself from other narratives that imagine, as Rachel Falconer has demonstrated, the western encounter with Africa as a journey into hell. The double Miltonic reference of writing about the nation and writing about the loss of Eden are elaborated through the author's representations of space. I suggest that in its depiction of the disintegrating domestic space of its American characters, the book brings together the personal and the political in order to show how the ideas of home and homeland may converge and diverge. In telling the story of a marriage that falls apart, the book also describes the story of the collapse of older certainties about the meaning of nation and the homeland.

Within the first few pages, Rush establishes some of the major themes and preoccupations of his novel: set in 1992, in a world coming out of the Cold War, the book opens with Ray Finch, the protagonist and central consciousness of the novel, realizing that something is wrong with his marriage. 'Anyway, he was home,' we are told. 'He loved this house' (3). Occurring as they do in the novel's very first paragraph, these seemingly innocuous phrases in fact announce one of the book's main concerns: the idea of belonging and the idea of home. The first sentence, 'he was home,' could well suggest that Botswana has become a home for this white American. However, the next sentence undermines the assumption by qualifying the notion of home and linking it to the structure of a house. Throughout the book, Rush proceeds to question these categories, painting a portrait of a man who does and does not belong in this African country; a man whose idea of 'home' is not firmly fixed, and one whose relationship with his 'real' home, the US, is also highly problematic. Ray Finch is neither an immigrant nor an expatriate. As a CIA agent, he is a duplicitous man who has to impersonate an expatriate (pretending to be a teacher) while forging links with the local community. His status as a secret agent prevents him from being integrated in any meaningful way, but at the same time his status demands that he give the impression of an integrated community member. The in-betweenness of his position is reflected in the description of his house and its surroundings: Ray's is one of a number of 'sumptuous' (3) homes built for civil servants and 'significant expatriates' (3). The properties are walled and gated on the street side, presumably to keep ordinary Batswana out, but also visually emphasizing their inhabitants' isolation from everyday life in Gaborone. Internally, the houses are also separated from one another, this time not by means of walls and gates, but through 'wire-mesh perimeter fencing that had to be constantly monitored and kept in repair because there was a network of footpaths through the area that the Batswana insisted on using' (3). The use of the word 'insisted' here serves a subtle reminder of the novel's white outsider's point of view, while the broken fences that allow the locals to take shortcuts speak of class and race issues that render integration extremely problematic. The fences, we are told, 'were constantly developing holes . . . and it was a fact that their African neighbors were consistently more lax that the expatriates who lived there about keeping the wire fences fixed up' (3–4).

In addition to highlighting the class and race divides in Gaborone, the image of the broken wire fence does of course also recall the idea of the national border as a space guarded by wire fencing. This, in turn, relates to Ray's status as a secret agent, and as an American in Botswana. Ray muses that if he'd 'kept on teaching in the US they might well have ended up in a university town someplace in the Southwest that looked pretty much like this part of Gaborone' (6). As we will see in Chapter 4, Dave Eggers makes a similar point in *You Shall Know Our Velocity*, where his two American travellers come to the conclusion that every corner of the world resembled a place in America. Whereas in Eggers this realization is meant to emphasize the hegemonic viewpoint of the American traveller, here the emphasis lies on the African country's lack of exoticism: this part of Gaborone doesn't look like a US South-western town because the US 'contains' all other countries, or because an African city can only be understood as a more colourful version of its closer US counterpart. Instead, this part of Gaborone resembles that imaginary university town because of its ordinariness, because it is unremarkable. Such a depiction of an African town in an American novel is very unusual, and Rush's subversion of his readers' expectations continues when Ray also reverses the familiar narrative of the dream of emigration to the US as a journey to success. 'I would have been nothing in America,' Ray admits, and with this admission he accomplishes two things: he introduces the unfamiliar, almost unsettling idea of the reverse journey, that from the US to Africa as a journey to prosperity. At the same time, he tacitly acknowledges the importance of his nationality: he would have been 'nothing' in America because he would have been a white American among dominant white Americans, whereas here he is the other; a powerful other who derives much of his prestige and privilege from his American passport; a man, in other words, who is valuable because he does not belong. Yet Ray also knows that he is not an outsider in the way tourists are outsiders. He loves Africa, he thinks, 'but not like the idiots who come over here and say Boy! Women with mountains of sticks on their heads. Look, an ostrich crossing the road!' (7). This distinction between the ordinary American tourist who marvels at the African country's 'exoticism' and Ray's more knowledgeable fondness for Botswana is developed throughout the book, and counter-balanced by Ray's wife's visit back to the US, where she has now become the tourist. Iris comes back and tells Ray of cosmetic dentistry that produces 'the most blinding white teeth' (255), thus reversing a racial stereotype. She is further disturbed by the perception that the US is 'in a religious frenzy of some kind', ruled by a kind of religion she describes as 'gruesome' (253).

The preoccupation with space and built structures that starts on the novel's first page continues when Ray sets off to be briefed about his latest mission by his boss in a meeting that takes place at the American Library. The library is located within a modern development known as the mall. The mall is described through Ray's eyes in significant detail, thereby expanding on some of the book's central preoccupations. The cement flagstones that were used to pave the mall, we find out, keep fracturing; there is soil subsidence and ants and termites underneath, and these factors conspire to produce 'a funhouse aspect to walking on the flagstones as one or another of them would sink or tilt underfoot' (68). The image of the unstable flagstones (which may also contain echoes of the flagstones Marlow sees in Brussels) metaphorically conveys the difficulties of 'paving over' an African culture by introducing western, and more specifically American, architectural practices. Borrowing from postcolonial discourse, Rush seems to be suggesting that underneath the cement, the African soil claims the space and exacts its revenge by refusing to be covered up and kept underground. This image also figuratively announces the arrival, later in the book, of Ray's adversary, the charismatic Davis Morel who campaigns to de-Christianize Africa, and whom Ray's bosses prefer, for nefarious reasons, not to designate a person of interest. As a potential threat to stability who is also not an official threat (not a person of interest to the CIA), Morel occupies an in-between position much as Ray himself does as insider and outsider. He is further made ambiguous by the fact that his mother is white American, and his father black Caribbean: a mixed heritage that plays upon the various meanings of African identities around the globe.

Moreover, Ray's secret intelligence work has uncovered among Morel's possessions a framed reproduction of Brueghel's *The Tower of Babel*. Ray thinks that the mall itself resembles the painting because it is half-finished, but what Ray doesn't also add is that it resembles the Tower of Babel in its confusion of architectural voices which create an incoherent structure. This structure is home to various shops, a hotel, the British and American Embassies, and the country's only cinema, and in their own way, each one of these structures says something about the colonial legacy in Botswana, and about this African country's continuing interactions with the West. The cinema, for example, shows kung fu movies that are popular with the Batswana six days a week, and on the seventh day it attracts the expat community by screening films such as *Tess of the D'Urbervilles* or *Chariots of Fire*. Those screenings are often marred by the jeers of the locals who continue with the audience participation atmosphere established the rest of the week. In this comical and joyful image of the native movie-goers who ruin the Anglo-Americans' pleasure, clearly borrowed from post-colonial discourse, Rush continues his subversion of hierarchies and assumptions about the West's cultural superiority. The clothing shops are also interesting in that they use 'faceless and raceless manikins' (70) originally pioneered in South Africa: 'They were peculiar. Their heads were like grapes. ... Most of the manikins were beige. Some were gray. Some were clear Lucite' (70). These uncanny creatures are so unsettling because they are 'other' to everyone: in their exaggerated non-humanity, they stand as reminders of the failures of blacks and whites to acknowledge each other's humanity fully, and to think beyond race and colour. With the British High Commission and the President Hotel 'looming', the latter 'dominating the whole left side of the plaza' (70), it is obvious that the mall stands as a monument of western intervention.

Ray witnesses daily the injustice and inequalities that are the legacy of colonialism, and yet on the whole he views the mall as a representation of the West's beneficence towards Africa. He thinks of the people 'only one generation away from herding cattle and chasing witches' who are now enjoying 'sanitation and technology', and considers the whole thing as 'a gift from the white West' (69). His love rival, Davis Morel, has similar preoccupations, but his take is slightly different: he believes that the white world has given Africa three poisoned gifts: plantation agriculture, the nation-state and the Christian religion (182). Of the three, it is only the Christian religion that Morel chooses to fight, realizing perhaps that the other two are now impossible to eradicate. Agriculture and the nation-state are also significant because they both relate to the idea of land as homeland and as physical space. Norman Rush uses images and metaphors of space, and of public and domestic structures, in order to interrogate the meaning of home and homeland, and the connections between the two. Published in 2003, the novel revisits the brief period between the end of the Cold War and the beginning of the war on terror. It suggests that in an increasingly radicalized world, we cling on to ideas about home and homeland that sustain outdated notions of nation and belonging. The book ends with the marriage falling apart. The American couple's African home is broken up, figuratively putting an end to stable narratives of belonging. Both husband

and wife step out of their old roles: the white American wife chooses the black Caribbean doctor who wants to rid Africa of Christianity, while the white American spy leaves the CIA to work this time as a real teacher in the new, post-apartheid South Africa. Though their choices do not represent any conventional happy ending, they are far removed from the narratives that lead their white characters into despair or death in Africa. In this respect, this book is typical of a new breed of American novel that redraws the contours and the colours of the old familiar literary map.

One of the novel's greatest strengths is the technical accomplishment that allows the third-person narrative to follow Ray's inner voice. Rather than having to use elaborate narrative tricks to emphasize the distance between himself and his creation, Rush simply sets his novel eleven years before the date of its publication. This is a time-span that might be deemed insignificant, but one that actually serves as a constant reminder of quite how much the world changed between the collapse of the Soviet Union and the declaration of the war on terror. An example of how this works on a textual level can be seen as Ray continues walking to his meeting and thinking about his job and what it means to work for the CIA: 'He would defend his country as a decent package of forces. . . . America represented a decent package of forces. Of course all governments were evil or had a level of evil in them, but in the case of America wasn't it fair to say that being evil was forced on it by lesser and more corrupt other governments . . . ? It was his feeling that now that it was over with Russia, America could relax into its natural shape, couldn't it?' (74). This simple use of dramatic irony allows Rush to highlight Ray's naïve devotion to his country's democratizing mission, and to point out that America's role as the world's policeman has been changing and evolving too rapidly for perceptions to catch up adequately with the changes. Ray also ponders the significance of the collapse of the Soviet Union, and tries to find an apt mental image to convey the sense of monumental change that this has brought on: 'He had an image of something like a metal claw sunk into half the planet suddenly disarticulating' (7), but he dismisses that as a weak image and considers instead 'a goliath . . . who sits down suddenly and looks faint' (7). Finally, he concedes that the event 'was too huge for any image he had been able to come up with' (8). Ray's inability to construct the right image 'right off the bat' (8) is of course not surprising, given the nature and extent of the change brought on by the collapse of the Soviet Union. What is important here is that Ray feels the impulse to create such images even though he understands that he cannot fully see the whole picture. The urge to construct a mental image that will capture the monumental changes happening in the world of 1989 has a triple function: it is an instance of dramatic irony (Ray doesn't know quite how much the world is about to change); it is a reflection on the difficulty of writing a spy novel in the post-Soviet era, and it is an example of Ray's need to understand and process the world around him by creating meaningful designs.

Ray's job as a spy is figured into the novel as an analogue for the job of the novelist: Ray thinks of himself not as a collector of facts, or a writer of 'Profiles,' but an author of 'Lives': 'They called what he wrote Profiles, but he called what he wrote Lives. He knew that his Lives had been used, at one time, as examples during agent training. . . . And his Lives existed materially and would be kept and someday might even be found, when the true history of the world was written, but that wasn't important' (75). Ray is not deluded to think his Lives will become important in the telling of 'the true history of the world'; instead, what is being highlighted in this ironic observation is the fact that history does indeed consist of those little narratives of not very powerful people in a small and not globally important country. The little narrative is contrasted with the big narrative of the US as policeman and saviour, as having global importance, unlike some of the little countries it spies on. This imbalance of power and influence is also explored in the novel through the thematic development of the disintegration of Ray's marriage to Iris.

The marriage is figured throughout the novel through references to the marital home, a home that sets the couple apart from their native hosts and prevents any meaningful integration. When Iris then falls in love with Davis Morel, Ray sees her feelings not only as personal, romantic emotions, but also as a switch in allegiance from the American to the African. The isolation of their home is further stressed through the first chapter's title, 'Paradise': Ray wonders how many people realize that the word derives from 'the Persian for walled garden' (6), and the image of the walled garden introduces not only the sense of a marriage that thrives in isolation, but also the sense of being in the wrong place that Ray feels throughout the novel. 'It always made him happy when the gate clicked shut behind him' (6), we learn of his return home, but the image of the gated house, or walled garden, serves as a reminder of his lack of integration. As that sense of not belonging grows throughout the novel, we come to see Ray as an American-in-the-world who is trying to sever the connections between self identity and notions of the nation-state. Yet he never feels a citizen of the world; rather, he feels permanently dislocated, always in the periphery rather than the centre of events. Ray feels there is very little magnificence in his life, by which he means 'external magnificence such as . . . being present for the Gettysburg Address.' He concedes that 1989 and 1990 had also been magnificent because of the fall of the Berlin Wall but 'then, of course, he hadn't been present, he had been in Africa.' Similarly, when Nelson Mandela was released from prison, he was in Botswana, 'onlooking from there' (155). This sense of missing out on great events, of being in the wrong place and being overtaken by history taking place elsewhere can be read as an analogue for Ray's country. He is not simply thinking about his personal distance from these events but also feeling, as an American spy, that his role in the world is changing.

This sense that as an American spy he is lacking direction and feels uncertain about his place in the world is developed elsewhere in the novel. Ray tries to rationalize his decision not to learn Setswana, the language spoken in Botswana, by reasoning that he might be posted to another country at short notice; however, he really knows that this is merely an excuse. Yet he also acknowledges that '[s]ome of his resistance to learning other languages could be attributed to chauvinism about English, some hard relic of his upbringing' (165). That chauvinism can be seen again when he reads reports prepared by his British colleagues at MI5. He finds the prose 'laughable,' and thinks that 'the British were losing their grip on the English language as fast as the colonials were' (90).

Throughout the novel Ray and Iris delight in linguistic games that are really designed to show off their superior grasp of the language. As English becomes the new *lingua franca* and its various permutations take it further and further away from Ray's understanding of 'correct' English, we also infer a sense that Ray as an American spy is being overtaken by other spies, other networks of power from which he is excluded. This exclusion is also reflected in his wife's affair with Morel, and in both instances it is the American male who is excluded. Ray realizes that at some point and signals his new-found knowledge with a symbolic gesture: he burns his American passport. The narrative explicitly links the crisis of masculinity with the crisis of national identity, as Ray muses that

> Iris wanted a different man. He could be a different man. Nothing could happen to him if he had his passport with him. That was factual. Nothing could touch him once whoever came to oppress him, as people liked to say, saw his passport. The iron wings of the United States were over him, gently beating, wherever he went . . . His passport made him a prince. (381–2)

Stripped of the privilege and security that his American passport offers him, Ray imagines that he can return to Iris a changed man: that a rejection of the hegemonic power his passport represents will somehow make him a better rival for Davis Morel. The reason why Ray thinks his rivalry with Morel has something to do with race and nationality is one that merits further scrutiny, because it helps to illuminate this novel's complex stance on interactions between the US and Africa. Davis Morel, we learn early on, is black, 'but lighter skinned than an African, in the medium range' (49). His father is from Antigua, his mother a white Quaker, and he himself a resident of Cambridge, Massachusetts. Raised and educated in the US, Morel is a new type of American whose 'unstable' national allegiance unsettles Ray. Morel comes to Africa in a mission to de-Christianize it: he is an inverted American missionary seeking to undo the effects of white colonialism and hegemonic power over Africa. At the same time, he is like Ray an outsider, rather than an African son coming home. He comes to Botswana on a working immigrant visa, but Ray cannot fully grasp why. He wonders why a man who is 'smart,' 'black,' 'presentable,' 'a man for all races so to speak, and a man in his prime, would want to work in Africa'. 'American professionals coming to Africa to perform benefactions during sabbaticals or when they were past their prime made one kind of sense,' thinks Ray. 'But Morel had to be in his peak earning period. And he appeared to be coming to stay. And he was . . . coming unsponsored, which meant that this was a personally driven and personally funded choice' (51). In many ways, then, Morel represents a new way of being in the world, unfettered by national allegiance or skin colour. His is a globalized identity that Ray cannot fully comprehend, and the burning of his own passport represents a feeble attempt to become more like his adversary.

The Finch/Morel rivalry explores different attitudes to the nation-state and to belonging, home, travel and dislocation, and these concerns are evident in almost every other aspect of the book's articulation. The intertextual web places the novel itself in a literary context that transcends national boundaries by actively evoking works of European literature in a way that not many contemporary authors do. Meanwhile, the narratives of adventure and descent into hell borrow familiar western tropes but use them to different ends. The pre-9/11 setting of the book sets up a contrast with the rapid changes of America's role, and as Ray starts to feel overlooked or even obsolete in his role as spy, so the book generally notes the demise of older traditions and hierarchies. The Batswana, we are told, prefer the racist attitudes of the British to the egalitarian spirit of the Americans (399). The former may be distasteful, but they carry with them the certainty of one's place in the world order. The American, on the other hand, has all the power but acts as if he doesn't, and that is harder to fathom. Harder still to fathom within the logic of American literature is Ray's decision not to leave Africa. Where the white American novel would have been expected to conclude with the hero's return from Africa to American soil, this one ends more unexpectedly with the move to a nearby African country. The American spy has lost his place in the new world order, and his country has symbolically lost its place as the destination of choice for a happy ending.

RUSSELL BANKS, *THE DARLING*

On 9 September 1990, Field Marshal Prince Johnson captured Samuel Doe, the Liberian dictator who had ten years previously overthrown President Tolbert's government. A videotape of the incident shows Prince Johnson seated at a large desk, with a picture of Christ carrying a lamb hanging behind him. 'I'm a humanitarian,' says Johnson, and then he orders his men to cut off one of Doe's ears. The ear is sawn off with a long knife and then handed on to Johnson, who proceeds to place it in his mouth and chew slowly. The tape then shows Doe being further tortured and humiliated until he concedes defeat and asks the armed forces to surrender to Prince Johnson. What does this brutal scene, described in accurate detail in *The Darling*, have to do with a narrative that reassesses a woman's involvement in American radical politics of the 1960s and 1970s? In short—a lot. Banks explains:

> It doesn't take long to go to Vietnam and cut the ears off the Vietcong, and heads, and other body parts. No, human beings do this. But it's particularly spectacular to Americans—white Americans particularly—we get a special frisson when we see Africans doing it. And we put them on the cover of a magazine, a kid in a dress with bandoleers of ammunition around his bony chest and paint on his face. (Birnbaum)

Leaving aside the cruel irony that the paperback edition of the novel did feature precisely such an African kid with ammunition around his chest, *The Darling* continues and amplifies Banks's preoccupation with the lasting effects of slavery on American life and culture. In his article on Banks's earlier novel *Cloudsplitter*, Anthony Hutchison has claimed that there are hardly any American writers who have 'negotiated the issue of race in as sustained, unflinching and intelligent a fashion as Russell Banks' (67). Indeed, Hutchison's subsequent analysis of *Cloudsplitter*, which paints a fictional portrait of the abolitionist John Brown, reveals many similarities between the 1998 novel and *The Darling*, which followed it. Hutchison calls *Cloudsplitter* a historical novel, and argues that in it Banks tells 'the story of race and the American Civil War'. In similar fashion, *The Darling* borrows from the historical novel in its seamless blending of fact and fiction, and in an update of the earlier book's preoccupations it tells a story of race, Civil Rights and the Vietnam War. As I will be demonstrating later on, the word 'story' is a crucial one; it appears on the last page of *The Darling*, where the narrator, Hannah Musgrave, takes stock of her eventful, highly politicised life. More pertinently for the purpose of my analysis, the word story is used by Hannah to contrast her past life with the unknown future heralded by the attacks of September 11 2001. Despite their many similarities and thematic and structural continuities, *Cloudsplitter* and *The Darling* are separated by the events of 9/11. The decision by Banks to mention the World Trade Center attacks on the last page of his novel alters the way we read the book, and opens up new ways of understanding his claim that 'the central narrative of the United States is the story of race': the novel does not engage with race only in its historical sense (the story of where African American slaves came from, and what happened when some of them got back), but also in its contemporary manifestations, where the war on terror has created new ways of understanding racial strife and questions of allegiance. *Cloudsplitter* dealt with the issue of race as an American concern, by which I mean that slavery and its legacy were examined for their lasting effect within the geographical limits of the US. *The Darling*, by contrast, seeks to understand the American story of race by exploring its transatlantic dimensions. Several American writers have of course used a similar mode of enquiry, but whereas they have concentrated on the slaveship journey from Africa to the US, Banks focuses on the largely overlooked history of a small country that was created in order to accommodate freed slaves returning to Africa. Banks therefore updates the transatlantic slave journey and brings it into the present, showing how contemporary Africa continues to be shaped by the US.

Banks's belief that the American public is fascinated by the spectacle of the murderous African explains why the Liberian setting is appropriate for this novel: it serves as a reminder that the horrifying spectacle of the African child soldier is not some kind of 'other' to the civilised American: their fates are linked in ways that most Americans would not suspect, and Banks is here able to explore the complex nature of this link. Banks's analogy between American brutality in Vietnam and African brutality in civil war reminds us that the US is no stranger to inflicting pain and torture, but more to the point it also emphasises the fact that the capacity for brutal torture is often projected on to the other; in this case, our understanding of the mindless killing of African civilians is meant to be juxtaposed with a false assumption of western superiority that would not allow such scenes to take place. It also helps us to read the novel in (or against) the context of the long literary tradition that has posited Africa as the other to the civilised and civilising colonialist and enabled writers to sketch character and create psychological depth by using Africa, as Chinua Achebe has powerfully argued, as the backdrop for their characters' unravelling. Moreover, Banks's comment about putting the image of a child soldier on the cover of a magazine also reminds us that the novel is concerned with representation; in this case, not the reproduction of images, but the telling of stories, and the intersections between the personal and the political which allow him to question the authority and authenticity of the stories and news reports that we do get to hear coming out of Africa. I will examine the intersections between the novel's three main concerns: the Liberian setting, the radical politics of the 1960s and 1970s, and the exploration into the female narrator's complex and often contradictory sense of identity. In so doing, I will argue that Hannah's sense of dislocation, which is underscored by her unreliability as narrator, is also physical, emotional and political. She goes to Africa as a traveller of sorts, a fugitive from justice seeking to lie low for a while, and ends up being embroiled in Liberian politics with a passion that replicates her earlier fervent desire to undermine the hegemony of her native country.

Banks writes about Liberia in order to write about the US. Unlike Rush, he has a protagonist who leaves Africa and returns to the US, and unlike Rush he also foregrounds the American context not only through the parts of the book that take place on US soil, but also throughout the narrative where Hannah's first-person voice asserts her Americanness in a way that

Ray Finch's internal voice never does. However, in using Liberia to write about the US, Banks does not render the former symbolic: Liberia is not used as backdrop, but as a credible means of enquiry into racial and international politics. In an interview Banks said: 'I do believe that the history of race in America is a central history and that it's our master Story' (Smith 2003). The Liberian setting allows him to demonstrate quite how relevant the 'story of race' still is today; by aligning the fate of a white American woman with the turmoil of an African country, he shows the effects of racial oppression and the displacement of peoples to be long-lasting, and stretching across the Atlantic from the Boston campuses where Hannah fought her early battles to the streets of Monrovia where child soldiers maimed, raped and killed their own people.

Twentieth-century Back-to-Africa movements are associated with black empowerment and liberation, but Liberia was conceived in the early nineteenth century as a dumping ground for freed slaves by an unholy alliance of Quaker abolitionists and Southern slave owners. Not only was this back to Africa movement not born of a noble desire to return people to the places their ancestors were snatched from, but it was also yet another manifestation of America's imperialist expansion and its disregard for those it displaced in the process. In his book *Back to Africa: A History of Sierra Leone and Liberia*, Richard West claims that 'Liberians . . . had no real right to the territory they had occupied, but justified their presence by their persecution abroad and by their claim to superior civilization' (124). This statement echoes the settling of the US itself. The settlers of Liberia not only displaced the indigenous population, but also created a new ruling elite whose superiority to the natives was taken for granted. In the same way that old American families could boast of a lineage that stretched back to the founding fathers of the nation, the Americo-Liberians of today are still considered part of the elite. In fact, this perceived superiority of the Americo-Liberians is often cited as one of the reasons that Samuel Doe overthrew President Tolbert's government in 1980. Doe was a member of the Krahn tribe, and his coup was at first seen as a welcome step in overthrowing a 150 year imposed 'foreign' rule and reclaiming Liberia for its indigenous population. The fact that after all this time the distinction between indigenous Africans and Americo-Liberians still exists and shapes politics shows that, just as in the US the effects of slavery have not yet disappeared, so too in Liberia its legacy is still going strong. In the US, civil war preceded the abolition of slavery; in Liberia, civil war erupted a century and a half after the first freed slaves were sent home. This neat analogy allows Banks to use Liberia as a mirror image of the US, at a time when the author would not have been able to predict that within a few years the US would have its first African American president, while Liberia would seek to heal the wounds of the past with the aid of a new president, US-educated Ellen Johnson-Sirleaf.

Within the novel, the narrator's changing descriptions of Ghana and Liberia also underscore the transatlantic connection that links the fate of

African countries today to slavery, imperialism and the Cold War. Upon her return to Liberia, Hannah finds 'a mingling of the known and unknown that greeted me when I made my first journey into the American South nearly forty years ago, when I was a college girl using her summer vacation to register black voters in Mississippi and Louisiana' (12) . The comparison between African and American spaces that we also see in Rush and Eggers is used here to question the meaning of spatial representation: Liberia and the American South are similar not because they look alike, but because they share the bond of slavery and a history of oppression. In Ghana, her description of the locals makes her sound like an updated version of Conrad's Marlow: 'They were excitable, loud, confident, and in your face, but in an engaging and good-humoured way, waving hands, gesticulating, bending, bowing, and spinning as they talked, haggled, hassled, gossiped, and sang' (67), yet there is a crucial difference. Hannah knows that this kind of description is exoticizing, and also willingly acknowledges the hidden reality behind the stereotype: 'when I looked beyond its exoticism to the day-to-day reality of people's lives, I saw that they were made poor and weak so that I could be rich and powerful' (69). Hannah's simple formulation has a two-fold effect: it highlights her own often simplistic moral principles, but at the same time it shows her to be aware of her own country's relations to the world. Where the American Dream has emphasized the idea of the US as the final destination of a journey, and where the land of opportunity is imagined as a static land mass with clearly defined borders, Hannah knows that her country's prosperity, as much as her country's troubles, are not to be separated from American foreign policy, or more generally from the historical and contemporary interactions between the US and the rest of the world.

Hannah is telling her story a year after her final return from Africa, and the date of her return, we learn on the novel's very last page, is 11 September 2001. Hannah's story is told from an all-female farm in the Adirondack Mountains where she has finally retired, and as the narrative moves forward and backwards in time and space, the reader actively has to reconstruct the chronology of events. In a narrative full of self-contradiction as well as temporal and spatial movement, Banks questions the notion of the continuity of *self*, while at the same time showing the very notion of the sense of self to be inseparable from the wider world of politics. Hannah is a reluctant and unreliable narrator; she begins by announcing that 'most of the time' she doesn't want to tell her story (31), and she goes on to say that '[t]here's much about that period you don't need to know, or perhaps much that I don't care to remember right now. Or *can't* remember. I was a different person then' (48). As she takes on different names and different identities, she actually asks 'who was I?', and once she has become a conventional African wife, she wonders whether 'when my politics disappeared, my only hope for an autobiographical narrative had disappeared, too' (165). More importantly, she goes on to say that a lot of the time in Liberia she felt like she was wearing a mask. The trope of the mask is of course a significant one; the wearing of masks may be associated with African art and ritual, or it may refer to white colonial representations of Africans, but it is unusual to find it used to describe a white American in Liberia in the 1970s. As well as highlighting the notion of racial identity as a disguise, the trope of the mask also links Hannah's sense of self with the causes she espouses.

Each political struggle she takes part in becomes a part of who she believes herself to be, but the fact that her sense of self is formed by external, political factors, also allows her to shed identities and put on different masks by taking on different causes. In her political involvement with the civil rights movement in the US, Hannah had forged a bond with oppressed African Americans, and got her sense of identity through fighting to promote their cause: to be American, for her, was to fight for the rights of her own fellow countrymen. In Liberia, though, her assumptions about race, democracy and hierarchy are destabilized, and it is in this temporary suspension of ideology that she finds a chance of reprieve: 'I was bone weary of my war against everything American,' she writes. 'American racism, the Vietnam War, even the Cold War and the System that fed off it, and my parents—they mean nothing to the Africans, I thought then. And, presumably, could mean nothing to me, too' (105). Hannah doesn't seem to know that Liberia was actually the second largest recipient of US foreign aid during the Cold War. As soon as the Cold War ended, the money dried up and the US left Liberia to its own devices. Charles Taylor actually launched his raid against Samuel Doe 45 days after the Berlin Wall came down. The ignorance and relative innocence of her first few years in Liberia are juxtaposed later in the novel with harrowing images of suffering, death and mutilation; as the civil war rages around her, Hannah once again has to shed an identity and the certainties that go with it, and reinvent herself.

As well as interrogating identity by highlighting its construction and showing it to be changeable, the novel, by engaging in great detail with recent political events, interrogates the process that turns these events first into news and then into 'history.' Throughout the narrative, Hannah interacts with real as well as fictional people; most notably, she claims that she helped Charles Taylor escape from an American prison, and that one of her sons was the man in the video who cut off Samuel Doe's ear. These overlapping inquiries into history, politics and identity allow Banks to question the grand narratives of history and the assumed superiority of the West. The intermingling of real and fictional characters is of course neither new nor unique to Banks, but what makes his contribution stand out is the fact that he deals with unfolding events rather than older historical ones. When the book was published, Charles Taylor's trial had not yet begun, and Ellen Johnson-Sirleaf had not yet been elected. Had Banks invented the story of the world-famous super-model who accepted a gift of dirty diamonds and testified during Taylor's trial, he would have been stretching the limits of our credulity. With no benefit of hindsight, he is better able to avoid passing judgment on his characters, and he can demonstrate how history is written and how people are judged for the outcome of their actions.

Hannah's unwavering belief in the causes she supports and her total devotion to radical politics are juxtaposed with her unstable, self-contradicting narrating and narrated self. In exposing and exploring these contradictions, Banks does not seek to diminish the vision or the achievement of his fictional heroine and her real-life counterparts. Rather, the novel encourages an assessment of the intersections between the personal and the political, and between dominant narratives and little stories. Hannah's story comes to an end on 9/11, and she concludes by admitting that her old life is now irrelevant; that hers is the story of an American darling that 'could have no significance in the larger world' (392). As a political activist, Hannah believed in the phrase 'by any means necessary,' but her concluding remarks suggest that the attacks on US soil are now forcing her to reconsider the totalizing nature of her own moral vision. It is here that Banks's use of the Liberian setting makes sense: Liberia exists today because slavery existed in the US, yet the link between the two countries has been growing weaker and weaker since the end of the Cold War. By bringing to the forefront the widely overlooked civil war of a mostly forgotten little country, Banks asks his readers to take the long view, historically and geographically. As narrator, Hannah looks back and explains to the reader an earlier version of herself; in the process, she inevitably selects, revises, and edits, just as Liberia has been 'edited out' of American public discourse. Her first-hand experience of the Liberian civil war suggests that the process that turns events into historical discourse is similar to the process of narrating the self. When Hannah helped Charles Taylor to escape from prison, she did not know that that escape was aided by the American government (which changes the nature of her actions), nor was she to know that Taylor would not turn out to be the Liberian saviour she had hoped he would become.

The Darling is a novel that explores identity in terms of gender, politics and narration. Hannah is shown to get her sense of self mainly from the various causes she espouses, and the people and ideas she opposes. The contradictions and occasional implausibilities in her behaviour may at first appear to be a failure on the part of the male novelist fully to imagine his female subject, but in fact it is these moments of incoherence, self-contradiction and multiplicity of motives that allow the author to link his concurrent investigations into the self, racial and sexual identity and the larger forces of history. In creating a white female American whose identity is partly shaped by African culture and African politics, Banks brings together the personal and the political. He emphasizes the dynamic contexts in which American identities are shaped, and he demonstrates that the transatlantic slave journeys to and from Africa continue to shape the world today.

Part II
Travel and Globalization

'Travel and the construction of American identity are intimately linked' (1) remark Judith Hamera and Alfred Bendixen. The editors of *The Cambridge Companion to Travel Writing* go on to claim that travel writing 'creates American "selves" . . . through affirmation, exclusion, and negation of others,' and it is some of these 'selves' that Part II examines. Hamera and Bendixen go on to note that 'the boundary between travel writing and fiction can be especially murky', and that '[f]act and fiction also intermingle in individual works' (2). These observations provide the conceptual link between Part I and Part II of this study: the 'murkiness' identified above has already informed my reading of the books in 'Africa and the Limits of Fiction', and it continues into 'Travel and Globalization'. Though the books discussed here are less troublesome when it comes to generic boundaries, and can easily be described as novels, they do acknowledge their debts to other types of discourse. Foer's book, for example, was initially conceived as autobiographical, as a travelogue-cum-family memoir telling the story of his search for his grandparents' history, a fact that survives in the metafictional naming of his American character, author Jonathan Safran Foer. Eggers's novel, meanwhile, contains pictures and drawings that inevitably draw attention to generic categorizations and constructions of reality. The novels by Keillor and Tan illustrate another point that Hamera and Bendixen make, though they make it about non-fiction: that 'the ways Americans viewed their own physical and cultural landscapes were, and remain, intimately linked to their real and imagined engagements with other places and times' (3). Tan in particular chooses a topic that has perhaps surprisingly not been much used in American literature: the ethnic subject as traveller *from* rather than *to* the US. Keillor repositions his local tales of small-town America by scrutinizing the formation of white American identities in the context of travel to Europe.

Alfred Bendixen reminds us that during 'the early years of the nation and throughout much of the nineteenth century, patriotic Americans often deplored the idea of foreign travel' (103). He cites Washington Irving, who, in *A Tour on the Prairies* (1835), laments the fact that American youths grow 'luxurious and effeminate' in Europe, instead of exploring the US in order to cultivate 'that manliness, simplicity, and self-dependence, most in unison with our political institutions' (103). Where Irving links American travel with the democratic values of his country, Thoreau also advocates simplicity and self-reliance, but he urges the exploration of a different kind of frontier: that of inner space. 'It is not worth the while to go round the world to count the cats in Zanzibar,' he writes in his Conclusion to *Walden* (1854). He continues:

> Is Franklin the only man who is lost, that his wife should be so earnest to find him? Does Mr. Grinnell know where he himself is? Be rather the Mungo Park, the Lewis and Clark and Frobisher, of your own streams and oceans; explore your own higher latitudes . . . Nay, be a Columbus to whole new continents and worlds within you, opening new channels, not of trade, but of thought. (353)

In typical Thoreauvian manner, travel is seen as frivolous, conventional and pointless, or as a capitalist enterprise driven by the desire for profit rather than self-improvement. Commerce and tourism are juxtaposed with inner exploration, which Thoreau considers the only kind of exploration worth embarking upon. He calls for the conquest of a new frontier, one that pushes ever westward, stopping not at the Mississippi, nor the Pacific Ocean, nor China or Japan, but continues in an infinite expansion which is the expansion of our inner horizons. His inspirational rhetoric combines the American values of self-reliance and the fashioning and re-fashioning of the self with the democratic spirit that inspires Americans not to feel inferior to the Old World, nor to be in awe of the past. Nearly two centuries later, travel in American literature is still bound up with many of the ideas put forward by Irving and Thoreau. The books I will be discussing engage with inner journeys, journeys of self-awareness and self-improvement. They explore familiar tropes of old and new world sensibilities clashing. They imagine the journey abroad as adventure, education, self-liberation, but also as philanthropic mission and as fraught with danger. All the books explore not only the ways in which an American can be a traveller, but also the ways in which the traveller understands and enacts his or her own Americanness.

Of course, between the pronouncements of Irving and Thoreau and the modern travellers discussed in these chapters lie the three authors who have done the most to shape the idea of the American abroad, and often more specifically the American in Europe: Henry James, F. Scott Fitzgerald and Ernest Hemingway. David Grant has argued that Henry James tapped into a rich cultural vein when he sent his Americans to Europe, not so much creating a literary tradition, as articulating a facet of American ideology that was already there. 'In grafting the American in Europe onto the literary consciousness of his country,' Grant argues,

> James himself was simply bringing closer to the surface a tradition that, because it is so tightly bound up with American ideology and the American sense of self, could never depend on a single writer to keep it alive . . . Europe traditionally represents to American novelists a life, or Life itself, that remains somehow unavailable back home. The paradox of Europe as both the antithesis of America and the only field upon which Americans can become themselves runs throughout [James's and Hemingway's] works. (267–8)

Nathalia Wright has further argued that of all European countries that American writers have visited or lived in, it is Italy that has most shaped the American literary self. She notes that, rather than travel writing or memoir, it is fiction that forms the 'most imposing body of literature produced by Americans as a result of going to Italy' (21). The Italy of American letters is a symbolic one, she writes:

> Historically or politically it is the epitome of Europe; intellectually and morally it represents experience not available in America. In any event it is a scene larger than the American scene, one where Americans may have intercourse with the world and the past, form fruitful attachments, or escape frustration. No other foreign country has figured so provocatively in American fiction. (29)

Where Italy has shaped American fiction by providing the setting and backdrop that Wright describes here, France, and more specifically Paris, has also largely shaped our understanding of the American modernist movement. In particular, the image of the expatriate author in Paris has come to encapsulate America's artistic interactions with Europe before WWII. J Gerald Kennedy has identified this movement as a kind of aesthetic and intellectual dislocation:

> Attempting to free themselves from the influence of familiar, native settings, writers and artists *underwent dislocation* to achieve a new relation to their work and to the verbal or visual language of its composition. The city of exile combined for them the strangeness of the foreign and the unreality of the modern, producing an alienation from the immediate environment while at the same time endowing it with the sort of imaginary power which only the unreal can possess. (192, added emphasis)

The dislocation identified here by Kennedy involves expatriation, which he defines as 'prolonged absence or even permanent exile from the homeland,' or 'a lengthy stay in an alien place' (25, 27). If these conditions came to define modernity, the postmodern authors I discuss here typically enjoy a more light-hearted and playful approach to the encounter between the old world and the new. The unreality of the modern has been replaced by the hyper-reality of the postmodern, so that the relationship that the fictional travellers develop with the countries they visit no longer pretends to contain any notion of an authentic encounter (and therefore no possibility of genuine alienation). Moreover, a lengthy stay is no longer necessary; the expatriate has been replaced by the author who can on the one hand transcend national borders, but who can also on the other hand bring to light the flimsiness of the notions of home and belonging in America itself. In other words, critical constructs of the modernist exile rely on assumptions about the Americanness that these authors were fleeing, whereas the novels examined here and in Part III also seek to demonstrate that 'the native' already contains its supposed 'other'. Finally, the authors I discuss also acknowledge the weight of literary history. Keillor, for example, knows that an American cannot easily write about Italy without acknowledging the debt to Hawthorne or James, and his playful allusions to *The Wings of the Dove* underscore the literary context of his transatlantic engagement.

Though expatriation in the shape of Americans in Europe has dominated the early part of twentieth-century American writing and has shaped our critical responses to that period and beyond, at the beginning of the twenty-first century this particular form of transatlantic exchange seems less significant. The rapid expansion of technologies and the spread of globalization have altered the very understanding of 'home' and 'abroad,' so that the engagement with other lands and cultures beyond the US's geographical borders has become more fluid, since it no longer has to depend on an extended sojourn abroad. At the same time, new American voices have altered our understanding of the native in American letters. They have also opened up American literature's involvement with the rest of the world beyond its traditional late-nineteenth and twentieth century parameters, which usually involved Africa, as the site of slavery, and Europe, as the seat of civilization, and have moved discourse away from the notion of the journey to Africa as a journey into the past, and the journey to Europe as a glimpse of the modern. Gertrude Stein embraced Paris because that was 'where the twentieth century was' (Kennedy 185), but the authors I examine find the modern, the present and the future, in places less likely and more diverse. From the satellite dishes in the Burmese jungle to the Budweisers served in bars in Dakar, the signs of capitalist expansion and globalization point to a different engagement with the world beyond America's shores.

The four books discussed in this section feature travellers and tourists who use the latest technologies to research their trips, to travel, to transfer funds and obtain local currencies and to communicate. At the same time, though, there is a sense of nostalgia for the older, slower-paced type of travel, seen in the old-fashioned epistolary exchange in Foer's book, or in Eggers's novel where information found through Google and travel books becomes obsolete before the travellers even reach their destination. This mixture of old and new styles of travel also prompts questions about encounters with the other: if the ways in which we organize and experience travel have changed dramatically, have our views of the people we encounter on our travels also evolved? The answer is far from clear or straightforward, and the evidence from these four books not conclusive. Dean MacCannell in *The Tourist: A New Theory of the Leisure Class* discusses tourism as a 'utopia of difference' and concludes that

> Whether or not tourism, on a practical level . . . , can ever be a "utopia of difference," ultimately depends on its capacity to recognize and accept otherness as radically other. To me, this means the possibility of recognizing and attempting to enter into dialogue, on an equal footing, with forms of intelligence different from my own. (xxi)

He also acknowledges that 'any celebration of "difference" is something insidious: that is, the sucking of difference out of difference, a movement to the still higher ground of the old arrogant Western Ego . . . , isolated by its belief in its own superiority' (xx–xxi). The novelists I examine here are perhaps not exempt from the arrogance of the old Western ego. However, coming as they do from ethnic and cultural places where that ego is contested (in their various positions as gendered and ethnic subjects, writers of regional literature or campaigners for social change) they combine positions of power and weakness: they are Americans, and therefore part of the global elite, but they are also engaged in forms of writing that seek to unseat the supremacy of that Ego through their exploration of different types of travel.

Amy Tan's novel satirizes the idea of travel as education and self-improvement. Despite being well-educated high achievers, her tourists are also ignorant and blind to the realities they encounter. Keillor's book sends a bunch of provincial innocents abroad on a mission to restore the name of a fallen soldier. Literally and figuratively, then, they are charged with improving the image of the American soldier abroad and, needless to say, their mission does not quite go according to plan. Foer's protagonist embarks on a heritage tour best understood as a dark pilgrimage: a journey to his ancestor's site of suffering that is meant to fill in the missing parts of his family history and thus restore to him a fuller sense of identity. The truths he uncovers disrupt rather than complete his family narrative, but it is in this way that self-awareness is finally realized. Eggers's characters are eccentric philanthropists on a mission to re-distribute wealth and forget their own grief. As well-meaning 'humanitarians,' they fail to do much good to the 'others' they encounter, but they do learn valuable lessons about themselves.

Chapter 3 focuses on Amy Tan and Garrison Keillor and examines some striking thematic similarities in two authors who appear to have very little in common. Tan is a Chinese American who has done much to promote the expression of ethnic identity and inter-cultural story-telling in her work. Keillor is associated with a home-spun, white American tradition of regional writing that appears to celebrate the local, the particularities of place, and a certain resistance to global change. Both are popular authors, though it is hard to imagine there is much overlap in their devoted readerships. With *Saving Fish from Drowning* and *Pilgrims*, though, they have produced two comic stories of travel, both loosely based on *The Canterbury Tales*: a context that is not closer to the white Minnesotan author than it is to the Chinese American one. Both novels employ the comic mode to say important things about the construction of American identities, and about America's place in a world shaped by globalization, but also producing new possibilities for cultural alienation. My analysis focuses on two issues that Keillor and Tan address in their novels: the construction of American racial and ethnic identities in the context of travel abroad, and the exploration of cultural contexts such as literary landscapes and mythical tropes. In chronicling the comic misadventures of groups of Americans abroad, the two novels also interrogate the notion of 'homeland security': whereas the American tourists are cautious and fearful, treating the rest of the world as dangerous and potentially hostile to Americans, they fail to see that their country is perceived as the aggressor rather than the victim.

Chapter 4 continues to draw on theories of travel, globalization and post-national studies in order to discuss how language, geographical space, ethnicity and cultural memory are brought into focus as the American travellers cross the Atlantic and come into contact with the world beyond their shores. Unlike Tan and Keillor's pilgrims, these American travellers find a world which is not sufficiently 'other' or different. This could be because both authors and travellers belong to a younger generation; one that has not lived through a time when the subaltern could not speak, and one that barely remembers a world without McDonalds, the internet or instant communication.

This chapter examines the meaning and symbolism of travel in two contemporary American novels by young male authors. *You Shall Know Our Velocity* and *Everything Is Illuminated* feature characters engaged in transatlantic exploration and adventure. Both novels scrutinize and thematize, through two personal and intimate journeys abroad, the ways in which young Americans perceive and are affected by the world beyond their shores at the beginning of the twenty-first century, as well as the ways in which America has gripped the imagination of those they meet on their travels. The two books engage with the issues of globalization and the Americanization of the world, and even though they may to some extent be read as continuous with the tradition of travel in American literature, they can also be read as reflecting new realities.

Foer's novel tells of a young Jewish American's search for his grandfather's history in Ukraine. It also tells the story of his Ukrainian translator, whose own grandfather turns out to have played an important part in the traumatic events of World War II. The novel concerns itself with the meaning of American Jewish identities; it also pokes fun at the heritage tourism industry that sees wealthy Americans 'returning' to Europe in search of their ancestors' hidden histories. Through the story of the Ukrainian translator, it also explores the existence of other Americas, such as the one imagined by would-be immigrants, and the one infiltrating other cultures and shaping popular culture. Dave Eggers's novel has two young males travelling to Africa and Eastern Europe to give money away to strangers. The half-baked, ill-executed scheme is neither genuine philanthropy nor self-indulgence, but it helps the reader to connect the theme of the American tourist with the questions raised by US humanitarian efforts and financial aid packages. The heritage trip and the philanthropic journey also raise important questions about the ethics of contemporary travel, and they serve as illustrations of what Fredric Jameson terms the 'dissymmetry' between the US and the rest of the world (Jameson 1998, 63). The world these tourists encounter is also notable for its sameness, but the people they meet do not always fully comprehend the power the US exerts over them. From Senegal to Estonia and Ukraine, the Americanization of the world forms a significant part of the narrative's background.

When Alex, the Ukrainian narrator of Jonathan Safran Foer's *Everything is Illuminated*, meets Jonathan, the American hero who has come to Ukraine to uncover his Jewish grandfather's past, he is unimpressed:

> He did not appear like either the Americans I had witnessed in magazines, with yellow hairs and muscles, or the Jews from history books, with no hairs and prominent bones. He was wearing nor blue jeans nor the uniform. In truth, he did not look like anything special at all. I was underwhelmed to the maximum. (32)

Alex's reaction is suggestive of the ways in which travel may excite and thwart expectations, while his disappointment at the American's ordinariness is indicative of the ways in which the myth of America has invaded all corners of the earth. At a time when the US makes its presence felt all over the world in ways that range from the relatively benign to the sinister or near apocalyptic, Foer's novel, along with Eggers's, present their readers with American travellers who are in many ways nothing special at all. This emphasis on the ordinary and the 'underwhelming,' though, does not seek to underplay the impact that Americanization has had on the world. Rather, both novelists explore intersections between the personal stories of travellers meeting people, using their American dollars and learning life lessons and the impersonal narrative of globalization as the mass movement of people, money and ideas.

Neither novel is primarily or explicitly concerned with Americanization, nor do they engage thematically with globalization in an overt manner. Dave Eggers's *You Shall Know Our Velocity* (2003) is about two friends, Will and Hand, who travel abroad in order to put emotional and physical distance between themselves and Chicago, scene of the tragic death of their best friend. Will, as the narrator, gives us access to his inner thoughts, and these are mainly related to his friend's accident rather than to the new lands and people he encounters. Michiko Kakutani, reviewing the book in *The New York Times*, described it primarily as one that combines 'the conventions of the buddy movie and road novel, and then glosses the whole thing with a dark, existential overlay' (7). Another *New York Times* reviewer, John Leonard, identified the novel's major themes as 'fear, violence, loss, death, unfairness, responsibility, community, redemption, self-aggrandizement and shareware' (9). Similarly, little critical attention was paid to Foer's preoccupation with circumatlantic exchange. Francine Prose wrote in *The New York Times* that Foer's was a book about 'the importance of myths and names, the frailty of memory, the necessity of remembrance, the nature of love, the dangers of secrecy, the legacy of the Holocaust, [and] the value of friendship,' and she only identified 'the confusions and collisions between American and post-Soviet culture' as one of 'a host of subthemes' (8). Chapter 4 argues that the transatlantic journeys undertaken in both novels are central rather than incidental, and the ease with which American critics have brushed away the significance of these journeys is perhaps in itself a symptom of the reception of such fiction in a globalized cultural environment.

In *Travel Writing: The Self and the World* Casey Blanton argues that travel writing and the theme of travel have had a great influence on American fiction, and he claims that '[b]oth American fiction and the American travel narrative that influenced it share a response to the *idea* of travel as a symbolic act' (15–6). The idea of travel in American literature manifests itself in different ways. It may refer, as Blanton notes, to Whitman's 'perpetual journey' of self-knowledge, or Thoreau's quest for life's meaning. Further, it may relate to narratives of immigration, to exploring and adventure and conquest, or it may relate to the Grand Tour and the idea of the journey as education and refinement. The novels under discussion here may fruitfully be read as belonging to several of the above categories, but the main difference between them and their predecessors is that these are books stemming from, and set in, a shrinking, homogenized world—a world in which maps as representations of space reflect even less than ever before boundaries of national belonging, or boundaries between traveller and host. As the nature and meaning of travel changes, so does its symbolism.

In her influential *Imperial Eyes: Travel Writing and Transculturation*, Mary Louise Pratt introduced the trope of the seeing-man, the one who sees with imperial eyes, and she defined her notion of the contact zone as a place where 'disparate cultures meet, clash, and grapple with each other, often in highly asymmetrical relations of domination and subordination' (4). The two novels I will be discussing test and redefine the notion of the imperial seeing eye and of the contact zone as a locus of power struggle. Coming out of a world where discourse has emphasised the ideas of the end of empire and the end of history, these books can help us to assess the extent to which the novel reflects a changed world, and how as a result the idea of travel has altered, and has in turn re-energised American fiction and its preoccupation with travel.

3 Amy Tan, *Saving Fish From Drowning*; Garrison Keillor, *Pilgrims*

AMY TAN, *SAVING FISH FROM DROWNING*

Saving Fish from Drowning tells the story of a group of American tourists who travel to China and Burma and are held captive by a remote tribe. The novel presents itself as a 'discovered' story. The 'author' begins with a 'Note to the Reader,' where she explains how she took shelter in the 'American Society for Psychical Research' to escape a sudden downpour, and came across the writings of a psychic medium who had the story we will read dictated by the spirit of Bibi Chen. Everything about this preface helps to create an impression of mystery and exoticism, thus parodically placing the text in the tradition of oriental-inspired tales of mystery. The 'author' begins by looking into the Society's archives, and describes a room 'jammed floor to ceiling with the leather and cloth spines of old books—little tombstones of ideas and history clothed in midnight blue, purple, brown and black, the titles imprinted in fading gilt letters' (xi). The atmosphere created here draws on traditions and tropes familiar from the stories of Edgar Allan Poe as well as television series that deal with the bizarre and the paranormal, and also from pulp magazines such as *Weird Tales* and its offshoot, *Oriental Stories*, that were popular in the 1920s and 1930s. This prepares the ground for the introduction of our dead guide and narrator, Bibi Chen. Significantly, Bibi is the owner of 'The Immortals,' a shop that sells decorative Asian antiques. The idea of the commodification of ethnic culture in the US, and the continuing lure of the 'oriental' style are therefore introduced from the outset, signalling the story's parodic intent. Bibi herself is described as exotic, 'wearing dramatic garb, along with a multicoloured braid and false eyelashes as thick as hummingbird wings' (xiii). Apart from aiding the creation of an atmosphere of parodic orientalism and mystery, the note to the reader also indirectly helps the author to engage with some of her critics. Amy Tan is a commercially successful author who has been criticized for commodifying her own ethnicity, and for misrepresenting her country of origin. By placing the frame at the beginning of her novel and introducing the dead narrator through the psychic medium, Tan seeks to create enough distance between herself and her fictional world so as to avoid the kind of criticism she has attracted in the past. In *Beyond Literary Chinatown*, Jeffrey F. L. Partridge quotes Koh Buck Song reviewing Tan's *The Hundred Secret Senses* for Singapore's *Straits Times*:

> If the joss-smoke of mystique that surrounds things Chinese is ever to clear, Amy Tan's new novel will offer scant assistance . . . This novel, while it will probably be snapped up by Tan's many fans, will unfortunately do little to help dismantle Western stereotypes of China and the Chinese. (55)

For her part, Tan has noted that she is

> alarmed when reviewers and educators assume that my very personal, specific and fictional stories are meant to be representative down to the nth detail not just of Chinese-Americans but, sometimes, of all Asian culture. (Gentz 106)

Saving Fish from Drowning is not a personal story, and it concerns several characters who are not even Chinese American. However, perhaps because the book deals with representations of foreign countries, Tan must have felt the need to emphasize the outlandish 'made-upness' of her story as a way of silencing those critics who crave authenticity and corrective representation in the work of the ethnic author. Our dead narrator, Bibi Chen, also bemoans the fact that she will not be able to act as docent for her group of friends as they set out for the trip she had planned for them. Tan here plays with the idea of the 'ethnic' author in American literature as a kind of guide, able to present and explain the mysteries of an unfamiliar culture to an audience eager for mind-broadening activity. The debate concerning the role of the ethnic author as tour guide, interpreter or translator has often been discussed, but it has rarely been thematized. In this novel, not only is the narrator as tour guide an image of the author as guide; the conceit is taken further, as Bibi is replaced by Bennie Trueba y Cela, and the group of travellers are (mis)led by a number of local guides in China and Burma. One of them is Miss Rong, whose comical name reveals not only her poor grasp of the English language, or the series of adventures and cultural blunders that she lets her group fall into, but also her own inability to speak other Chinese dialects: a native guide with no local knowledge. Their last guide, Walter, speaks excellent English and is very efficient. The plot 'rewards' him for being so Westernized through the offer of a scholarship to study journalism at Berkeley and a generous donation of 25,000 dollars. However, before Walter can take up his place at University, 9/11 happens and visas for foreigners like him are indefinitely suspended. This recipient of American benevolence is therefore denied the opportunity to live his American dream; as the US discovers and creates new enemies, Walter becomes collateral damage by losing out on a cancelled offer of a better future.

The 'Note to the Reader' is followed by a newspaper story from the *San Francisco Chronicle* that reports on the eleven missing American tourists who are the focus of the novel and comically highlights the blurring of fact and fiction and the role the media play in the spread of globalization, which are issues that will become central to the rest of the novel. Immediately after that, Bibi Chen starts narrating the main body of the story. She begins by describing the journey she had planned, starting in the southwestern corner of China, and continuing south on 'the famed Burma Road' (1). The famed Burma Road carries strong connotations of empire, and helps to draw parallels between the colonizing missions of the British in the nineteenth century and those of the US today. Bibi calls the trip 'a fabulous journey into the past' (1), thus confirming a commonly held view of the Western traveller, that to travel to the countries of the East is also to travel back in time. Walter D. Mignolo has examined this popular stereotype, claiming that this denial of coevalness is typical of the ways in which the West seeks to affirm its cultural superiority over the rest of the world (35). Later in her narrative, Bibi makes a more explicit reference to the denial of coevalness and to Burma's colonial past when she writes of her friends crossing the border into Burma, a crossing that makes her feel 'plopped in the past' as if she had traveled in H. G. Wells's time machine. She thinks of Orwell and Kipling, 'the chroniclers of old colonial Burmah' (145), and professes a liking for the 'exotic and languid life' (146) depicted in 'the literature of yesteryear' (145). Against tales of 'intoxicating ... perfumes' (145–6), she finds that recent stories about Burma 'pale' in comparison. Who wants to read about 'sacrilege, torture, and abuse'? (146), she asks as the sarcasm in her voice grows. She wants 'the funny monkeys chattering in the tree branches and not the poachers and their empty shell casings below' (147). 'That's what we visitors love,' she concludes. '[A] rustic romanticism and antiquated prettiness, no electric power lines, telephone poles, or satellite dishes to mar the view. Seek and you shall find your illusions through the magic of tourism' (147). By pitting the harsh realities of Burma's repressive regime against the old colonial tales of dreamy exoticism, Tan is also exposing a dichotomy and defending her own craft by indirectly reflecting on her own enterprise: the creation of a light-hearted, romantic comic adventure that engages with serious political issues.

The early parts of the novel take place in China, and they are rather predictable, as they consist of light-hearted tales of cultural misunderstandings, uncomfortable hotel beds and that ultimate symbol of the clueless tourist, the tour bus. However, what sets these pages apart is the narrative voice. Being dead as well as Chinese American, Bibi has access to the thoughts of many characters, and is able to reverse the point of view, seeing through the eyes of the Chinese guide, for example, who 'stands in' for her, the guide of the original trip and our guide through the story. When Miss Rong, their first tour guide, counts the people on the tour bus, it is not faces or names she remembers, but types. She sees 'the black lady, the plump man, the tall man with horsetail hair, the kissing girl, the man who drank too many beers, those with three baseball caps, another with two sun hats, and so on' (74). Her description is a good illustration of the fact that nationality and ethnicity are not fixed categories, but fluid ones that change depending on the setting and context. For example, not much is made of the 'black lady's' blackness throughout the story. Her status as American tourist overrides her ethnic heritage and skin colour, so that when she is abroad she is American more than she is African American. This suspension of racial and ethnic categories, or the suspension of marginalization more generally, has been dealt with in other American narratives. Leslie Silko's *Ceremony* and Walter Mosley's *Easy Rawlings* series, for example, highlight the plight of the Native American and the African American male who become temporary unhyphenated Americans when they go to fight in wars, but then return home to their old categories and are marginalized once again. Tan implies that it is not only patriotic duty that 'promotes' the individual to the status of unhyphenated American. Being a tourist, and therefore engaging in monetary transactions and seeking services from those less fortunate than one's self, can also lead to a temporary suspension of ethnicity.

The ways in which ethnicity is partly determined through the gaze of the outsider are also explored when Bibi informs the reader that Esme, Marlena Chu's daughter, 'could easily have passed for a child from Lijiang' (64–5). It is tempting to interpret that as simply meaning that she looks Chinese, but Bibi is able further to qualify that statement by explaining that the locals 'were the result of centuries of bedtime mergers among Han Chinese, a dozen Yunnan tribes, and over the ages, British opportunists' (65). To be Chinese in Lijiang, therefore, can denote different categories and relate to various historical circumstances that are not obvious to the western visitor. Thanks to her own duality, Bibi is able to highlight the double-standards involved in constructions of identity. Marlena speaks with an accent 'shaped by her Shanghainese birth, her childhood in São Paulo, her British teachers, and her studies at the Sorbonne' (33), while Wendy's mother is called Mary Ellen Brookhyser Feingold Fong, the series of surnames taken from her various husbands reflecting a multi-cultural approach that led to her American daughter receiving presents for Christmas, Chanukah, and the Chinese New Year (44). The novel highlights the fact that whereas the US is increasingly aware of its own multi-ethnic makeup, the tendency still exists to view non-Western cultures as monolithic and ethnically and racially lacking in diversity. The comic reversal continues when the travellers see a water buffalo, blindfolded, with mud up to its belly, being whipped. Miss Rong explains what the buffalo is doing (softening the mud to help make bricks and tiles), and further informs her group that 'This is karma ... Past life this buffalo must be doing bad things. Now suffer, so next life get better' (77). Her views are contrasted with those of wealthy Americans 'who bought organic-buckwheat pillows for sitting on the floor, who paid experts to teach them to empty their minds of the noise of life. This was quite different from the buffalo-torture and bad-karma Buddhism found in China' (77). This passage pokes fun at the commercialization of cultures and religions that Americans often engage in, but it can also be understood as a kind of meta-commentary on the novel itself. Amy Tan's version of China is a China that exists primarily for American readers. It is not sanitized and re-packaged in the same way as the organic buckwheat pillows, but it is of necessity shaped by the experience of writing in and for the West. It is, above all, shaped by the culture that gives voice to the hyphenated American author.

Tan continues knowingly and playfully to explore the constant border-crossings that the hyphenated American performs as subject, as author and as global traveller. When the group approach Burma, they stop at a tourist spot where there is a white wooden post 'where you could stand with one half of your body in China and the other half in Myanmar. . . . So without going into Mayanmar, you could claim you had been there' (125). Later on, when the group have crossed the border, their guide informs them that they have not yet arrived in Burma. To 'leave one place is not the same as entering another', she says, prompting Bibi to observe that this was 'exactly how [she] felt. In between' (141). The reader naturally assumes that Bibi is referring to her ethnic heritage, but she is in fact speaking about being in limbo. She explains Buddhist beliefs about the afterlife, and notes that she probably has another month in her peculiar, suspended state, though she cannot be sure. Limbo therefore joins the other non-sites and liminal spaces in the novel as spatial representations of transactions, imaginings, fears and desires about the 'other' encountered when West travels East.

Another, more unexpected instance of in-betweenness occurs when Bennie compliments the Burmese guide, Walter, on his linguistic prowess. 'Have you noticed his English is better than mine?' he asks. 'He's more American than I am' (161). What makes this observation surprising is that Bibi goes on to explain that what Bennie meant was that Walter spoke with a British accent, which to Bennie's ears sounded 'more high-class than his American mid-western one' (161). This complex hierarchy of accents seems very confusing, but what Bennie is implying is that the WASP, the American most closely related to the old British colonizer, is also the 'true,' authentic American, with all other regional variations resulting from immigration and intermingling seen as of lesser value. Walter, on the other hand, has a very different understanding of Americanness. Being American, he notes, 'has less to do with one's proficiency in English and more with the assumptions you hold dear and true—your inalienable rights, your pursuit of happiness' (161). Walter's understanding of American identity is tied in with ideology and not with language, thereby emphasizing that an American identity is open to anyone willing and able to embrace that ideology even if their linguistic heritage disbars them from membership of that select group, the American. Bennie calls Walter an honorary American, to which Wendy responds: 'Not everyone wants to be an American' (162). Wendy's sensitivity to issues of patriotism and belonging is yet another instance of in-betweenness, given further weight by the fact that Wendy is also partly an image of the author of the novel. Wendy, we learn, 'wanted to fight for Burmese rights, for democracy and freedom of speech. She could not tell anyone that, however. That would be dangerous' (44). Wendy therefore has to 'masquerade' (46) as a tourist while seeking opportunities to gather facts and talk to local people. In an interview appended to the paperback edition of the novel, Amy Tan has spoken of her own dilemmas in travelling to Burma and writing a light-hearted novel about it. She explains how she went to Burma for a week and took copious notes, trying to imagine what life was like for the locals, rather than interviewing anyone and risking having her cover exposed. Writers are not allowed in Burma, she pointed out. 'Horrors, we might write about the place' (6). In that interview, as well as another one she did with Lisa Allardice in *The Guardian*, Tan also spoke more generally about the dilemmas surrounding the decision to write a comic novel about a country best known for its repressive regime. She told Allardice that she thought about the ethics of her choice and went to Nadine Gordimer

> with that very question. I asked, "Can you take a very dark serious subject about human rights abuses and write it as a comedy?" She said, "Absolutely—sometimes it's the only way." I thought about doing it in a darker way, but I decided it would border on being moralistic, rather than using the seduction of fiction to do what it can best, which is to be subversive.

That subversiveness was further aided by circumstances beyond Tan's control. Allardice notes that

> [i]t is tempting to read this morality tale about a group of well-meaning Americans and their hapless "group leader", blundering into a foreign country, as a satire on the Bush administration's gung-ho foreign policy. Tan seems pleased by the idea, but it wasn't deliberate. She started the novel well before 9/11, but as she got to the end she was struck by how much it reflected world events.

Saving Fish from Drowning can easily and fruitfully be read as a novel responding to George W. Bush's policies after 9/11, but to find out that the composition of the novel pre-dated 9/11 does not diminish its importance. Rather, it is a useful reminder that 9/11 did not represent the break from the norm that it was initially seen as. True, an attack on US soil in post-war years was unprecedented, as was the visual spectacle accompanying the crime. However, what was neither new nor discontinuous was the strained relationship between the USA and large parts of the non-western world. While it is obvious why politicians would want to present 9/11 as an aberration, novels such as this one remind us that American foreign policy already employed, pre-9/11, the rhetoric and tactics also adopted after the attack. This is clear in the novel's title, which is explained twice.

The first explanation for the paradoxical phrase 'saving fish from drowning' comes before the narrative proper begins. The book opens with two epigraphs which can be understood as related, even if their true significance is not clear until the end of the novel. Saving fish from drowning, we learn, is a 'pious' man's way of reconciling his belief that it is 'evil to take lives and noble to save them' with his interest in catching fish. It is, in other words, a piece of sophistry where the pious man disguises his self-interest as charity and benevolence. The other epigraph, taken from Albert Camus, speaks of good intentions which may 'do as much harm as malevolence if they lack understanding.' The American tourist is a useful and easily recognizable cultural stereotype of the well-intentioned traveller who is oblivious to the consequences of her or his actions, and Tan's novel does indeed mine that vein. However, as the story of the pious man illustrates, her target is not so much the clueless American tourist—though that figure is shown to be complicit—as it is US foreign policy and its rhetorical and ideological justification. The story of the pious man is taken up again when Walter, the group guide, explains that butchers and fishermen are usually not Buddhist, but when they are, fishermen can justify their actions by claiming they are saving the fish. Heidi is shocked, and Dwight responds: 'No worse than what we do in other countries' (162). There follows a brief discussion among the group, where they try to establish whether interventionist policies are desirable or morally justifiable, but no consensus is reached. Later on, the travellers come across a group of horribly mutilated people. One of the locals (who will later kidnap them) explains that they are made to walk in front of soldiers in order to locate landmines. Marlena mutters that they shouldn't have come to Burma because it is wrong to witness such suffering, and the group all feel 'uselessly sympathetic' (288). Soon enough, though, the group will be abducted by the Karen tribe, and they will indeed be able to help, not so much through any particular actions as by virtue of being Americans in peril: no expense is spared in trying to locate them, and their plight catches the attention of the media world-wide. This, in turn, highlights the plight of their abductors who throughout the period of the tourists' confinement show themselves to be surprisingly media-savvy and able to use modern technologies to draw attention to their predicament.

Tan is therefore able to use the metaphor of saving fish from drowning to comment not only on interventionist US foreign policy, but also on the ethics of travel, and more specifically what has become known as 'dark tourism'. Though the term normally denotes travel to sites of death and suffering, such as concentration camps or slavery memorials, I use the term more loosely to apply to countries with poor human rights records as well. John D. Barbour notes that

> [o]ne of the most interesting issues raised by increasing global travel is the ethics of cross-cultural travel. Do travel and travel writing perpetuate exploitative, hierarchical, or unjust relationships of power, or do they suggest alternative ways of encountering other cultures? (15)

His question is further complicated by the fact that cross-cultural travel often effectively means that those who are better-off visit those who are worse-off, and those who enjoy freedom of movement visit those who do not have that choice. In other words, it is not simply a clash of cultures and values, but a clash of ideologies and political regimes. Tan is careful not to paint a picture of the strong visiting the weak, or of the enlightened visiting the benighted. All these modes of tourism are facilitated by globalization while they also raise new ethical questions created by that same process. For instance, as the case of Walter's post-9/11 cancelled visa demonstrates, Americans are not always able to return the hospitality they receive abroad, and this is another example of what Fredric Jameson would call the dissymmetry between the US and other countries, even China (Jameson 1998, 63). When Tan's novel was published, Chinese tourists were not allowed to visit the US. The ADS scheme, which regulates Chinese tourism and approves which countries the Chinese can visit, only added the US to their list in 2008.

The study of American literature often involves a scrutiny of the ethnic writer as outsider and insider in their own country, and Tan takes advantage of that position by sending her Chinese American narrator (albeit post-mortem) to China and Burma. By setting her novel abroad, she can highlight how power relations are transformed when re-contextualized. Further, Tan herself occupies a position of duality: marginalized as representative of the 'ethnic' author, but also commercially successful and very popular. This ambivalent position of weakness and strength is replicated in the power relations within the novel, and further amplified by the intertextual allusions to places real and imagined that are sites of competing ideologies.

The travellers start their journey in Lijiang in China, a place believed to be 'the fabled city of Shangri-La that James Hilton described in his novel *Lost Horizon*' (42). Bibi reflects on the myth of the 'ethereally beautiful, hard to reach' place (43) and bemoans its commercialization. Her own travellers will later stumble upon another Shangri-La which will turn out to be a place of illusions:

> They had entered a green-veined new world, a vibrant, single-hued world of wildlife that quivered and breathed. Everywhere the travelers looked, it was choked with creepers, vines, and liana hanging, winding, and snaking their way through, making it seem that the jungle ended only a few feet in front of them. . . . With small intakes of breath, my friends registered their astonishment. "Amazing." "Heavenly." "Surreal." (238–9)

This place, they learn, is No Name Place; a joke at their expense that, in recalling the notion of Utopia, foreshadows the perils and difficulties the travellers will encounter (after all, this is a small patch of 'paradise' in Burma, a country that stands for everything US rhetoric abhors). The event gains further comical value from the fact that the group does not realize that they have been kidnapped by a tribe that believes one of them is their long-awaited saviour. When the bridge they crossed to get to No Name Place is secretly lowered, they accept the fact that they are completely cut off from the world, but find little solace in the fact that they have thus achieved the wealthy, stressed-out tourist's dream: an 'escape from it all'.

The references to Shangri-La and Utopia allow the author to amplify the theme of international travel in the age of globalization. Can there still be secret, 'undiscovered' corners of the world when GPS has mapped the world, and Google Earth can show us what it looks like at the click of a button? And can sinister, repressive regimes cut themselves off from the rest of the world? Benign Edenic places and ideologically suspect 'non-places' alike have been mapped, commercially exploited, and connected to the rest of the known world through media and technology. These are the issues that the second half of the novel explores as comedy, romance and satire are all stepped up. One of the novel's great jokes is that the abducted group do not realize they have been abducted. They believe they have been cut off by a collapsed bridge, and throughout their ordeal they remain kindly disposed and sympathetic toward their hosts. During their first night, they are surprised to hear a strange sounds accompanied by flickering light. This turns out to be a TV set broadcasting 'good old GNN' (294), Global News Network. They soon discover that there is a satellite dish, and a car battery powered by a bicycle they take turns to pedal. The Lord's Army's ability to appropriate technology presents them as resourceful *bricoleurs* who attempt to guarantee their own survival by using the very technology that, by spreading globalization, threatens their existence. This is further underscored by their avid watching of the Australian reality show *Darwin's Fittest*. The tribe, we learn, 'had fantasized they might one day have a TV show . . . then SLORC would be too ashamed to kill a tribe that was number one' (295). The show they dream of is called The Lord's Fittest, but when they finally have their wish granted, the 'studio execs' rename the show to Junglemaniacs! The sensationalization of the Lord's Army's fight for survival represents a victory for capitalism and market forces; the *bricoleurs* are finally defeated by the engineers, and their little narrative is absorbed into a bigger one that flattens and caricatures the thing it calls reality. However, the abducted Americans are not immune to this distortion of reality either. While still in captivity, they watch old friends and relatives being interviewed about them on TV, and they see versions of themselves that they don't quite recognize. They soon become 'The American Eleven' (426), and there are vigils and fasts in Tokyo, Oslo, Madrid and Rome, while in Germany a candle-lit rally celebrates not only the

American Eleven, but also Burmese students, journalists, and supporters of the National League for Democracy (426). The speed with which a local event becomes a media circus and a global phenomenon is of course an easy target for the satirist, but what makes Tan's exploration of these issues more interesting and original is her insistence that the forces of globalized media do not necessarily make distinctions between the powerful and the powerless. The American tourists end up misrepresented and swallowed by a bigger narrative as well.

The novel therefore offers a complex picture of the American traveller. The comic elements are derived by the workings of the plot and the narrator's tone, and there is a strong element of parody of the nostalgic tourist gaze. These are juxtaposed with the feelings of fear that the travellers experience: the fear of undemocratic, repressive regimes, the fear of offending locals, and the fear of being victims of abduction. However, alongside these more conventional fears, Tan shows them also to fear living in a world that is not connected, a world where the television set and the satellite phone are not controlled by the Americans but rather by their captors. Garrison Keillor is concerned with similar aspects of contemporary travel, and it is a well-timed phone call that saves his gullible American tourist from the scheming Italians she encounters.

GARRISON KEILLOR, *PILGRIMS* (2010)

Garrison Keillor's Lake Wobegon series has been running since 1985, the year *Lake Wobegon Days* was published, while the related radio series, *A Prairie Home Companion*, started life in 1974 and despite some intervals, still continues today. In the quarter of a century that Keillor has been chronicling the rather uneventful lives of small-town America, many of the issues and concepts associated with his writing have been transformed. The very notion of regional writing has come under close critical scrutiny, as scholars have sought to reconcile the pull of the global with the appeal of the local, while also questioning the validity of such dichotomies in the first place. The idea of home, so central to the Lake Wobegon series, has also been transformed since the mid-1980s, through changes in the world order as well as through the accelerated development of technologies and the spread of globalization. Notions of whiteness, and of cultural and racial identities, also continue to be questioned as it becomes clearer that there are other world views that do not consider the white Anglo-American the 'golden standard' against which to measure 'other' identities. Home is an important concept in the Lake Wobegon series: *Lake Wobegon Days* opens with a section entitled 'Home,' and Keillor's next book is called *Leaving Home* (1987). However, as we shall see, home becomes a problematic concept in *Pilgrims*, where ideas of home as property and home as national allegiance are brought together and placed under scrutiny. The motto on

Lake Wobegon's town crest reads 'Sumus quod sumus': we are what we are, a gentle joke on the pragmatism and down-to-earth philosophy of the town's inhabitants, but also a kind of shorthand for the nostalgic and almost certainly false notion of simpler lives in a simpler time: the kind of America that everyone assumes has always existed, and the kind that everyone assumes no longer exists.

Keillor enjoys great popularity and has a devoted band of followers who listen to his radio shows and who read his books, but he has not attracted the critical attention he deserves. Bob J. Frye implicitly acknowledges this when he attempts to position the Lake Wobegon novels into the context of literary satire, arguing that 'Keillor is more than a folksy humorist dealing in nostalgia. He is an artful satirist' (122–3). *Pilgrims* is certainly satirical, and it does not even keep up the pretence of nostalgia that one may have found in earlier books in the series. In telling the story of an American war hero who turns out to have been a lot less heroic than his townspeople had supposed, Keillor makes nostalgia itself the target of his satire. At the same time, by setting his story in Rome, he indirectly asks his readers to re-examine their assumptions about US regional writing. *Pilgrims* alludes to *The Canterbury Tales* through its title, and it borrows the trope of the story-telling traveller. More importantly, all the characters who travel to Rome tell stories about their lives back home, thus filling in gaps in our knowledge of the Lake Wobegon characters from previous novels. In this sense, the novel may be set in Rome, but at the same time it returns to the familiar setting of Lake Wobegon, placing it in a new and different context. Moreover, the contrast between the sophistication and the weight of history associated with one of the great cities of the old world and the folksy simplicity of the relatively new immigrants of Lake Wobegon allows Keillor to question and vex our perception of regional writing. Michael Kowalewski argues that, in American letters, the 'overly dramatic attempt to establish regional distinctiveness often seems to prompt a response in the opposite direction,' leading to a 'kind of antimythic puncturing of regional stereotypes' (11). This can be seen in the novel much more clearly than in others in the series: by taking his characters out of Lake Wobegon and across the Atlantic, Keillor punctures national stereotypes at the same time that he gently mocks the provincialism of his pilgrims. His satire also has a political edge. At a time when the myth of America as world liberator is being emphasized by politicians eager to justify their incursions abroad, the story of a celebrated World War II hero whose exploits were far from heroic speaks to contemporary anxieties about the US's role on the world stage.

Kowalewski further argues that there is 'still often an undeniable thread of antimodernist (or antipostmodernist) recoil in much contemporary regional writing' (14). That thread certainly exists in earlier Wobegon novels, but here Keillor offers a more critical engagement with the (post)modern. The Italian setting places the novel within a long tradition of American writing that engages with the old world, and the presence of 'Garrison

Keillor' as an author character in the novel, slightly alienated from his characters, aloof and detached, comically conjures up images of the iconic expatriate author. Meanwhile, the intertextual weaving of *The Wings of the Dove* draws attention to the book's engagement with the American authors who have shaped our view of the interactions between European and American selves. The intertextual references are light-hearted in tone, as the comic resolution of the plot amply demonstrates, but they nevertheless acknowledge the recoil that Kowalewski writes about. The references to Henry James further serve to highlight the novel's knowingness about identity construction. Margie Krebsbach is not just a typical midwesterner; she is also a Milly Theale who has the last laugh, providentially saved from the cunning plots of her Italian associates. Apart from the comic potential of Margie's triumph against the scheming Europeans, the acknowledgement that literature shapes rather than just reflecting regional identities is crucial here. Lori Robison examines the local colour writing of the American south and concludes that by 'nostalgically investing in a place in which heterogeneity is contained and made safe, local color literature has in the past created an imagined community, a nation that need never fully recognize its racist present' (62–3). Her essay suggests that 'our ways of representing regional identity have been inextricably caught up in the construction of national and racial identities' (67), and though her conclusions are largely drawn from the study of the literary south, it is obvious that her remarks apply equally to other regional literatures. Keillor distances himself from such constructions of regional and national identities; by creating a rich intertextual web, he foregrounds the artifice and artificiality involved in identity construction. By uprooting his characters and taking them to Rome, he is better able to point up their whiteness, the mid-western Americanness and their insularity; qualities that would have been invisible in the more familiar setting of Lake Wobegon.

To study the work of an author so closely associated with regional literature is also to ask questions about a sense of place, and about the meaning of regionalism in the age of globalization. Krista Comer asks, '[h]ow might we in regional studies pursue *post*national thinking?' (116). She goes on to discuss Judith Freeman's *The Chinchilla Farm* (1989), arguing that its feminist re-appropriation of male Western regional convention allows the author to point up the global in the local. Borrowing her terminology from James Clifford, Comer concludes that the novel reminds us that 'roots' come from 'routes': that '[r]egional identities do not exist . . . before they encounter "others" against whom they define themselves' (12). This point will be taken up further in Part 3 of this study, but it also has a place here: the regional identities of the Minnesotan pilgrims can more easily be appreciated as comic constructs when placed against a background that renders their familiar homeliness suddenly quaint, provincial and obsolete. However, to argue this point is not to concede that Keillor has somehow rejected the characters he has always treated with fondness and respect.

Rather, *Pilgrims* demonstrates that even though an authentic regionalism may no longer be a viable concept, an inauthentic one is just as good. This point has been made in sociological research that has sought to understand the meaning of regional identity in an age where hardly anyone stays put. Wendy Griswold and Nathan Wright argue that a 'dynamic social context' produced by the movement of people, money and culture, 'far from chipping away at enduring regionalism, actually produces it' (1421). They conclude that 'regional culture endures in America, despite mobility, despite homogenization, despite electronic media, despite swatches of sprawl, despite globalization, and despite the peculiarities of each region' (1443). Their findings are further qualified by the observation that under such conditions, regionalism is not 'authentic'. It is, they write, 'indeed a hybrid, . . . a product of movement, a result of dynamic rather than static populations' (1443–4). *Pilgrims* is such a hybrid; it is a regional novel, but it makes no claim to authenticity. When Margie first receives the phone call from the Italian daughter of August Norlander, she thinks of her as a mythical creature, belonging to two worlds that are incompatible: 'Roman woman half Minnesotan. A sort of mermaid' (41), she muses, and the image of the mermaid perfectly captures the sense of hybridity and the rejection of authenticity that become such important features of this novel.

Keillor's novel takes the familiar characters of Lake Wobegon and transports them to the unfamiliar cityscapes of Rome, where they travel in order to restore the neglected grave of a World War II soldier. Keillor's usual brand of humour is once again evident in this book, further amplified through intertextual references ranging from Chaucer to Henry James. In addition to telling the story of a hapless group of 'pilgrims' from the new world encountering the mystifying ways of the old one, the narrative also tells the story of a female subject transformed by the experience. Keillor playfully acknowledges the uses and limitations of stereotypical images of Italy, and he explores his American tourist as gendered and ethnic subject transformed through the experience of travel. Travel is viewed in its traditional sense as a form of education and an opportunity for personal growth, but is also explored for the comic potential of the loosening of inhibitions that often accompanies the American tourist coming in contact with Europe.

While Amy Tan used the title concept of saving fish from drowning to think about the place and the role of the US in the world today, Keillor chooses the title *Pilgrims* with similar parodic intent. A pilgrimage will normally involve as its destination a specific place associated with a person or event; it will produce a deepening of one's faith through the undertaking of such a journey, and the journey will largely be institutionalized and prescribed. The site in this case, is not simply the city of Rome, but more specifically, the grave of an American soldier. More to the point, this is a much-mythologized soldier whose story is told to schoolchildren and who is set up as representative of the US's role in the war. In undertaking to find the untended grave and restore to it the dignity and recognition it is thought to deserve, the 'pilgrims' essentially undertake a journey aimed at glorifying US military actions, and a journey that aims to reinforce the dominant ideology of the American soldier as an agent of liberation, a force for good. The journey is not designed to produce spiritual enlightenment, but to strengthen faith in the country's military might and the righteousness of its position. This pilgrimage is neither prescribed nor institutionalized in any conventional sense; however, it partakes of the educational and aspirational values of the grand tour that saw American travellers come to Europe in search of culture, refinement and education.

The pilgrims go to Italy to tend the grave of an American soldier, but it take days before they get around to fulfilling their mission. Having arrived in Rome, their traveller's excitement has overtaken their sense of patriotic duty. As they wander around Rome trying to take in its sounds, smells, sights and tastes, their own provincialism is thrown into relief. As William Merrill Decker has noted, America's involvement in the two World Wars 'diminished the American's sense of cultural inferiority. . . . A heroic self-regard encouraged Americans to look upon the world . . . as theirs to possess' (Bendixen 136). Culturally, the US emerged from World War II with a feeling of superiority; where once an American might have suffered from cultural inferiority complex, now they could hold their heads up high and remind their European cousins that they liberated them and helped preserve their culture. The story of the restoration of the grave plays upon and subverts this perception by exposing the lack of authenticity of this particular story of American heroism. It turns out that August Norlander was no hero. He had an affair, he fathered a child, and he died an accidental and undignified death rather than dying heroically in battle. While the US's role as heroic liberator is undermined through Norlander's story, Italy itself affords a different kind of liberation. Throughout their stay in Rome, all the pilgrims tell an important story and make a confession about themselves. Travel appears to produce a temporary suspension of the ordinary rules of behaviour within the group, and Italy seems to enable them to loosen their inhibitions.

Pilgrims is subtitled 'A Lake Wobegon Romance'; the word romance serves to highlight the light-heartedness of the book, and its theme of marital love, but it also has another function: it inevitably calls to mind Hawthorne's Romances. *The Marble Faun* may be the most relevant because of its Italian setting, but Hawthorne's views on the romance more generally are also useful here. In his famous Preface to *The Marble Faun*, Hawthorne wrote of the difficulty of being an American author, living in a land of 'commonplace prosperity' and trying to compose a romance in a land of 'no shadow, no antiquity, no mystery, no picturesque and gloomy wrong' (4). Keillor comically juxtaposes the complex moral universe of Rome with the direct simplicity of the mid-westerners, but like Hawthorne, he does not write *about* Italy. Hawthorne acknowledged that 'a foreigner seldom acquires that knowledge of a country at once flexible and profound, which may justify him in endeavoring to idealize its traits' (4). The romance, Hawthorne further explained in the 'Custom-House,' afforded the author more freedom by laying no claim to a faithful representation of reality, leaving him free to accentuate, amplify or dim certain aspects of the 'real' world, creating a space 'somewhere between the real world and fairyland, where the Actual and the Imaginary may meet' (28). While clearly useful to an author interested in the possibilities of the symbolic, this strategy, applied to *The Marble Faun*, freed Hawthrone from the obligation to represent Italy in faithful or meticulous detail. That impulse in fiction to describe foreign locales in minute, historically accurate detail is also mocked by Mark Twain in his 'Whisper to the Reader' at the start of *Pudd'nhead Wilson*. He writes of his friend William Hicks who helped him with the legal aspects of the case the book deals with and who now lives in a shed

> which is up the back alley as you turn around the corner out of the Piazza del Duomo just beyond the house where that stone that Dante used to sit on six hundred years ago is let into the wall when he let on to be watching them build Giotto's campanile and yet always got tired looking as soon as Beatrice passed along on her way to get a chink of chestnut cake to defend herself with in case of a Ghibelline outbreak before she got to school, at the same old stand where they sell the same old cake to this day and it is just as light and good as it was then, too, and this is not flattery, far from it. (v)

This delightfully parodic passage reminds us that demands for authentic travelling experiences are not new, and that some kind of obligation on the author's part faithfully to represent foreign lands has long been with us. Additionally, the Twain passage highlights another aspect of the American journey to Europe: all too often, such a journey is imagined as a journey to the source. Where Umberto Eco and Jean Baudrillard see in travel from Europe to America a journey from the real to the hyper-real (see Holland 161), the American conversely conceives of the journey to Europe as a return to authenticity, to a place where history comes to life, where notable people really lived and notable buildings were really erected.

Keillor mocks this impulse by weaving into his novel references to fictional and mythical places that highlight the ways in which every culture builds stereotypical images of another country. Margie is partly inspired to organize this trip through her reading of *O Paradiso*, the memoir of a Minnesota farmwife who finds a new lust for life after her husband dies and she moves to Italy. The success of books such as Elizabeth Gilbert's memoir *Eat, Pray, Love: One Woman's Search for Everything Across Italy, India and Indonesia* (2006) clearly demonstrates that there is a large market for the type of book that imagines the female subject's journey to emancipation and emotional peace in terms of an 'educational,' self-improving journey through the world, but Keillor's comic juxtaposition of the mundane represented by the Minnesotan farmer's wife and the sophisticated exoticism of the title *O Paradiso* betrays his parodic intent and serves as a knowing nod to the reader of this story about a frustrated Minnesotan wife. The author of *O Paradiso* describes her transformation by employing a series of stereotypes associated with Italy: 'I got to Rome and learned to live with gusto and express joy and grief, to dance with my arms in the air, to throw my head back and laugh, to frankly explore my own passions and desires' (28), and it is this Italy, the one constructed through the American imagination, that Margie hopes will help to rekindle the passion in her marriage. Further references to Paradise serve to promote the idea of Italy as a kind of paradise for the repressed American who would like her horizons broadened, while they also continue to highlight the ways in which Italy has been constructed and promoted for the tourist market. In Rome, Margie meets a handsome stranger, Paolo, who invites her for tea in his hotel room. The hotel is called Il Paradiso, but it is a false paradise, because Paolo turns out to be a con man, trying to extract money from Margie in league with Maria.

The references to Italy as Paradise punctuate the narrative and draw attention to the creation of national myths, but the notion of Italy as paradise is also inverted. Maria, the American soldier's Italian daughter, speaks of growing up hearing stories of her late father's homeland. In her imagination, she has reconstructed Lake Wobegon as her 'El Dorado,' her *'paradiso'* (66). In one of the novel's funniest passages, Maria goes on to describe her imagined Wobegon as a place where 'everybody was full of love and sunshine and told jokes and poured syrup over their cakes and danced the hopping dance'. Her description becomes increasingly fantastical as she goes on to talk of 'Big fish the size of trucks leaping from the water . . . enormous pumpkins that people carve doors and windows in and live inside.' When she comes to the description of birds 'who make a wild warbling sound like a woman crying,' Marge interrupts her: 'They're called loons,' she remarks coolly. 'And they're real?' comes Maria's response (66–7). This seamless blend of the outrageous (people living inside giant pumpkins) and the real (the loons in the lake) shows Margie how her own hometown can be re-imagined by an outsider, and invested with the same mythical aura that she associates with Italy.

Margie's romantic image of Rome comes not only from *O Paradiso* but also from her favourite movie, *Roman Holiday*. Margie carries with her images of Audrey Hepburn and Gregory Peck on a Vespa, 'buzzing through the ancient streets and around the stone-paved piazzas.' She associates the film with the 'love of life. *La dolce vita*. Buoyant personalities, high-wattage conversations with big gestures, the spirit of carnival and dancing in the streets and the frank enjoyment of the flesh' (44). The spirit of carnival that Margie associates with Italy is the opposite of what she has been raised to expect from life. Margie recalls her mother advising her that life 'is what it is. People want to make it into a carnival and it just isn't' (146). Margie has spent her adult life being the stoical, practical person her mother had wanted her to be, but now 'Margie thought that there was something to be said for carnival going' (146). The potential that carnival holds to free a person of their inhibitions and release their suppressed desires has been explored elsewhere in American literature, most notably and provocatively by Robert Coover in *Pinocchio in Venice* (1991) where the distinguished American professor undergoes a carnivalesque, grotesque transformation from model of industry and civility to an uninhibited, mischievous Pinocchio. Like Keillor, Coover was aware of the constructions of Italy as the antithesis of the puritanical American, and even though his technique and subject-matter rendered the novel an experimental curiosity read and admired by few, it nevertheless expressed cultural anxieties and desires that were common currency in American culture.

Margie emerges from her first encounter with Paolo feeling 'a new woman.' 'Buried all her life in Lake Wobegon, now she had (sort of) shacked up with a man she'd just met—sat on his bed and let him touch her in the Hotel Paradiso' (165). She imagines staying in Italy forever, forging a new identity and a new life for herself, much like the Minnesotan farmer's wife in *O Paradiso*. She further ponders what the Audrey Hepburn character from *Roman Holiday* would have done in her place, and concludes that she would have acted in the same way. Striving to find an image to describe her awakening, Margie thinks that '[s]he'd had the meat loaf and gravy and now someone offered her the shrimp appetizer and the spring roll and the wonton soup' (184). Margie doesn't choose an example from Italian cuisine to complete her analogy, but no matter: one exotic dish serves just as well as another to highlight the boring predictability of meat loaf and gravy.

Margie's inability to think beyond stereotype and cliché provides a lot of the comic material in the novel, but we don't necessarily laugh *at* her, because she has control over her cultural references, her chosen intertext. At the same time, though, she is a character in a novel driven by another intertextual presence, one to which she is oblivious: the story of what happens to her in Rome is clearly modelled on *The Wings of the Dove*.

The plot of *Pilgrims* features an American heiress who is tricked out of her large fortune by two scheming lovers (in this case Italians).[1] The man seduces her and the woman offers her friendship, and Margie falls for their plot and only realizes she has been deceived when she returns to America at the end of the novel. However, the book ends happily for Margie in a way that figuratively and playfully celebrates the triumph of provincialism over the forces of globalization. The Italian con involves Margie being enticed to buy an apartment. Capital can move freely in a global economy, and all she has to do is instruct her bank to transfer the money over to Italy. By the time she finds out she has been tricked, she assumes that the money has been transferred with the speed that one imagines money travels these days. However, she then receives an unexpected phone call. Rather than being contacted through a remote and anonymous call centre, she is greeted by a bank employee she has already met at her local branch who explains he has not yet sent the money to Rome because she had not specified a delivery date. He explains that he was reluctant to send such a large amount of money without further confirmation from her, preferring to be 'safe than sorry' (285). Thus, the triumph of the plot is not just the triumph of the simple, honest American over her sophisticated seducers, but also the triumph of the small, local branch of the bank over global capitalism and technology. Margie goes on to send Maria 50,000 dollars along with a note thanking her for the 'invaluable' experience (286), thus acknowledging that despite being the victim of deception, she is also a winner because she has reached a new level of self-knowledge and self-realization. Michael R. Martin reads *The Wings of the Dove* as a novel that exposes 'how capital shapes the possibilities of human self-realization within the urban spaces of modernity' (105), and in its own comic way *Pilgrims* updates that notion. It retains the central idea of the connection between money and self-realization (further amplified through a sub-plot in which 'Garrison Keillor' accidentally offers to pay for the whole town to travel to Italy), but it also transforms the urban spaces of modernity into the non-spaces of post-modernity. From the inconveniences and the practicalities of air travel, to the central plot device of personal banking, the novel examines the gaps and ruptures in our narratives of postmodern hyper-, virtual- or non-space. Plane journeys do not abolish space: they are long and boring. Emails from the Roman bank remain unanswered until Stan Larson has had a chance to make an old-fashioned phone call to his client. In other words, the local persists and has not been bulldozed by the global.

Where the novel makes a significant contribution to our understanding of American engagements with the global is in highlighting the ways in which local, regional identities are neither autochthonous nor insular. The novel shows the Lake Wobegoners to be just as made-up and culturally constructed as the stereotypical scheming Italians, while nationality itself is a commodity that can be bought and sold. The con involves Maria convincing Margie to buy an apartment for half a million dollars. The apartment in question, Maria claims, is in a building that used to be the hotel where she was conceived. It is therefore sold to Margie not only as representing the dream of emancipation and freedom from a life of mundane drudgery back home, but also for its nostalgic associations with the past through the dead American soldier. When Margie finally agrees to buy the property, Maria embraces her and says 'now—you are a Roman. One of us' (255). Maria's easy equation of home-ownership with national belonging underscores the importance of capitalism in the construction of ethnicity by suggesting that you can buy your way into a country, a culture, or a way of life. Her rejection of authenticity may be cynical, but it teaches Margie an important lesson about who she is and where she belongs.

Pilgrims and *Saving Fish from Drowning* share an unusual feature: they both have two endings. One is comical and in keeping with the light-heartedness of the plot, the other much darker. Tan's American travellers mostly find happiness in their lives, and their earlier entanglements and misunderstandings are happily resolved, while the mystery of Bibi's death is also cleared up. The Lord's Army, on the other hand, does not fare so well. They jump into a swollen river, pursued by their enemies, and all we know is that they are now 'Somewhere Else,' a split that divides Life from Death (440). Margie forgives Maria, inherits the money, and uses it to save her husband from his financial troubles. At the same time though, the person who had started out so full of hope and dreams of *Roman Holiday*-type adventures concludes that the potential of travel to transform the individual is over-stated. 'Nothing changes . . . You go to Rome for the experience of a lifetime and then it's time to go home and put in the tomatoes,' she muses near the end of the novel (238). That sense of disappointment and anti-climax is one that we find in Eggers's and Foer's novels in the next chapter. Like the novels discussed here, *You Shall Know Our Velocity* and *Everything Is Illuminated* do not just thematize travel abroad. They also position themselves at the crossroads where regional literature meets globalization, and where teleological stories of immigration to the US are rendered obsolete by modern technologies and patterns of migration. They also take up the idea of the journey as pilgrimage and as a kind of sentimental education, and in many ways offer a twenty-first century version of the grand tour.

4 Jonathan Safran Foer, *Everything Is Illuminated*; Dave Eggers, *You Shall Know Our Velocity*

DAVE EGGERS, *YOU SHALL KNOW OUR VELOCITY*

In *You Shall Know Our Velocity*, Will and Hand's adventures are driven by their desire to give money away and to grieve for a lost friend, but the broader picture that emerges from their story is one of an Americanized, homogenized world in which escape may no longer be an option, because the US is ever-present wherever they go. Still, in the spirit of old-fashioned travel, Will and Hand do learn lessons from their journey, but what prompts them to reflect and learn is not the difference they encounter, but rather the degree to which difference is disappearing in a shrinking world. Sixteen years before Eggers wrote his novel, Jean Baudrillard wrote in *America* that '[i]n reality, you do not, as I had hoped, get any distance on Europe from here [America]. You do not acquire a fresh angle on it. When you turn around, it has quite simply disappeared' (29). Eggers's novel powerfully demonstrates that, unlike Baudrillard's vanishing Europe, the US is omnipresent when an American goes abroad; everything from the language people speak and the goods they consume to the houses they live in and the land that surrounds them bears the imprint of the US's domination of the world, both in real political, economic and cultural terms and in terms of other countries' *imagined* relation to the US. In such circumstances, the very idea of travel as education for a young American is necessarily altered. Rather than being exposed to instances of otherness which either reinforce one's sense of superiority or provide aspirational and inspirational models, Will and Hand see images of their own country, and learn what lessons they learn through an encounter with sameness as much as difference.

The purpose of their trip is two-fold: Will and his friend Hand want to give away Will's 80,000 dollar windfall, but as the narrative unfolds it becomes clear that they are also travelling in order to cope with bereavement following the accidental death of their best friend Jack. Travel, then, becomes a means of escape from their feelings. They hope to leave their grieving selves behind, and they subscribe to the notion that travel allows one to 'get away from it all'; that by immersing themselves into other cultures, they will lessen the pain associated with their hometown of Chicago.

But what if the world you escape to is no different to the one you leave behind? Will and Hand find too many similarities between the world they leave behind and the worlds they encounter, so at some point they realize that the escape they had hoped for is not really possible. However, this is not to say they do not derive a degree of comfort from their travel. Their journey does turn out to have healing potential, and that comes from their developing sense of connectedness. Will and Hand start out their journey as two isolated figures whose money-giving mission places them on an unequal footing with the people they meet. Gradually, though, as they hear other stories and interact with people who dress like them, eat the same food as them, and speak the same language as them, while also telling them stories of different lives, they begin to develop a sense of travel as an expanding web that connects those disparate individuals. If this realization verges on the sentimental or the naïve, it is also undermined from the very beginning of the narrative, where we find out, as we do in Tan's novel, that our narrator is already dead.

The story concerning Will's money is one that indirectly allows Eggers to pose questions about his country's financial relations with the rest of the world. Will considers the money ill-gotten, since he earned it for posing for a commercial drawing rather than for doing any 'real' work, and that appears to be his main motivation for giving it away. Will therefore combines an American work ethic with a typically American philanthropic impulse, and in this sense he can be seen as representative of his country's dominant ethos: a celebration of hard-earned money, and an often misguided attempt to help the less fortunate; to save, perhaps, some more fish from drowning. However, his ill-conceived—and, as it turns out, rather badly executed—scheme is neither entirely philanthropic nor driven by a genuine belief in America's role as benefactor. At the same time, neither is it driven by a Marxist desire to undermine the American ethos of capitalist gain by re-distributing wealth, and it is precisely this ambiguity of purpose that allows Eggers to raise questions about how America 'pays for the world' (71), as a French sailor in Dakar puts it to the two friends.

You Shall Know Our Velocity borrows from the genres of the road novel and the Bildungsroman and creates a parodic twenty-first century version of the Grand Tour. In keeping with generic conventions, the two main characters learn a lot about themselves and their place in the world as Americans and as individuals, but their overall experience is one of displacement and dislocation. Instead of progressing through a teleological, paced journey (real and metaphorical) to knowledge, refinement or maturity, they get caught up in a fast-paced itinerary directed by air ticket availability, flight connections and the demands of work back home. Unlike the fictional road trip or the Grand Tour, Will and Hand's journey is characterized by its urgency and short duration. This paucity of leisure time is contrasted effectively in the novel with the perception that modern travel annihilates distance and makes the rest of the world almost instantly accessible to an

American. Even though Hand can only take one week off work, the two friends' initial plan is to make a round the world trip in seven days. Soon, however, it becomes clear that this isn't as easy as they had imagined. Crossing time zones means that they will get less than a whole week, while visa requirements make some countries out of bounds; but most worryingly they soon find out that not every country is connected to every other country they want to visit: 'nothing from Greenland to Rwanda,' says Will as they're planning their plane reservations. 'Why wouldn't there be a flight from Greenland to Rwanda? Almost everything, even Rwanda to Madagascar, had to go through some place like Paris or London' (8). When eventually they make it to Senegal, they come across the same problem: 'Online we checked planes leaving from Dakar. Nothing, almost nothing, without Paris first. . . . Could we just drive from Dakar to Cairo? We couldn't' (51). At this point, the narrator loses his patience:

> This was fucked up. Why wouldn't there be planes going from Senegal to Mongolia? I'd always assumed, vaguely, that the rest of the world was even better connected than the US, that passage between all countries outside of America was constant and easy—that all other nations were huddled together, trading information and commiserating, like smokers outside a building. (52)

Will's formulation perpetuates the familiar American notion of the US as 'not other' and the rest of the world as 'other,' but the novel suggests that the rest of the world, this 'not America,' is a complex geo-political entity formed by historical forces the narrator does not fully comprehend. That every flight out of Senegal has to go via Paris is of course the legacy of French imperialism, while the people outside America do turn out to be 'huddled together,' but not for the reasons the narrator had supposed. Though often united in their dislike for American expansionism, they are at the same time brought together by their ability to communicate in English, use computers, and find common cultural referents that more often than not relate to American popular culture. The arrogance implicit in Will's outburst serves to parody the image of the American as rightful beneficiary of the whole project of modernity; it pokes fun at the notion that all the struggles for democracy, independence, freedom and self-rule have existed for the benefit and comfort of the American tourist.

There is further evidence that Will is ignorant of the historical forces that have shaped the modern world and have determined which airports serve as hubs or stopovers. The book he takes on his travels is a biography of Winston Churchill; a book, in other words, associated with WWII history. Because the book is very big and Will wishes to travel light, he tears out the first 200 pages he has already read before the start of the trip, and also the last three hundred, presumably because he knows he will not have the time to read them. Both the vandalism of tearing up a book and the symbolism of an incomplete book of history become symbols of the two friends' incomplete experience of the world they encounter, and their limited understanding of the forces that shape it; they are travelling light in more ways than one.

Their first destination, Dakar in Senegal, is an early lesson in displacement: the airport is likened to a shopping mall. On the way to the hotel, on a road busy with BMWs, they pass what Will describes as 'condos next to shanties, the condos given ears by hundreds of small satellite dishes' (45). Their hotel, described as 'cool, safe, immaculate,' (47) is the kind of generic hotel that could exist almost anywhere. They go to an Italian restaurant where they eat fettuccine and sip Senegalese beer while listening to pop music, and they seem not at all surprised by that. This image of Africa painted at the beginning of the twenty-first century could not be further from Joseph Conrad's images of primeval forests and dream-like, unearthly landscapes. Yet the two images are far from unrelated, since the capitalist project that fuelled the ideology of colonial expansion in the nineteenth century is not to be separated from the market forces that brought satellite dishes, cell phones, BMWs and pop music to Africa. To the Western reader, the world that Will and Hand encounter in Dakar is as confusing and disorienting as Conrad's Africa, but not because of its difference, but because of its sameness. They appear to be able to get on with their lives exactly as they would have done back home, only in hotter and sunnier surroundings. In addition, the narrator's blasé attitude suggests that for a younger generation global sameness is no longer surprising, but rather the norm. As their travels continue, the two friends find that Tunisia looks like the Balkans, Casablanca resembles Chicago's North Side, and Marrakesh could be Arizona. 'Growing up,' says Will, 'I thought all countries looked, were required to look, completely different. . . . But every country now seemed to offer a little of every other country, and every given landscape, I finally realized, existed somewhere in the U.S.' (253). Even though this passage makes the point that every *landscape* exists in the US, Will and Hand's experience of Europe and Africa highlights the ways in which American cultural and financial imperialism is homogenizing the world.

The people they meet on their journey also reinforce the notion of displacement, allowing the author to ask questions pertaining to national identity, politics and history. In Dakar, they meet a Chilean with a house in Florida, who tells them that Star Trek can be read as a paradigm for American foreign policy during the Cold War. Here is a minor character who makes a brief appearance, and yet manages to introduce into the novel, and to the minds of the two travellers, a host of issues relating to nationality and belonging. Also in Dakar, they meet two refugees from Sierra Leone. In Morocco, they meet a French woman. In Latvia, they meet Russians. At Heathrow airport, they buy a guide book from a Pakistani clerk, and they eat at an Irish diner staffed by a Dutch waitress, a Swedish busboy, and a Korean bartender. These experiences seem to confirm Will's earlier theory that the rest of the world, the non-US, is better connected. However, that connection is not what he had expected it to be in that citizenship, ethnicity, nationality and migration all turn out to be shifting concepts that challenge and destabilise Will's notions of identity and belonging. In dominant American ideology, ethnicity and nationality may be defined according to the competing theories of the melting pot or the salad bowl or the mosaic, but all these different models share the assumption (in the dual sense of the word) of an American identity. In Europe, Africa and the former Soviet Union, Will and Hand are challenged to accept a different model of ethnicity that relates to forced migration, persecution and shifting borders, as well as the free movement of citizens of the European Union. The difference of the American model of understanding ethnicity is also highlighted through references to the two main characters' own origins. When Hand points out that Will is a Pole, Will replies that he's a 'fourth Polish,' but it 'might have been less. It was my father's name, which diminished my attachment to it, to its origins' (294). Similarly, when Will points out to Hand that he ought to be able to speak French because his father is French, Hand replies, 'Not, like, *from France*' (48). These two examples show that for white, young Americans ethnicity can be a take-it-or-leave-it affair; a question of choosing and emphasizing or de-emphasizing one's origins. The reverse position is seen when Will and Hand meet people from other countries and cultures whose priority is not to construct an American(ized) identity.

In Estonia, Will and Hand pick up Taavi, a hitchhiker on his way to Tallinn. He is dressed in a generic uniform of jeans and black jacket with rock group patches sewn on the breast, and he introduces himself as the drummer of a rock band. Will wants Taavi to tell them about Soviet tanks, revolts, riots and underground resistance, but Taavi is much keener to talk about making music, hiring recording studios, and drinking vodka with his friends. The narrator concludes: 'That Taavi Mets seemed in every way someone we knew in high school was a natural thing and a reductive and unfortunate thing—or maybe this was good. What did we want? We want the world smaller and bigger and just the same but advancing. We don't know what we want' (273). Will's, and Eggers's, inconclusive reaction to the Americanized Taavi echoes Fredric Jameson's views on globalisation. Jameson claims that 'one can deplore globalization or celebrate it, just as one welcomes the new freedoms of the postmodern era and the postmodern outlook . . . , or on the other hand, elegiacally laments the passing of the splendors of the modern' (Jameson 1998 55). Jameson goes on to note that one of the most significant aspects of globalization is 'the sense in which globalization means the export and import of culture' (58), but he makes the point that there is no balance or symmetry in this exchange, since the US has a disproportionate influence on the rest of the world, both linguistically and culturally. Responding to those who would claim that at the level of culture globalisation is a force for good because it encourages 'the proliferation of new cultures,' Jameson argues that this argument lacks 'economic specificity' and more importantly, 'is rather inconsistent with the quality and impoverishment of what has to be called corporate culture on a global scale' (66). Of course, the difference between a philosophical enquiry into the effects of globalisation and a novel is that the latter concerns itself with the private sphere and the diversity of individual characters. Taavi's Americanized frame of reference may be a 'reductive and unfortunate thing' when viewed as symptom of a global phenomenon, yet on a private and intimate level it allows a connection between him and the two Americans that might otherwise not have been possible. More generally, the novel engages with questions similar to the ones that Jameson poses, but it links Will and Hand's discovery of the effects of globalisation and post-national identities with the private story of their grief and loss. Will notes that in escaping Chicago and travelling abroad, he and Hand are looking for connectedness:

> [W]hen we landed in Estonia, or any of those other places, there was nothing, of course, no one waiting, and no one wanting us there, no one needing us. There wasn't one thread connecting us to anyone and we had to start threading, I guess, or else it would be just us, without any trail or web and if it was just us, ghosts, irrelevant and unbound. . . . Then there was something wrong. (303)

It is ultimately this realization that concludes the hero's education on his Grand Tour and enables him to come to terms with his grief; he reaffirms his commitment to the present and the living through his idea of threading or connectedness. If this version of globalization is too cheerfully optimistic or reductive, it is counter-balanced by the novel's genuine and complex engagement with issues of identity, and also by the narrator's death: Will begins his narrative by announcing on the book cover his death in a burning ferry 'with forty-two locals we hadn't yet met,' thus putting an end to his quest for connectedness.

In *You Shall Know Our Velocity*, Will tells of his encounter with a 'busboy' and a 'bartender' at Heathrow airport. These words are not used in British English, but Will does not seem to be aware of the fact, just as he does not seem to realize that the word 'condo,' used to describe the buildings in Dakar, sounds peculiarly American to other English speakers. By assigning names familiar from his own culture, Will is translating and making sense of the new and the different, but at the same time he is seen to be either unwilling or unable to recognise difference. In this, he is perhaps closer to Pratt's imperial traveller, for whom the worlds he encounters are there for him to colonise, linguistically and culturally. However, the assumed superiority that his naming implies is counter-pointed by his genuine amazement that English is spoken everywhere. Will, at least, is aware of his shortcomings. He is amazed that everywhere they travel most people's English is 'seamless.' 'I had sixty words of Spanish and Hand had maybe twice that in French, and that was it. How had this happened? Everyone in the world knew more than us, about everything and this I hated then found hugely comforting' (220).

Will is also deeply embarrassed when Hand speaks in broken English to non-native speakers. In Dakar, he communicates in what Will identifies as a Senegalese accent which was 'almost a British accent, but then a slower version, with him nodding a lot' (48). Why then would Will take comfort in Hand's condescending attitude, or in his own realisation that the rest of the world knows more than he does? It could be due, in part, to a sense of guilt: if the two travellers to some extent feel they are becoming ambassadors for their country, then some of the hostility they can expect to encounter by those suspicious of America's foreign policies can at least be mitigated by a relative ignorance which renders them harmless and blameless. It could also be that there is comfort to be had in a world that conforms to stereotypes and preconceptions: the sophisticated, cosmopolitan, multilingual inhabitants are the other to the American traveller who knows little and cares even less about the rest of the world, and even if by accepting this simplification Will has to concede his own inferiority, he can at least draw comfort from a world in which stereotypes are reinforced rather than challenged. To Eggers's credit, if communication in broken English is used for comic effect, it is always at the Americans' expense, which as we shall see is not always the case in Foer's novel.

Questions about the construction of identity and space, and about geographical and historical accuracy, preoccupy Will and Hand on their travels. When Hand is surprised to find that Morocco is not all desert, Will remarks that this 'demonstrated the great gaps in knowledge that occur when one gets most of one's information from the internet' (162). And when Taavi gives them a version of life in Estonia that does not tally with what their guidebook says, they are upset: 'Nothing was true. Nothing in the guidebook was true but the maps. Are maps true? Nothing else was true. The word *fact* could not exist. All facts changed on the way to the printer' (271–2). Theories of the post-national and of globalization may well describe a changed world, but *Everything is Illuminated* and *You Shall Know Our Velocity* demonstrate that for individuals who are 'nothing special at all' these changes have not yet altered the older categories and concepts of ordering and making sense of the world.

In *Postmodernism, or, The Cultural Logic of Late Capitalism*, Fredric Jameson prefaces his discussion of the Westin Bonaventure Hotel in Los Angeles with the following observation:

> My implication is that we ourselves, the human subjects who happen into this new space, have not kept pace with that evolution; there has been a mutation in the object unaccompanied as yet by any equivalent mutation in the subject. We do not yet possess the perceptual equipment to match this new hyperspace, as I will call it, in part because our

perceptual habits were formed in that older kind of space I have called the space of high modernism. (38–9)

Jameson's remarks on postmodern architecture apply equally to the experience of globalisation as investigated by the two novels. Ideas about language, the notion of identity being tied to space and borders, and the conflation of history with geographical space are concepts that the characters in the two novels find it hard to abandon, even as the new space around them suggests to them that the world has moved on. This notion is also exemplified in Hand's fascination with quantum physics. He tells Will about 'this guy named Deutch' who argues that 'everything exists in a bunch of places at once. We're all made of the same electrons and protons, right, so if they exist in many places at once, and can be teleported, then there's gotta be multiple us's, and multiple worlds, simultaneously' (111). In reality, what Will and Hand encounter is not so much multiple selves and multiple worlds, but rather a sameness that they cannot fully comprehend or describe. Ultimately, the travellers are disappointed because the world they encounter does not live up to their expectations of discovery, escape, adventure or wonder. Will and Hand cross the Atlantic only to meet people very much like them, while Jonathan, as we shall see next, returns from Ukraine having failed to find the place and the people who in his imagination made up his grandfather's past. Instead of learning more about his own family, he comes home having learned the terrible secret of Alex's Ukrainian grandfather. For his part, Alex gives up on his dream of emigrating to America, and stays home to look after his family.

Finally, the enigmatic title of the novel turns out to be related to notions of travel and space. Eggers's title comes from a story that the Chilean Raymond has told Hand about his ancestors, people who believed in

> the impermanence of place.... They had a curiosity about place, knew there were other places to go, and so when these guys [the Spanish conquistadors] are after their land, they're not thrilled about it, but they also don't feel like they own it or anything either, so ... They moved on. They kept moving. There was a lot to see. (326)

Before moving on, they leave a message behind for the conquistadors, which reads 'YOU SHALL KNOW OUR VELOCITY'—a message that brings together the ideas of space, movement and importantly, change. When the real Jonathan Safran Foer's grandfather fled the Nazis, his village was in Poland and not Ukraine. When these two novels were published, Latvia, Estonia and Ukraine would best be described as former Soviet republics. Today, Latvia and Estonia can properly be described as European countries by virtue of their admittance into the EU. Ukraine has had its Orange Revolution and will be looking to strengthen its ties with the West. Maps and affiliations change all too quickly, so that maps and guide books can no longer aid the traveller. As Will would have it, 'All facts changed on the way to the printer' (272).

JONATHAN SAFRAN FOER, *EVERYTHING IS ILLUMINATED*

In Riga, Will and Hand come across a Jewish Museum. 'I didn't think there were any left here', remarks Hand. 'The Germans killed every Jew in the Baltics. I thought so at least. . . . I could never walk in that place. Can you imagine coming back here? Being Jewish and coming back here? Fuck. No way' (313). Whereas Hand cannot imagine why an American Jew would want to return to a scene of trauma in Europe, Jonathan Safran Foer's *Everything Is Illuminated*, published in the same year as Eggers's novel, concerns itself precisely with the kind of journey that Hand finds so shocking. The semi-autobiographical novel tells the story of Jonathan Safran Foer, a young Jewish American who travels to Ukraine in search of Augustine, the woman who saved his grandfather from the Nazis. In dramatizing a personal search for family and identity, the novel also takes on the growing industries of dark tourism and heritage travel, both of which ultimately offer the American tourist an incomplete and at times distorted image of the US's relation to the countries they visit.

In his role as translator, Alex assumes the role of cultural mediator, but finds also that he cannot remain detached from the words he needs to translate. When it comes to translating an account of the annihilation of Trachimbrod by the Nazis, he feels uncomfortable: 'You cannot know how it felt to have to hear these things and then repeat them, because when I repeated them, I felt I was making them new again' (185). Yet ironically Alex is in the business of making these things new again. His father works for a tourist company called Heritage Touring, and here is Alex explaining the company's mission:

> It is for Jewish people, like the hero, who have cravings to leave that ennobled country America and visit humble towns in Poland and Ukraine. Father's agency scores a translator, guide, and driver for the Jews, who try to unearth places where their families once existed. . . . I will be truthful again and mention that before the voyage I had the opinion that Jewish people were having shit between their brains. This is because all I knew of Jewish people was that they paid Father very much currency in order to make vacations *from* America *to* Ukraine. (3)

Of course, what Alex does not realize until he meets Jonathan, and what the tourist company glosses over with its genteel name, is that those Jewish people make the journey to Ukraine not simply to find the places where their relatives once lived, but more specifically, and more traumatically, to re-visit the sites where their ancestors suffered the effects of Nazi persecution. Throughout the novel, Alex invests America with an almost mythical status, dreaming the typical immigrant dream of unlimited freedom and prosperity, but what he learns from Jonathan is that America is real, and therefore imperfect, while his own country, Ukraine, also carries connotations in Jewish American minds that seem as strange to him as Alex's America seems to Jonathan.

Heritage touring may be an entirely pleasurable experience involving journeys to Ireland or Scotland, for example, and opportunities to sample local food and drink, research the family tree, and return laden with souvenirs. However, heritage touring may be much more unsettling when it crosses over to the realm of 'dark tourism,' a term given currency by John Lennon and Malcolm Foley in their 2000 study *Dark Tourism: The Attraction of Death and Disaster.* Dark tourism describes travel to sites of suffering and death; these may be primary sites, such as Concentration Camps or Ground Zero, or secondary sites, such as Holocaust museums or slavery memorials. It is a sad reflection of the history of the past couple of centuries that in the case of Jewish American and African American travellers, heritage and dark tourism more or less coincide. Though in literary studies this area remains underdeveloped, it is a rewarding way of understanding constructions of ethnic and racial identities in the US, and of illuminating transatlantic imaginings and the forces of history and ideology that underpin them. In 'Transatlantic Dreaming: Slavery, Tourism, and Diasporic Encounters,' Bayo Holsey discusses African Americans who 'return' to Africa in search of ancestors and more improbably living relatives as well. She uses the phrase 'fantasy trope of transatlantic reunion' (166) to refer to stories of African Americans who travel to Ghana to search for their roots and supposedly come across relatives they physically resemble. The reality is more likely to involve 'tension and misunderstanding' (167), she claims, because those with the means to travel abroad and the people they meet and claim as long-lost family 'occupy radically different positions within the global economy' (167). Her conclusions are very relevant to the main themes in Foer's novel:

> pilgrimages are contested by many local residents because the slave trade, as the diaspora's origin, occupies a marginalized and stigmatized place in public memory. Instead, for Ghanaians, these tourists conjure images of wealth and mobility that fuel their imaginations of homes elsewhere that they have little chance of ever experiencing. Thus, I argue that both African Americans and Ghanaians participate in simultaneous yet reverse imaginative processes or transatlantic dreamings that converge within sites of painful memories of slavery's past. This encounter provides an apt example of the 'power geometry' of late capitalism, which, as Massey notes, describes not only differential access to travel but also varying levels of control over the nature and meaning of that travel. (167)

A similar power dissymmetry exists between Jonathan in the novel and his Ukrainian guide, Alex, who dreams of emigrating to the US, which he imagines as a consumerist paradise. Further, Alex is ignorant of his country's involvement in the extermination of the Jews during WWII, and denies the possibility of such involvement when Jonathan refers to it as well-known historical fact.

Craig Wight and John Lennon have studied the memorialization of the holocaust in Lithuania and have concluded that 'the "dark" heritage landscape that exists in Lithuania is dominated by moral complexities surrounding the commemoration of the nation's tragic past' (528). Their research uncovers convincing evidence that Lithuanians are very reluctant to admit the existence of Nazi collaborators in their midst, and prefer to imagine and remember what happened as a Jewish tragedy rather than a Lithuanian one. Much of the interpretation, they write, 'points to Lithuanian Nazi collaborators including policemen, doctors and other professionals. It is this "real" interpretive setting that the manager believes may repel indigenous Lithuanian visitors, who may prefer to avoid any level of engagement with the issues presented.' (524). The evidence from the novel suggests that the Ukrainian Alex feels much the same way as the Lithuanians in Wight and Lennon's research. When Jonathan tells him what happened to his ancestors, Alex replies that surely their Ukrainian neighbours must have helped them. Not so, replies Jonathan. He goes on to upset his host and guide by pointing out to him that some of his fellow-countrymen were so hostile to the Jews that the latter actually felt safer around German Nazis than they did around some Ukrainians. Alex refuses to believe the story, claiming that it is not to be found in any history books. This early confrontation between the two young men becomes key to our understanding of the novel's symmetry. Jonathan does not find what he came to look for, but he does learn things about his grandfather's past. Alex did not set out to learn anything, and yet by the end of the novel he is the one who has learnt a bitter lesson about his country's history and about his own grandfather. The grandfather, who pretends to be blind and figuratively represents his own and his country's deliberate 'blindness' in relation to the past, turns out to have betrayed his best friend, a Jew, by pointing him out to the Nazis. This confirms Jonathan's point of view, and shocks Alex who was genuinely ignorant of his countrymen's involvement. In other words, though it is Jonathan who crosses the Atlantic in order to learn something about his past, it is Alex who never leaves his country who ends up learning something important.

Alex's ignorance of his own country's recent past is matched by Jonathan's complete lack of interest in Ukraine's present. Engaged in his monomaniac search for Augustine and Trachimbrod, he displays no curiosity and expresses no interest in the country he is visiting. In this, he is typical of the heritage tourist whose travel to another country is also an imaginative journey into the past. Paulla A. Ebron recounts the experience of taking a McDonald's (yes, *that* McDonald's)-sponsored tour to Senegal and the Gambia, and is struck by her fellow-travellers' lack of interest in contemporary African politics:

> we were on a pilgrimage to Africa. Such a journey takes place in mythical time; in this case, it involved a temporal displacement of the current moment in which the international representation of an actual place, Senegal, and contemporary African political culture could only be (at worst) a Eurocentric distortion and (at best) an irrelevant waste of time. (920)

Jonathan's trip is also one that takes place in 'mythical time;' the country he is visiting is of interest to him primarily as a container for his ancestors' past, rather than a modern country with its own history, politics and culture. The mythical qualities with which Jonathan invests Ukraine are further underscored by the magical-realist account of the shtetl that he is busy writing. Beginning in 1791 with the story of the founding of the shtetl in Trachimbrod, the narrative comes up to 1942, when the shtetl is bombed by the Nazis. Some of the stories of the generations from the late 18th century to the middle of the 20th are based on Jonathan's knowledge of his grandparents' past, but the narrative he produces is his own imaginative and often fantastical creation: a fiction of an imagined past, a made-up family history through which Jonathan attempts to find his own place in the world.

Two-thirds into the narrative, a woman who may or may not be Augustine gives Jonathan a box labelled IN CASE. Inside it lies a map of the world dated 1791. Alex, Jonathan's Ukrainian interpreter and narrator of the novel, is much taken with this find:

> 'This is a premium thing,' I said. A map such as that one is worth many hundreds, and as luck will have it, thousands of dollars. But more than this, it is a remembrance of that time before our planet was so small. When this map was made, I thought, you could live without knowing where you were not living. This made me think of Trachimbrod, and how Lista, the woman we desired so much to be Augustine, had not ever heard of America. It is possible that she is the last person on earth, I reasoned, who does not know about America. (223)

Geoff Ward has written that 'it is not entirely clear where America might be located. A glance at the atlas does indicate a sizeable chunk of the earth. More importantly, America's economic world-dominance . . . has made of it something monstrously ubiquitous' (11). His point about the ways in which America is dominating the world today is echoed in Alex's musings about the 1791 map, but Foer's novel reminds its readers that through its historical immigrant status, America itself shifts and changes shape in its interactions with the world. The main story of Foer's novel (for it contains two distinct narratives) is set in motion by Jonathan Safran Foer's decision to travel to Ukraine in search of his family's past. It is significant that we learn early on that his grandmother may have known some of the answers he is after, but never did tell: 'her memories of the Ukraine aren't good,' Jonathan explains. '[a]ll her family were killed, everyone, mother, father, sisters, grandparents' (61). For the young Jonathan, second generation immigrant, the trauma of the Holocaust resides in Europe, and he feels he must get there to find it. In this, Jonathan is typical rather than unique: he conceives of his family's wartime past in terms of actual geographical space, rather than imagining it in terms of psychological trauma, or memories handed down through generations. His desire to uncover his grandfather's past and thus complete the picture of his family history shows that even a young American, born in the late 1970s, cannot have a complete sense of his identity and his place in the world while he remains ignorant of how European history affected his own forefathers. To be Jewish American, the novel suggests, is to be somehow incomplete, since part of the meaning of that identity is linked with a past that happened elsewhere.

In its structure and form, Foer's novel is more complex and sophisticated that Eggers's in that all the peculiarities of its formal articulation are put to good use and are never divorced from the main theme of circumatlantic exchange. There are three narrative devices interwoven throughout the novel. Some chapters are narrated by Alex, and they deal with the events surrounding Jonathan's visit to Ukraine. Other chapters take the form of letters written by Alex to Jonathan after the latter's return to the US. It transpires that Alex is sending Jonathan the chapters we have been reading, and the letters often contain Alex's responses to Jonathan's criticisms and editorial suggestions. The third part of the book is made up of the story that starts in 1791 in Trachimbrod, with chapters sent by Jonathan to Alex. Though Alex is the main narrator, he announces from the start that Jonathan is the 'hero' of his narrative, and it is significant that the American traveller is depicted indirectly, through Alex's impressions of him, and through his own fictional story of Trachimbrod. With his decision to create an American hero who is only glimpsed through other narratives, Foer has found a formal analogy for the issues of identity that his book explores. Further, as Alex notes in the epistolary part of the novel, he and Jonathan have 'always communicated in this misplaced time,' a comment which is not only a self-conscious acknowledgement of the nature of the epistolary novel, but also one that can be read as continuous, in its interrogation of temporal difference, with the book's interrogation of spatial difference as well.

Alex's narrative, related in his imperfect English, adds another layer of complexity to the novel by showing that to be Ukrainian, to be 'other' to the American visitor, is also to have an unstable identity. Alex, who dreams of going to the US to study accountancy, begins his narrative with evidence of the Americanization of everyday life in Odessa: he likes American movies, he 'digs' Michael Jackson and other 'Negroes,' he watches adverts for McDonald's on TV and can carry a conversation on the price and relative merits of cappuccinos, mochas, lattes and mochachinos. The meaning of his Ukrainian identity, however, is not modified only by the influence of American culture, but it is further interrogated as the narrative unfolds. Travelling in the countryside with Jonathan, they stop to ask directions, but Alex finds that he is afraid to approach the farmers:

> But in truth, I was also afraid of the men in the field. I had never talked to people like that, poor farming people, and similar to most people from Odessa, I speak a fusion of Russian and Ukrainian, and they spoke only Ukrainian, and while Russian and Ukrainian sound so similar, people who speak only Ukrainian sometimes hate people who speak a fusion of Russian and Ukrainian. (112)

This example of linguistic conflict reveals the Ukrainian identity to be unstable in two ways: it shows the legacy of the Soviet past and the difficulty a 'new' nation has in extricating itself from a forced union, while it also reveals internal conflict within Ukraine itself, where loyalties are divided and being Ukrainian can have different meanings and connotations. Like most Ukrainians, Alex is annoyed when his country is referred to as 'the Ukraine,' because the definite article is seen as an attempt by the Soviet regime to suppress national feeling by relegating a country to the status of a province, but the language he speaks further problematizes the issue: not only is it a fusion of Russian and Ukrainian, but it is also a language that is absent from the text, which he narrates in English.

Both novels display a heightened awareness of the fact that the English language is now firmly established as the new lingua franca, and by foregrounding its uses and misuses they highlight an important aspect of cultural globalization and the Americanization of the world. Walter D. Mignolo argues that even though there are more speakers of Chinese than of English in the world, English is more important because 'the question is not so much the number of speakers as it is the hegemonic power of colonial languages' (41), a view that echoes Jameson's point about the dissymmetry between the US and every other country in the world. Fredric Jameson takes a slightly different line of argument by claiming that English 'is the lingua franca of money and power, which you have to learn and use for practical but scarcely for aesthetic purposes' (59). Mignolo further asserts that in the early modern period 'languages were taken as one of the foundations upon which to enact identity politics; language served to define the boundaries of a community by distinguishing it from other communities' (38). Migration and the global economy may have rendered this particular form of identity politics no longer viable, but perceptions and ideologies often take longer to adjust to new realities, and language still has its function as a marker of identity and difference, even if its use and appropriation has changed beyond recognition since the early modern period. Both novels link the act of linguistic translation with that of cultural translation; in both cases, they suggest that translation highlights difference as much as it serves to create common ground and make communication possible. To different degrees, both books insist that language not only shapes but also narrows the way we view the world, and the inventive use to which this issue is put in the two narratives highlights this issue at the same time as it re-energizes American literature.

In Foer's novel, it is at times hard to decide whether we should be laughing at or with our Ukrainian narrator. Laura Miller described Alex's version of English as resembling 'an out-of-control garden hose turned on full-force and allowed to thrash away on a summer lawn. He's got a thesaurus and he'll be damned if he's not going to use it.' Yet Miller went on to argue that by the end of the novel Alex comes to be a much better writer than Jonathan, and 'his stumbling English incandesces into eloquence.' Similarly, Francine Prose began her review by calling attention to the novel's 'hilarious prose,' but went on to claim that 'not since Anthony Burgess's novel *A Clockwork Orange* has the English language been simultaneously mauled and energised with such brilliance and such brio' (8). It seems odd that the English language should be energized by an American writer speaking in the voice of a fictional Ukrainian who is writing in English, and yet the gamble pays off because this device is fully supported by, and in turn enhances, the novel's major thematic concerns. Reviewing the novel for *The Guardian*, Mark Lawson noted that 'Safran Foer is transmitting linguistically a message that lesser writers might have conveyed editorially: the unreliability of reconstructing foreign events.' The same effect is achieved in the sections of the novel dealing with the fictional Foer's imagined chronicle of Trachimbrod: where Alex is seen to struggle to find the right word, Jonathan allows his narrative to disintegrate altogether: as his story reaches the Nazi destruction of Trachimbrod, it ends with pages of ellipses and a collapse of syntax and punctuation. Both narrators' language, then, suggests that there are things for which they have no words. This may be a commonplace, but it is saved from cliché because it asks to be read within the wider frame of reference that the book employs. In other words, the novel does not simply make the well-rehearsed point that language may be an insufficient vehicle for expressing memory and trauma: it goes a step further to suggest that not only our language, but also our cognitive skills and our cultural frames of reference can no longer help us to comprehend a world that is changing faster than we can adapt to it.

Alex's idiosyncratic use of the English language, coupled with his bragging and his general air of buffoonery, are also reminiscent of a literary antecedent: Tonish, 'the squire, the groom, the cook, the tent-man, in a word, the factotum, and I may add, the universal meddler and marplot, of our party' (4) in Washington Irving's *A Tour on the Prairies*. Tonish is 'a little swarthy, meager, wiry French creole' who speaks 'a Babylonish jargon of mingled French, English, and Osage' (4). Though well liked by the party, he is clearly a figure of fun, and the comical value of his Babylonish jargon is a useful reminder of the ways in which mastery of the English language confers feelings of entitlement and superiority; an issue seen in Amy Tan's novel in the previous chapter as well. Irving, as we have seen, promotes travel within the US and denigrates the traveller abroad. In this novel, it may be Alex who is presented as the buffoon because of the way he speaks English, but Jonathan is the one who is ignorant on a bigger scale.

When Alex and Jonathan find the woman who may be Augustine, they ask to be taken to Trachimbrod.

> 'There is no Trachimbrod anymore,' she replies. 'Take us there,' Grandfather said. 'There is nothing to see. It is only a field. I could exhibit you any field and it would be the same as exhibiting you Trachimbrod.' 'We have come to see Trachimbrod,' Grandfather said, 'and you will take us to Trachimbrod.' (154–5)

If Trachimbrod has been wiped off the map, isn't Augustine right to say that one empty field is as good as another? And if the place has been obliterated, can Jonathan still claim that he can trace his ancestry to a place that no longer exists? Jonathan's inability to separate space from history explains his trip and it also explains the failure of his trip. His transatlantic imaginings involve a return to origins, a return to sites of authentic history and ancestry, but the reality he discovers is that the world has moved on. Several of the trips away from the US that Part II has examined did rely on the idea of the journey abroad as a return to the past and a return to authenticity, but all of the narratives ultimately rejected the falseness of this conception.

Part III
Dislocation and/at Home

In *Globalization: The Human Consequences* Sygmund Bauman writes: 'Nowadays we are all on the move ... even if physically, bodily, we stay put' (77). Part III examines the ways in which fiction engages with Americans who 'stay put' when the concept of home is challenged and redefined at a pace that even Bauman, writing in the late 1990s, could not have predicted. 'There are no "natural borders" any more,' he writes. 'Wherever we happen to be at the moment, we cannot help knowing that we could be elsewhere, so there is less and less reason to stay anywhere in particular (and thus we feel often an overwhelming urge to find—to compose—such a reason)' (77). Bauman goes on to define the outmoded world, the world as a 'state of rest,' as a place 'with solid walls, fixed roads and signposts steady enough to have time to rust' (78). The novels I discuss here re-examine the attachment to place that accompanies conceptions of nationhood and state. As Bauman astutely observes, the state is conceived as a physical location, and figured through the familiar structures of houses and roads. Chang-rae Lee, Ethan Canin, Dinaw Mengestu and Jhumpa Lahiri all show a great interest in the relationship between these solid structures and the multiple meanings of home and belonging. They all write about dislocation at home, by which I mean that they write about their characters' relationships with their places of residence (houses, towns, roads) and use the opportunity to explore the ways in which these concepts have evolved and acquired new meanings under the spread of globalization. Their characters have homes to which they feel varying degrees of attachment, but that does not mean that they feel 'at home': part of their identity, part of their sense of self and their sense of national allegiance, lies elsewhere, in time and in space.

When travel 'becomes a kind of norm,' writes James Clifford, 'dwelling demands explication. Why ... do people stay home?' (5). Part III engages with this question by examining four novels that deal with the notion of 'home' and its various meanings. Canin and Lee write about older Americans who appear to be assimilated immigrants, but whose relationship to the US as 'home' continues to be shaped by events in their past lives, some of them prior to arrival in the US. The relationships between subject, subjectivity, home and nation are figured as familial relationships centered around American houses and domestic spaces which are haunted by events that took place in other continents and previous lives. Franklin Hata, Chang-rae Lee's narrator and protagonist, attempts to tell a story of successful integration into the small community of the fictional town of 'Bedley Run,' where he buys his big house in the early 1960s. However, as Hamilton Carroll argues, his narrative of assimilation is disrupted and ultimately undermined by events that took place during World War II, when Hata was still called Kurohata and served in the Japanese army. Because the trauma experienced during that time still shapes his life in the US, Hata is unable fully to assimilate. Dismissive of his neighbours' casual racism and xenophobia, he firmly believes it is the immigrant's responsibility to adapt to the host culture, and not the other way round. Despite his best efforts, though, despite his seemingly successful mimicry of local customs and behaviour, he remains a dislocated person, emotionally and ideologically living elsewhere: one whose sense of self and ethnicity was shaped elsewhere and now refuses to be erased. 'Doc' Hata has the obvious external markers of successful integration: a business and a beautiful house in the suburbs. Yet the business (now sold to a younger couple) is floundering and the house is damaged by fire, and as the commercial and domestic spaces he has created around him lose their solidity, so his identity unravels. An American immigrant identity defined not by one, but by two traumas is the subject of Ethan Canin's *Carry Me Across the Water*. August Kleinman, a refugee from Germany in the 1930s, fights as an American soldier in World War II and remains haunted by his actions during active service. Images of Kleinman travelling on planes frame the beginning and the end of this novel, reinforcing the notion that this is a man on the move, suffering a sort of temporal dislocation. He travels to the future, represented by his three-month old grandson, whom he visits in Brooklyn near the beginning of the novel, but he also travels to the past, represented by another small boy, the one referred to in the Japanese soldier's letters, and whom he meets in Japan, now a grown man. Like Chang-rae Lee's Hata, Kleinman is a successful man. He makes a fortune, collects Francis Bacon, Morandi and Jasper Johns and flies first-class to the scene of his trauma. Yet neither his material wealth nor his privileged position in his society allow him to belong.

A Gesture Life and *Carry Me Across the Water* illuminate the concept of dislocation through their extensive reliance on two seemingly unrelated tropes: the family home(s) and the ageing protagonists' relationships with their grandchildren. The two are of course connected to the extent that they stand for family, but they are also unrelated both through the necessities of the plot (the children and grandchildren live elsewhere) and through the different attitudes to roots and routes that they represent in relation to the protagonists. Where the home never quite manages to contain the whole self, which has never been fully Americanized or suburbanized, the grandchildren enable the main characters to achieve some sense of connectedness deeper than the one their homes ever afforded them. It is people, the books suggest, not houses or street addresses or zip codes that shape these two ageing figures into better versions of themselves and finally give them a grounding, even if not quite a home.

Reviewing Canin's novel for *Salon*, Amy Reiter noted that Kleinman 'seems to be watching his life unfold as if it were happening to someone else,' a predicament he shares with Franklin Hata. Both men are now old and looking back, unlike the protagonists in Mengestu and Lahiri's novels, who are young and try to forge their lives and shape their American selves. Lee's and Canin's novels tell familiar immigrant stories of flight, settlement and conflict, but neither ends in resolution. These two novels differ from other immigrant narratives in two ways: their protagonists have multiple allegiances signified by their military service: one has fought for the Americans, the other for the Japanese, yet both have an equal claim to an American identity, and both become American patriots of sorts. Both novels also end with the ageing protagonist in flight, not at rest. A more familiar and comforting type of narrative would have an elderly man coming to terms with the past and accepting his place in the world as an American; these novels refuse to do that. Hata doesn't go back and doesn't try to trace the family of the woman he feels responsible for. Kleinman does go back to make amends of sorts, but his atonement does not help him come to a resting place he can call home. *A Gesture Life* ends with Hata selling his house and dreaming of going far away, while *Carry Me* closes with the image of Kleinman reclining on his seat as the plane takes off: the last words of the book are 'the lightness of escape, then lift' while Lee's ends 'almost home'. It is this condition of 'almost home,' a home conceived as a metaphor for the nation, and one containing internal rifts, contradictions and clashing cultures, that these books examine: the sense of belonging and not belonging, of being here but also elsewhere. Of course, American literature, like American life, has always relied on this sense of dislocation: Americans have always come from elsewhere so they are already dislocated (with the exception of Native Americans, whose dislocation is of a different nature). However, these two novels are not typical of the tradition of immigrant fiction. They do not narrate stories of origins and settlement, or do so only marginally, and their formal structure emphasizes the ways in which the past continues to live in the present where other immigrant fictions look ahead to the future. The fact that they both conclude with ageing immigrants who do not settle, compromise or attain a sense of belonging also indicates that these books do not conceive of the immigrant journey as a teleological one, and it is this idea that links them to the novels studied in Chapter 6.

Mengestu and Lahiri are also representative of a new kind of immigrant author; they write about home and belonging in national as well as domestic space, but they write about transnational subjects who no longer conform to the older pattern of immigration and assimilation. Where Chang-rae Lee and Ethan Canin write about older immigrants looking back and taking stock of their lives, Mengestu and Lahiri write about young *Americans* who are the children of immigrants. Both *How to Read the Air* and *The Namesake* can be said to have a clearly defined protagonist (Jonas Woldemariam and Nikhil Ganguli respectively), yet both also devote extensive passages of their narratives to the story of the protagonists' parents. In Lahiri's novel, the parents' story is rendered in third person, emphasizing a certain distance between the generations. Mengestu, on the other hand, has Jonas narrate the story of his parents. More specifically, Jonas narrates two stories: one is the 'official' version of his mother and father's road trip from Peoria, Illinois to Nashville, Tennessee. Though the journey takes place while he is still in his mother's womb, Jonas tells it with authority. As he retraces his parents' journey, both physically and as narrator of their story, he attempts to discover who he is. In Part I of this study I looked at stories of Africa, while Part II considered the importance of the ethnic journey of origins. This novel can be read within those parameters because Jonas is of African origin and undertakes such a journey to his roots. However, in this case his roots really are routes, because he does so not by travelling to Ethiopia, but rather to Tennessee. The second story of origins he tells is openly made-up. This is the story of his father's misadventures in Africa and his escape to Europe and then America, as told by Jonas to his school pupils who should be studying American literature instead. The double narrative of the immigrant parents and their children is in both novels supported through an extensive imaginative engagement with representations of domestic space. Alongside this emphasis on domestic spaces, both novels also feature journeys, and in their juxtaposition of stasis and movement, routes and roots, they explore new ways of being American, and create new stories that enrich and enlarge our understanding of the immigrant novel that has dominated the second half of the twentieth century. Another important aspect of the book is the two characters' different places in society. Though both are college-educated, Jonas is a self-sabotaging underachiever, while Nikhil is a high-flyer. Read alongside one another, the novels suggest that race or country of origin alone cannot account for one's position in life. Nikhil is the son of parents who came to the US to study; he embraces and embodies the narrative of success even as he understands that some sacrifices have to be made. Jonas is the child of an unhappy, turbulent relationship between two people who emigrate to escape poverty, and he lacks Gogol's sense of entitlement and ambition.

Three of the four novels studied in Part III are narrated in a fragmentary, non-linear fashion. David Cowart notes that '[i]mmigrant writers display a proclivity for narrative fragmentation' (86). However, as the case of Ethan Canin demonstrates, an author does not necessarily have to be an immigrant to find this sort of structuring amenable to their plots. It is, rather, the act of narrating the immigrant experience that lends itself to fragmentation. By dislocating the temporality of their plots, these authors question the concept of the self as a continuous, coherent entity. They also move away from the conception of the immigrant story as one of linear progression from old country to new, and in seeking to abolish categories such as narrative past and narrative present, they show their characters to be *simultaneously* self and other, to occupy imaginary spaces that are both here and there.

5 Chang-rae Lee, *A Gesture Life*; Ethan Canin, *Carry Me Across the Water*

CHANG-RAE LEE, *A GESTURE LIFE*

Franklin Hata's narrative opens with the phrase 'People know me here' (1). This simple statement of assimilation and belonging, however, is soon qualified by the next sentence: 'It wasn't always so' (1). Hata recalls the early days of his arrival in Bedley Run, when he was not treated in an overtly racist manner, but made to feel not '*un*welcome' (3, emphasis in the original). The rest of the book ostensibly tells the story of his trajectory from tolerated immigrant to venerated community member. However, the cracks in this narrative soon appear, and then accumulate throughout the story. His daughter claims that people laugh at him behind his back and use racist language to talk about him, and she further accuses him of worrying too much about his image and about how others perceive him. Those who treat him with respect, like estate agent Liv Crawford, have an ulterior motive. Though various critics have written about the discrepancies between Hata's aspirations and his views of himself on the one hand and the way he is treated by and treats other people on the other, there has been no acknowledgement of the fact that the book challenges not only narratives of assimilation but also narratives of dominant belonging. Hamilton Carroll, for example, repeatedly refers to Hata's desire to assimilate, to render his otherness invisible and to become fully Americanized. However, the novel shows that dominant American identities change, too, and they change not only because ideologies shift over time, but because changes in the economy produce changes in attitudes to race and ethnicity. When Hata arrives in Bedley Run, he is accepted because the town has dreams of prosperity and growth, and 'pretty much anybody new to town was seen as a positive addition to the census and the tax base' (3). Later on, though, he becomes the victim of casual racism and this coincides with the town's economic decline and the country's recession. The novel goes to great lengths to show that the extent to which America embraces or rejects its newest arrivals and its ethnic others is not determined by some unchanging notion or narrative of Americanness, but rather that it is contingent upon a number of factors, some of which have to do with the national and global economy. It is fair to assume that, as American literature continues to be energized by authors who are or become American in new and unexpected ways, this concept will replace the older understanding of the immigrant other arriving in an America shaped by its dominant ideology.

Young-Oak Lee speaks of Hata's 'ultimate goal of attaining an American national identity' (146), while Hamilton Carroll speaks of Hata's 'narrative of successful assimilation' (592). In two similar readings of the novel, Lee and Carroll go on to demonstrate that it is Hata's relationships with the women in his life that disrupt the narrative of successful assimilation. Though this reading is largely convincing and illuminating, it relies on a false assumption: that Hata does aspire to perfect assimilation and comes close to achieving it, that his self-construction as 'Doc Hata,' a valued community member who truly belongs in Bedley Run, goes unquestioned by him. As the title of the novel makes clear, this is but another pretence: Hata is able to *mimic* the natives, to appear as an assimilated American as far as his Asian looks will allow, but it is just that: an imitation, a life composed of gestures that mirror the gestures of others; the show of assimilation through an enactment of an Americanized identity. A careful reading of the book shows that from early on in the narrative Hata feels dislocated, alienated, not belonging. He has a sense of detachment from his own life, and a sense of a dislocated national subjectivity. Carroll argues that Hata attempts to 'constitute himself within the bounds of hegemonic US citizenship' (593) and is thwarted through his abjection of K and Sunny. However, this reading does not take into account the extent to which Hata is aware of a layer of selfhood that eludes such self-constitution. This elusive self, the part of Hata that cannot be accounted for through the traditional modes of enquiry into ethnicity, is figured through his relationship to his house, and the depiction of domestic and suburban space plays a large role in illuminating the complexities of Lee's engagement with ethnic belonging.

The centrality of the house in the narrative links gender, race and nation and de-stabilizes Hata's self-construction. His house is described as 'one of the special properties in the area' (16), a two-story Tudor revival house on Mountview, one of the town's most desirable neighbourhoods. Rosemary Marangoly George suggests in *The Politics of Home* that 'the basic organizing principle around which the notion of the "home" is built is a pattern of select inclusions and exclusions. Home is a way of establishing difference. Home . . . acts as an ideological determinant of the subject' (2). *A Gesture Life* not only shows an awareness of the politics of home but also actively engages the narrator protagonist in contemplation of the meaning of home. Early in the narrative, Hata begins to describe his sense of detachment from his home, suggesting that he is a dislocated person, caught in the wrong place. Displaying Duboisian self (double)-consciousness, he thinks of his seemingly perfect family home as 'discomfiting': 'I keep stepping outside my house . . . looking at it as though I were doing so for the very first time, when I wondered if I would ever in my life call such a house my home'

(22). Though he cannot fully grasp what he is feeling, he knows 'something is afoot' (22), this something being the unravelling of his identity that the reader will witness by the end of the story. In addition to having his narrator explicitly talk about the meaning of home, the novel further engages with the question through its intertextual weaving of a story that has emotional geography and the meaning of the suburban home at its very heart. In a perceptive and nuanced reading of the importance of the house in *A Gesture Life*, June Dwyer notes that Chang-rae Lee 'addresses issues of housing and the reception of upwardly mobile ethnic Americans by the Anglo-dominated middle and upper-middle classes' (167) and goes on to argue that Hata

> wants nothing more than acceptance in America and an escape from his past life as a Japanese citizen of Korean parentage. His wish to fit in and deny any tension or trouble in his life dictates the way he conducts himself in Japan as well as in the US. His home reflects his obsession with propriety and acquiescence to the norms of the dominant group. (173)

Despite the many strengths of her explorations of the ethnic suburban home, Dwyer commits an error by not making a distinction between Hata's narrative discourse and the discourse of the novel. What Hata says is not necessarily what the novel says, and it is by looking at the cracks, at the discrepancies between the two, that we can gain a fuller sense of Hata's attitude toward his ethnic identity.

One of the crucial episodes in Hata's narrative is the small fire that damages his home. The story begins with Hata taking a swim, then going indoors and making a log fire to warm himself up, all the while thinking about his life and his place in the world. As he plunges into the cold water at the beginning of the scene, Hata has a sudden feeling that he is not in his own swimming pool but 'someplace else'. Shaken by this brief feeling of dislocation, he goes inside the house to warm himself up, and as he gathers the kindling he finds himself recalling a story he had once read in one of his daughter's books: 'The story ... is about a man who decides one day to swim in other people's pools, one after another in his neighborhood and town, which, as described, seems very much like Bedley Run' (23). Though it is not named, this is of course John Cheever's 1964 story 'The Swimmer.' Joseph Berger describes Cheever as 'America's foremost chronicler of suburbia,' and his work is studied alongside that of John Updike, John O'Hara and Richard Yates, all of them authors interested in white suburban masculinities. What is of particular interest, and revealing about the intertextual presence of 'The Swimmer' here, though, is not simply the thematic link to another story of suburbia, but rather the fact that 'The Swimmer' is not really set in a neighbourhood and town like Bedley Run in any obvious way that Hata would be able to recall years after reading it. There are, however, sufficient similarities to make the analogy instructive. Neddy Merrill is eight miles away when he decides to swim all the way back home to Bullet Park. Along the way, there are descriptions of the people he meets and parties he gatecrashes, but very little actual description of the town or neighbourhood that Hata appears to recall. References to Lisbon and Hackensack place the story in Connecticut or New Jersey, familiar Cheever territory. Other than those place names, the story relies on Neddy's 'remembered or imaginary' maps and charts (777); in other words, an inner, psychological geography. Alongside this inner landscape, the story creates a sense of space not by engaging with external, topographical detail, but rather by describing a set of people and their elaborate shared codes of inclusion and exclusion: the 'life composed of gestures' that Hata's daughter so despises. The swimmer's arrival at the Biswangers' is instructive and worth quoting at length:

> He crossed some fields to the Biswangers' and the sounds of revelry there. They would be honored to give him a drink, they would be happy to give him a drink. The Biswangers invited him and Lucinda for dinner four times a year, six weeks in advance. They were always rebuffed and yet they continued to send out their invitations, unwilling to comprehend the rigid and undemocratic realities of their society. They were the sort of people who discussed the price of things at cocktails, exchanged market tips during dinner, and after dinner told dirty stories to mixed company. They did not belong to Neddy's set—they were not even on Lucinda's Christmas-card list . . . Grace Biswanger was the kind of hostess who asked the optometrist, the veterinarian, the real-estate dealer, and the dentist. (785)

It is, then, a world defined by party invitations, a world where social success is measured by one's inclusion on the right Christmas card list, a world where it is vulgar to discuss the price of things. Rather than describing an actual place that sounds like Hata's neighbourhood, Cheever describes the conditions that produce such zones of exclusions and the symptoms by which we identify them. We don't know if Hata sends any Christmas cards, but he derives a sense of pride and satisfaction from the fact that he has been able to crack the code in his neighbourhood. He measures his own success as an immigrant by recounting how he was able from the start to read correctly the elaborate rules of behaviour, and to mimic them so well that he was not marked out as a foreigner. He sees around Mountview 'an unwritten covenant of conduct,' a 'signet of cordiality and decorum' (44). However, he does not simply congratulate himself for his ability to decipher the secret code. He internalizes his own exclusion from the set and believes that his success lies not only in his unobtrusive presence, and the absence of markedly 'ethnic' modes of conduct, but more to the point it lies in the ways it reinforces his white neighbours' feelings of secure superiority: 'I must have given them the reassuring thought of how safe they actually were,' he writes. He does not mean that they're safe because he blends in;

they are safe, rather, because 'an interloper might immediately recognize and so heed the rules of their houses' (44). It is this extraordinary sense of almost perverse pride in one's marginalization that his daughter Sunny rages against in the passage that gives the novel its title, accusing her father of making 'a whole life out of gestures and politeness' (95).

Interviewing Chang-rae Lee, Dwight Garner asked him whether, 'on some level, he has set out to reimagine Cheever country':

> "Well, I grew up in Cheever country," he said, laughing. "And I've always felt that Cheever country is surprisingly amenable to a man like Hata. There's a point in the book where a real estate agent says, 'Franklin Hata is our town. He's what this place is all about.' That has a lot to do with being successful and unperturbed in a way, at least on the surface. I don't think I'm reimagining Westchester as any kind of literary landscape, but I do think in some ways I'm rediscovering the kind of people who live there."

The 'kind of people' who live in Chang-rae Lee's suburbs are people like Henry Park's father in *Native Speaker*, who work hard to dim the outward signs of their racial difference, and people like Hata, whose quiet life contains horrors and traumas that cannot be guessed at. 'The Swimmer' ends with Neddy Merrill pounding on the door of his locked-up house; the story concludes just before the moment when the realization must come that his home is no more, that his paradise is lost. Doc Hata's narrative, on the other hand, acknowledges the loss, or absence, from the start. It begins (as well as ending) with the feeling of dislocation in time and place, the feeling of not being in the right place, of not being 'at home' in one's house or home-town. In his swimming pool Hata experiences a sort of epiphany that reveals the falsehoods his American identity has been built upon:

> It is an unnerving thing, but when I was underneath the water, gliding in the black chill, my mind's eye suddenly seemed to carry to a perspective high above, from where I could see the exacting, telling shapes of all: the Spartan surfaces of the pool deck, the tight-clipped manicures of the garden, the venerable house and trees, the fetching, narrow street. And what caught me, too, was that I knew there was also a man in that water, amidst it all, a secret swimmer who, if he could choose, might always go silent and unseen. (24)

It is important to note that in transcending his bodily self and seeing his world as if from above, Hata links the secret swimmer with the regimented structures of the pool, the lawn, the house and the street: the suggestion seems to be that these structures, which are meant to denote order, safety, home, can be destabilized through the presence of silent, unseen inhabitants: those whose outward lives appear to conform to the narrative of success and nationhood, but who secretly hold on to other identities, in this case identities that could not be accommodated under the banner of 'suburban American'. Trauma, this novel suggests, unseats the self, and a traumatized self is in a permanent state of dislocation, since some of that self will always belong and return (or try to resist returning) to the scene of the trauma.

Unlike August Kleinman's in *Carry Me Across the Water*, Hata's trauma is not an American one in the sense that it takes place in his former life in the Japanese army during World War II. His assimilation into mainstream American society, then, is hampered by that past, but Chang-rae Lee does more than write a story in which a quiet suburban life hides un-American secrets: he also reverses the point of view to show that the keeper of these secrets is rendered homeless. In other words, the beautiful house on Mountview is not a façade concealing horror and abjection from the all-American neighbours. It is a disguise, a false place of refuge that unsettles the individual as much as it would unsettle the neighbours were they to find out what the mock-Tudor special property contains. A little reminder of the past comes back to haunt Hata when his daughter rummages through his personal belongings and comes across a piece of silk, like a woman's scarf, 'though it was completely black' (147). He tells her it is a flag from the war and changes the subject, so the reader only finds out the true significance of this piece of silk seventy-seven pages later. The flag was one that Captain Ono, the doctor on the camp where Hata was posted, used in order to issue covert instructions relating to K, the comfort woman. Hata, we learn, means flag, and Kurohata, which was Hata's 'original' name, is a black flag, used 'in olden times to warn of a contagion within' (224). Hamilton Carroll notes that this passage prefigures what Hata will become as an American citizen: a contagion, though a hidden one. Carroll sees the trauma of Hata's Japanese identity bleeding into his new life (600) and hampering his attempts to assimilate, and Hata himself uses the image of the flag once more in order to signal not simply his otherness and foreignness, but also his immense guilt and remorse. In a passage filled with self-pity as much as self-awareness, he realizes he is 'at the vortex of bad happenings,' and he thinks he ought to 'festoon the façade of [his] house and the bumpers of [his] car and then garland [his] shoulders with immense black flags of warning, to let everyone know they must steer clear of this man' (333). The flag that warns of contagion is of course never displayed in the American suburb. It is kept in a box, to be discovered by an American daughter. 'What if I had stored a pistol there,' asks her father (148), but what he has stored is equally dangerous and destructive even if it goes unnoticed. In 'Ethnic Home Improvement,' June Dwyer praised Sandra Cisneros for painting the front of her house a bright colour, one that upset the genteel tone of her neighbourhood. Hata's house connotes ethnic difference in ways that are hidden: the lacquered box containing the piece of silk, the swimming pool containing a hidden swimmer, and finally the idea that this mock-Tudor house imitates more than an architectural period.

Early in his narrative Hata admits that he is almost ready to give in to the realtors who are pressing him to sell a home that is no longer appropriate for him (too old, no family), but does not make that decision for the reasons the realtors suppose. The time feels right to him, he says,

> not so much from a financial viewpoint but from a sense of one's time in a place, and that time being close to done. It's not that I feel I've used up this house, this town, this part of the world . . . but more that . . . this happy blend of familiarity and homeyness and what must be belonging, is strangely beginning to disturb me. (21)

Whereas other readings of the novel suggest that Hata wants to assimilate, and fools himself into thinking he has succeeded, this passage shows that in fact he does not think of his life in Bedley Run as the pinnacle of success. It is not the place where he can live out his days, having fulfilled his American Dream. The phrase 'one's time in a place' is telling: it suggests that Hata is rootless, and that what others may see as a permanent settling in to a suburban American life is for him but a stop along the route. Chang-rae Lee further reveals Hata's rootlessness through the choice of words to signify allegiance and assimilation: 'familiarity', 'homeyness' evoke the family home as microcosm for the nation, or as a metaphor for successful citizenship. The third ingredient, though, is not simply belonging, but rather 'what must be belonging.' The phrase suggests that Hata has no direct experience of this sense of belonging; he may recognize it as an abstraction, but is unable to relate it to his own life as a person born to Korean parents, raised as Japanese, and settled in a typical American suburb.

As is often the case with immigrants, Hata's sense of belonging is also tied in with the rejection and assumption of different names. He claims to have forgotten his original Korean name, though he contradicts himself sufficiently for us to infer he does know it. His Japanese surname is shortened from Hirohata to Hata when he comes to the US, and Franklin is his ironically chosen first name. The reference to Benjamin Franklin is hard to miss; it is ironic because Hata creates the outward appearance of a man who lives the American Dream in all its glory, while at the same time he remains detached from the persona who achieves this: he is hiding behind his assumed name, masquerading, playing the part of the good immigrant. His Japanese name further vexes the transnational parameters of his multiple identities, as we learn when he recounts the story of what happened in World War II that resulted in his traumatic encounter with a Korean comfort woman. The woman, "K", sees him for the ethnic Korean that he is, but he plays down that identity, asserting his desire to be, and to be seen as, Japanese. The story of his rape and betrayal of K is also the story of suppressed ethnic identity and the embrace of dominant male imperialist narratives. Their relationship is one between the powerful and the subjugated, and it is his maleness and his Japaneseness that give him the upper hand, whereas his suppressed Korean self represents a weakness.

The various names that Hata has used and discarded throughout his life have built up layers of identity that have created a sense of distance and detachment. Throughout his narrative, he gives strong hints that he has suffered a permanent dislocation from his own sense of self. Recollecting his affair with Mary Burns, he thinks that even though his memories are happy ones, 'there is an unformed quality to them as well, as if they were someone else's memories and reflections, though somehow available only to me, to keep and to hold' (41). This feeling of detachment is further intensified when he returns home from the hospital. During his absence, Liv Crawford, the realtor who wants to sell his house, has been supervising the restoration of the fire-damaged interiors. As she shows him around the rooms that have been repainted the same colours as before, he gets the feeling that the house is and is not his own: 'I have the peculiar sensation that this inspection and showing is somehow postmortem, that I am already dead and a memory and I am walking the hallways of another man's estate,' he writes (139). This feeling matches the earlier epiphanic moment in the swimming pool where he saw the other man, silent and detached alongside his bodily self. Now, as the author continues to elaborate on the connections between house, home and self, Hata uses language that describes him as much as it describes his property:

> This is my very house, my Mountview house in Bedley Run, understated and grand and unsolicitous of anything but the most honorable regard, and despite how magnificently Liv Crawford has directed its exacting restoration, I cannot escape feeling a mere proximateness to all its exhibits and effects, this oddly unsatisfying museum that she has come to curate for this visitation and the many that will someday follow. (139)

The image of the house as museum, as a structure containing representations of other lives rather than actual residents, is reinforced elsewhere in the text through Hata's growing sense of detachment from his actual surroundings. Hamilton Carroll, who argues that Hata has emigrated to the US in order to reconstitute himself, sees in this detachment 'the failure of this recuperative project.' Hata 'cannot escape the events of the past,' he writes, and 'cannot erase his history' (607). For Carroll, this signifies the novel's resistance to 'hegemonic US citizenship' (593), though I argue that Chang-rae Lee does not tell the story he does in the way he does it in order to pit Hata as an individual against the strictures of hegemonic US citizenship, but rather in order to add texture and nuance to the very understanding of US citizenship. Hata, in other words, does not fail to become a good American because he did bad things as a Japanese soldier. Though he may not know it himself, he *is* American, one of very many Americans with lacquered boxes in their attics, hidden relics in their drawers and shortened names that disguise their origins. The otherness he carries within him does not mark him as not belonging; rather, it describes him perfectly as an American citizen in the late twentieth century, a rootless man dislocated at home.

To read the story of Franklin Hata as the story of a failure to assimilate is to accept that Hata's world is the world of the novel, which is not the case. Hints and reminders that other layers needed to be heeded can be found occasionally in the text, prompting us to see from the outside, as Hata himself does. 'I sometimes forget who I really am,' starts Chapter 14. 'I forget what it is I do,' 'I forget why it is I do such things' (285). 'Then I might get up in the middle of the night,' he continues, 'and dress and walk all the way to town, to try to figure once again the notices, the character, the sorts of actions of a man like me, what things or set of things define him' (285). The image of the night-time walker who haunts the streets of Bedley Run looking for his daytime double, and the rare shift from first to third person that carries on for only a couple of lines, enable us to relate the theme of dislocation that runs through the book to its actual articulation: just as Hata tries to get a glimpse of his self in the street, so the reader must remain aware of the gaps between Hata's narrated and narrating selves. Therefore, when Hata goes on to describe his house as a 'lovely, standing forgery' (352) we can both appreciate that he is talking about himself as an immigrant and see that he fails to realize that the forgery does not mark him out as 'other': the forgery is his true home, an American home that contains his multiple identities in a way that is uniquely, typically American.

The exploration of multiple identities, and the ways in which American ideology is or is not able to support them, is evident in the novel, and its preoccupation with names as signs of identity and with structures as containers of multiplicity also manifests itself in a different context, that of business and commerce. Hata's medical supply store is named after his daughter Sunny. The store and the daughter are meant to be outward signs of success and markers of nationhood and belonging: alongside the family home, Hata has a family and a business. However, as the naming of the business after the adopted daughter implies, family and business are not proof of success, but rather constructed so as to give the appearance of success. Sunny grows up to reject her father's false narrative and moves away from him. The store is bought by a young couple whose family unit is also falling apart, and this causes Hata to consider the possibility that the store will no longer exist. He had hoped to leave behind 'a humble legacy that a decent man had once begun and built up and nurtured' (192), but now he is worried that 'the memory of the store will fade away,' and 'the appellation of "Doc Hata" will dwindle and pass from the talk of the town' (192). In the same way that Hata had hoped to leave his mark on the town, he had also once hoped that the adoption of a daughter would accomplish two things. For one, it would confer upon him the air of respectability that belongs to a family man, and it would also somehow help him to come to terms with his guilt over the treatment of K.

The story of the murdered Korean comfort woman and that of the Korean American daughter contain similarities that emphasize the extent to which Hata's conception of self-identity and nationality is also bound up with his sense of masculinity, as Carroll and Young-Oak Lee have both shown. Regarding K, Hata realizes the consequences of his actions too late. In one of the book's most harrowing scenes, he comes across her murdered, mutilated body in a clearing, and as he gets to work recovering her remains he sees a 'tiny, elfin form, miraculously whole, . . . [i]ts pristine sleep still unbroken' (305). The loss of the foetus may partly explain his desire to adopt despite not being married, and therefore not an obvious candidate for adoptive parenthood. Yet this does not stop him from more or less forcing his own daughter to have a late termination. The pregnant body, and the pregnant female's potential to subvert or undermine dominant ideologies, are recurring tropes in the book. Hata is disappointed when he sees Sunny for the first time because he can tell immediately that she is not racially 'pure'. He realizes immediately that there will never be an easy affinity between them, nor any assumption made by others that they are 'of a single kin and blood,' because of the other colour or colours that 'ran deep within her,' and he understands that she must have been the product of 'a night's wanton encounter between a GI and a local bar girl' (204). As a Korean man who became Japanese and then became American, Hata ought to have a rather more enlightened understanding of the importance of 'blood.' Yet his fear of miscegenation also plays a part in his decision to encourage Sunny to have a late, illegal abortion. Though a racist motive is never acknowledged explicitly, the baby has to be aborted because it is a threat both to Hata's masculine authority (as symbol of the daughter's defiance and disobedience) and a further threat to the bloodline.

Despite being a first-person narrator and the centre of consciousness in the novel, Hata does not always come across as a sympathetic character, but the novel derives a lot of its emotional and intellectual power from the lessons he appears to learn by the end of the book. Lee borrows some of the conventions of the Bildungsroman and applies them to the story of an old man, showing that his journey through life, through different countries, ethnic identities and names, continues to shape and affect him. Hata does find peace of sorts, and like the Bildungsroman hero he does understand his place in the world, even if what he understands is not quite the same as belonging. In the end he learns that familial blood does not matter in the way he thought it would. Though he loses his markers of success as a family man, his daughter and his store, Hata finds redemption through his grandson. When he sees him for the first time, he is surprised that the boy isn't darker, but he notes his black hair, 'tightly curled, near-Afro' (208). He is soon touched by the boy's easy affection for 'Mr Hata,' and when he shakes his hand goodbye, Hata has another epiphany. He understands that he is old, and that his time with his grandson may be limited. More importantly, though, he realizes that 'all these years alone' he had never thought of 'the larger questions' (219). Like the Bildungrsroman hero, he has reached the point where he understands something important about his place in the world and the extent of his familial relations. Unlike the Bildungsroman hero, though, his findings do not bring a sense of completion. Instead, Hata feels that his life 'had all at once become provisional again, the way a young man's might be, open to possibility and choice and then vulnerability as well' (220). By admitting his love for his grandson, who is neither related by blood nor 'racially pure,' Hata opens himself up to the possibility of becoming vulnerable again, but he gains a strong sense of kinship that finally allows him to act with kindness and compassion. By interrogating family structures and showing that much of what is considered natural (the love of parents for their children, for example) can also be acquired, the book suggests that nationality and belonging can also be acquired through custom and not birth.

The second lesson that Hata learns is that ideas of nation and home do not have to be tied in to a specific place. In fact, one could argue that what he learns at the end of the novel is not only that he has treated K and Sunny badly, but also that as a man embodying the dominant ideologies of the 1940s and the early postwar years, he has been caught in outmoded ideas of home and belonging. He talks to Liv Crawford and Renny Banerjee about the 'question of feeling at home in a place' (135), but he learns at the end of the book that feeling at home is not tied in to place any more than it is tied in to blood. Stepping out of his house to look for a fleeting apparition, a reflection that catches his eye, he looks back across his property and sees the routes in his roots: 'it seemed I had traveled for miles to the place I was standing, as if I had gone round and round the earth in an endless junket, the broad lawn a continent, the pool a whole ocean' (289). It is only when he acknowledges the transnational makings and remakings that have fashioned his identity that he sees the world for what it has become: not the nation-states that World War II was fought over, but a different world where home and place are negotiated rather than fixed or given. This 'almost home' is good enough for him in the end. The narrative ends not with rest or stasis, but with the idea of flight and return:

> Let me simply bear my flesh, and blood, and bones. I will fly a flag. Tomorrow, when this house is alive and full, I will be outside looking in. I will be already on a walk someplace, in this town or the next or one five thousand miles away. I will circle round and arrive again. Almost home. (356)

By bringing together the ideas of blood, place, travel and home, Lee shows the connections between the various thematic strands in this novel, and shows them to be provisional and unresolved rather than fixed categories.

In some ways, the ending parallels the idea in Eggers's *You Shall Know Our Velocity* that all facts changed on the way to the printers; that to write about ethnicity and nation and the beginning of the twenty-first century is to embrace provisionality. It is a similar provisionality that Canin explores in *Carry Me Across the Water*, a book that suggests oceanic crossings in its very title, and one that ends with its ageing protagonist on a plane feeling 'the lightness of escape' (206).

ETHAN CANIN, *CARRY ME ACROSS THE WATER*

Canin's novel tells the story of August Kleinman; German Jewish by birth, American citizen and soldier, who in his old age travels back to Japan to atone for a 'crime' he committed during World War II. As I shall demonstrate later, the criminality of his actions at a time of war is of course questionable, but the matter of his guilt is further complicated by another crime he may or may not have committed as an American citizen after the war. The journey from the US to Japan and the crime against the Japanese soldier are the two events highlighted in the narrative, while the (unrelated) stories of the journey from Germany to the US and the possible murder of an American gangster remain relatively underdeveloped. The novel is narrated in the third person but closely follows Kleinman's point of view, thus allowing an insider as well as an outsider perspective. The narrative's temporal frame is fractured, and the reader has to reconstruct the chronology of events in order to get a clear sense of cause and effect, of actions and consequences. By amplifying some events while allowing others that might have been equally life-defining to slip into the background, and by vexing the chronology of his text, Canin actively interrogates the markers and the makings of an American identity. All the while, Kleinman's success as well as his personal failures and small tragedies are figured through the trope of houses, and more specifically the idea of the family home.

Kleinman is shaped by two crossings: one trans-atlantic, the other trans-pacific. He leaves Germany as a well-assimilated Jew, and then he fights for the US in Japan as an assimilated American of German Jewish origin. The two crossings de-stabilize his identity and undermine the narrative of success, signified by his material wealth, which he becomes increasingly indifferent to. August Kleinman flees Germany with his mother in 1933, months after Hitler becomes chancellor. Apparently unmoved by news of his father's and grandfather's death by lynching back in Hamburg, he goes on to forge a good relationship with his stepfather, Hank Kleinman. Hank was 'something of a miracle, an optimistic bear of a man,' 'a religious Jew but a man of unparalleled joy' (59). Hank gives August a regular American boyhood, teaching him to play stickball, coaching him on his grammar and accent, and generally facilitating his entry into American citizenship. Yet August feels that those happy years were 'tainted by the long shadow over them' (59). The shadow was not his father's fate, but more generally a feeling at once childish and mature that 'in America only he and his mother understood the truth about the world,' that beneath their regular American happiness lay 'a knowledge of the world' (60). This knowledge of the world is of course common to all refugees, though obscured by the American narrative of integration and success. Valentino Achak Deng also discusses his knowledge of the world in *What Is the What*, and Franklin Hata knows things that seem incompatible with his quiet life as a respected elderly man in a beautiful house in the suburbs. Kleinman, however, is unable to settle down and enjoy his new American identity not so much because of the childhood trauma, but because of his own actions. In other words, it is not the shadow of anti-semitism in 1930s Germany, or retrospectively the shadow of the Holocaust, but rather his own involvement in World War II as an American soldier. What he did in Japan haunts his successful, prosperous postwar years, and the beautiful, comfortable houses that signify his success in America can never quite offer the security and contentment he may have wished for.

Kleinman's first significant home is the one he buys in Squirrel Hill in Pittsburgh. He recalls the city being cleaned up and rebuilt around the time that he decides to buy the family home. Noting the 'great towers rising, the ash-filled air cleaned' (94), Kleinman sees the city's renaissance as a manifestation of American ideology, the 'marvel of human endeavor and recompense' (94). The purchase of the house allows him to participate in that narrative of endeavour, of America building and re-building itself, though at the same time he knows that he cannot erase his past or 'clean up' his own deeds. Later in the novel, Kleinman recalls how the outskirts of his chosen neighbourhood of Squirrel Hill were still 'cloaked in a haze of industrial ash' when he first arrived there (140). It didn't take long, though, for the clean-up to be completed, the district made safe and desirable, and by choosing an up-and-coming location for his family home, Kleinman showed the same kind of vision that allowed him to become a pioneering and successful businessman. Descriptions of the house and hints about its importance are sprinkled throughout the narrative. On p. 97, it is 1992 and the Kleinmans 'still' live in the same four-bedroom Tudor at the edge of Squirrel Hill. Eight pages later, we are back in 1953 and he is 'contemplating the purchase of a home at the edge of Squirrel Hill' (105). Then, after we've read about his wife's death, about the Newton house and the Back Bay condo, we go back to seeing his wife at the early stages of senility recognizing 'the brown-roofed, triple-gable Tudor three blocks ahead' on the way back from the neurologist (140). By dislocating the family home and disrupting narrative continuity, Canin is able to emphasize the accumulation of life experiences that shape Kleinman. By abolishing the narrative distinction between past and present, Canin shows that his protagonist is not haunted by the past so much as he is condemned to live in it, not as memory or trauma but as his present.

Moreover, in Squirrel Hill Canin has made a choice of location that enables him to emphasize some of the novel's main thematic concerns. The 2002 Pittsburgh Jewish Community Study, compiled by the United Jewish Federation of Greater Pittsburgh in partnership with the Jewish Healthcare Foundation, notes that Squirrel Hill contains 28% of all Jewish households in Greater Pittsburgh, and that 78% of Squirrel Hill respondents 'definitely view Squirrel Hill as the center of their family's Jewish life' (35). More recently, the *Wall Street Journal* has described the area as a 'Jewish enclave' (Ansberry). However, one wouldn't know any of this by reading *Carry Me Across the Water*. The narrator does note the presence of the Jewish Community Center (140), but other than that there is little to suggest that Kleinman has settled into a Jewish area. His neighbours, we learn, were 'dentists and accountants and the superintendent of schools, men with plenty of money but with nowhere near, he calculated, what he himself had socked away' (97). In other words, to Kleinman the Tudor house represents Americanization, assimilation and success rather than retreat to an ethnic enclave. It is perhaps important that the house is repeatedly described as being on the edge of the district, creating an analogue for Kleinman's own Jewish identity, which exists on the periphery of his self-perception. Unlike Hata's Tudor revival house that fails to live up to its image of a happy American home, Kleinman's does contain a typical American family of ambitious overachievers. And yet this home does not represent the end of his life-journey; it is not the culmination of his successful American life. There are two more houses after the Tudor family home that shape and reflect Kleinman's identity.

After his children leave home and the mental health of his wife deteriorates, they move to Boston in the hope that a return to Ginger's home city will revive her spirits. The house they settle in, though, has no emotional investment and is rather described entirely in terms of financial and practical arrangements. It is a house made into a home with the aid of 'a telephone and a checkbook' (129), painted a bright barn-siding red not in order to express any notion of individuality or non-conformity, but simply so that Ginger can recognize it from a distance. In a sense, then, the move to Boston represents a failed homecoming. Kleinman realizes too late that his wife had wanted to live there all her life, but now that she is back she is barely aware of her surroundings. Ginger is an Italian American; her marriage to Kleinman and move to Pittsburgh symbolically represent a change in her ethnic identity, and yet her homecoming does not restore her to her former self. The day after her funeral, Kleinman moves out of the Newton home and pays cash for a condominium in the Back Bay. The emphasis placed on the easy availability of money in the purchase of the two Boston properties suggests that there is no emotional involvement. The house on Squirrel Hill was the subject of contemplation, and contained the fears and dreams of the self-made, up-and-coming immigrant businessman. The two Boston homes, on the other hand, signify an emotional hardening, a need not to connect self with home. By moving out of Newton so soon after his wife's death, Kleinman seeks to escape the memory of his wife's declining years, yet the new condo in the Back Bay contains mementoes of all his former lives.

The novel opens with a letter written by the Japanese soldier that Kleinman killed and addressed to his wife, whom Kleinman will later attempt to trace. The first thing we learn after reading the letter is that Kleinman has a copy of it in his condominium in Boston (5). More importantly, we also learn that this is 'one of the few items he brought with him from the house in Newton when he moved' (5–6), though this early in the narrative we have no idea what this means. The other items described in this scene are two paintings by Francis Bacon and one by Morandi, a porcelain cup containing several gold teeth and an alabaster brooch. The paintings are mementoes of his prime, in life and in business, and the ones he keeps in the condo are the very first ones he acquired. The Bacons and the Morandi were later followed by a Mark Rothko and a small Jasper Johns, and Kleinman's collection represents both his forward-looking vision, and his unwillingness to conform (the businessmen he is forced to mingle with 'stared, perplexed, at the walls' (131)) and thus assimilate into his professional class (amongst the businessmen who don't appreciate his art collection 'he understood himself to be an outcast' (131)). The meaning of the gold teeth in the porcelain cup is revealed on p. 53, in a flashback to his time in the war. The narrator describes Kleinman coming upon the bodies of half a dozen Japanese soldiers. Another GI, a 'friendly Italian from the Bronx,' uses his knife to pull the gold teeth out of the dead men's mouths, but his gruesome task is cut short when he steps on a mine and is blown to pieces. The teeth, therefore, are a terrible souvenir from the war, a reminder of greed and death; a memento mori. The brooch, we later learn, is a memento of his wife who, in the early stages of her decline, gets confused and wears the brooch on her 'pants leg' (152). The condo with its sparse furnishings and few possessions represents Kleinman's need to transcend the past, as well as his inability to do so. Most of the things from the Newton house have gone into storage, but the few remaining ones are reminders of the events that shaped his life.

The way that Kleinman experiences his integration and his success as an American, not an American Jew or a German Jew, can be seen when he visits his old family home in Queens for the first time in almost twenty years. He finds the neighbourhood changed, the old businesses not just closed but 'razed'. Here, one would expect the immigrant to reminisce about his childhood, to show some nostalgia for those early American years, and some regret for the complete destruction of the places associated with his childhood. Not so Kleinman. He thinks that '[t]here was enough in the world to feel sorry for without mourning the change of one small neighborhood. People came and went; buildings fell and rose. Here was the newest wave in the world's endless tide of aspirants' (191). He realizes that his mother and step-father, who still cling to the past, have been 'left behind by the world' (193), so that now that the neighbourhood was no longer Jewish 'their lives had been drawn like nooses around them. Hank Kleinman ... would not, somehow, cross a border' (194). Kleinman, on the other hand, 'always looked forward in his life' (194). His embrace of the dominant ideology of always looking ahead, of welcoming change and envisaging a better future, seems almost complete, and yet there is one thing that stops him from always looking forward, and never looking back: it is the memory of what he did in World War II.

The wartime events are narrated in short chapters interspersed through the narrative of Kleinman's late years, and the full extent of what took place is not revealed until the end of the novel. Stationed in an island beachhead near Okinawa, in the East China Sea, Kleinman is given the task of securing caves where Japanese soldiers may be hiding. Entering one such cavern, he is confronted by an unarmed Japanese soldier. Kleinman suspects a trap and kills the man, who then turns out to have been alone, and anxious to show Kleinman his wall paintings, rather than to cause him any harm. Though he couldn't have known the Japanese soldier would turn out to be harmless, Kleinman remains haunted for the rest of his life by the thought that he has killed an innocent person. Amongst the dead soldier's possessions he finds a bundle of letters addressed to a woman called Umi and containing references to their baby boy Teiji. The story of how he tracks down Teiji, and what transpires when he meets him, amplifies the themes of nationalism, the morality of war, and the changing face of ethnic belonging at the end of the twentieth century. At the same time, a firm intertextual nod to Joseph Conrad once again (as in Norman Rush) places the novel within a continuum that stretches from the end of the nineteenth century to the present and allows the author to highlight the legacy of imperialism in the shaping of national identity, and the changes brought about by what Kleinman perceives as 'the malignancy of international capital' that moves the world (130).

Kleinman arranges the journey with typical late-twentieth-century ease. He makes the necessary arrangements and hires a guide who helps him to track down the dead soldier's family. Umi is dead, but her son Teiji, an aspiring painter who works as a banker in London, had come home to look after her and is still there. The encounter with Teiji and his wife shows Kleinman a world that has changed significantly since the end of the war. Teiji's profession and the overseas posting are obvious markers of the international capital that is re-shaping the contours of Kleinman's map. Teiji's wife is also not typical; she speaks with a British accent, has Asiatic hair, eyes with a suggestion of the East, and a nose that might be Semitic (165). Though she remains a peripheral character with a short appearance in the novel, the author uses her racially mixed appearance as shorthand for the crossings and inter-minglings that go into the making of new identities. In his quest for atonement and forgiveness, Kleinman has not even entertained the idea that Umi might be dead, let alone that her son might be a banker living in London, rather than a provincial Japanese man staying at home. Teiji turns out to be ignorant of his real parentage, so Kleinman has more explaining to do than he was prepared for. Rather than apologizing to the son for killing his father, now he has to tell him who his real father was to begin with. He hatches 'an obscure plan of charity' (181) and tells Teiji that his father died uttering his son's name, and predicting that the boy will grow up to be an artist (181). Just as the heavens didn't fall when Charlie Marlow lied to the Intended, so here the narrator notes that '[o]ne did not change the world with a few words' (181).

This intertextual hint encourages a reading of the novel that questions empire, morality and redemption, but also brings to the fore questions of allegiance. When Marlow returns to Brussels knowing what he does about Belgian imperialism, he feels like a stranger who does not belong there; his experience has unravelled his sense of nationality and Europeanness. Similarly, then, can Kleinman ever be a good American, knowing what he has done in the war? The ways in which a traumatic past, American and otherwise, erupts into the present allow Canin to investigate Jewish postwar identity in a new context which is neither part of the earlier immigrant narratives nor Holocaust survivor/refugee tales. The novel was published in the months before 9/11 and stands to gain from contextualization that was not available to the author at the time: the stories of American soldiers fighting today will perhaps in a few decades' time also interrogate the meaning of an American identity. The questioning of the morality of Kleinman's actions is further complicated by another crime he commits in peacetime. When his brewing business takes off, he receives a threatening phone call from a gangster called Meyer Sharp who presumably means to sell him protection. They arrange to meet at a promontory where Kleinman charges into the gangster, causing him to fall into the rapid waters below. Afterwards, he cannot find any evidence of a man called Meyer Sharp, nor is a body ever recovered, so that he convinces himself that perhaps the man had crawled out of the river. Yet he is tormented by guilt; more specifically, he feels a guilt that brings back 'memories of standing in a dark cave in the East China Sea' (109). The killing of a soldier at war and the killing of a gangster in self-defence are not morally equivalent, except that they both ensure Kleinman's survival and prosperity. In this sense, Kleinman is also a symbol for his adopted country: he is both a man whose identity is conflicted and multifarious, and a typical American at the same time, in the sense that his story exemplifies the story of America's ascendancy after the bombings in Japan and the end of World War II.

The memory of the Japanese soldier he killed comes back to Kleinman twice more in the narrative. The first time, and the first one narrated in the novel, is when he is starting out as an American businessman and family man. He worries about his business failing, and in those moments of fear and insecurity 'his mind sometimes returned him to the cave on Agunijima'

(95). Later, when he takes a rare holiday to Barbados (rare because he has never been able to enjoy all the money he has amassed), as the small plane from Miami approaches the island he feels tears forming in his eyes, realizing that the last time he'd seen an island was in the China Sea (98). The guilt that he feels in both instances is that of the prosperous man who knows others have died so he can prosper. However, the acknowledged guilt of killing a Japanese soldier is also matched by the unacknowledged guilt of having fled Germany before Hitler took control. Kleinman thinks of his life as 'the Flight, the Battle, the Riches, and the Decline' (40), a life that corresponds with the great upheavals of the mid-to-late twentieth century and shows how the insignificant story of one man whose identity is not fixed is also the story of his adopted nation.

Kleinman's identity is figured through the houses he buys and inhabits, but also through a series of images that emphasize both continuity and slippage. Since boyhood, we learn, he has been unable to keep a yarmulke in place: 'something about the shape of his cranium: an irreligious skull' (24), and this image captures his ambivalent feelings towards his ethnic and religious identities. His son Jimmy marries a woman who converts to Judaism for his sake, and ends up a 'better' Jew than Kleinman. She has to remind her father-in-law of crucial religious holidays and practices, and admonishes him when he pronounces the Americanized 'Yom Kipper' instead of 'Yom Kip-*pur*' (54). The notion that Claudine, who has freely embraced her Jewish identity, is more authentic than Kleinman is further reinforced in the novel through the recurring images of originals and copies: he commissions a copy of one of the Japanese letters, and he flees Germany with two Peccatte bows, one original and one a copy. He sells the counterfeit one to gain passage to the US, but it later transpires that that had been the original; a small detail in the novel, but one that emphasizes the 'counterfeit' identities that refugees from Europe created for themselves in the New World.

Alongside the images of originals and copies, and the probing of notions of authenticity in identity formation, the novel further underscores the idea that identities are made and remade, fashioned and undone, through a series of small images that echo one another throughout the disjointed narrative and show how the past lives in the present. The condo in Boston, for example, turns out to have the same veined marble staircase that he remembers from his father's house in Hamburg. The condo manager is unable to shed any light on this, and Kleinman feels 'shaken' because memory 'seemed like an unfamiliar companion' (135). Just as he has successfully repressed the memory of Meyer Sharp falling into the river, Kleinman has also repressed the memory of his German past, except for those moments of haunting that produce temporal and existential anxieties and force him to admit that the world turned through cycles (116). When his daughter is three years old, she starts tugging at her earlobes in exactly the same way that Kleinman's father had done, showing to her father that though he has turned his back on his past, the bloodline lives on. When he takes his son camping, he finds himself repeating acts he remembered from his stepfather in Queens, and finds it 'miraculous' that a motion of Hank Kleinman's is now repeated in his own limbs. The two companion images relating to the father and the stepfather prompt questions about Kleinman's composite, if not hyphenated, identity, and are further amplified by another set of mirroring images in the novel that question the wisdom of tying identity to place.

Standing on his son's porch in Brooklyn, Kleinman looks at the Brooklyn Bridge, noticing the lights shining in one direction, and 'the shadows of its cables a dark ghost in the other' (112). To the symbolism of the bridge Canin adds further symbolism when Kleinman proceeds to plant some tulip bulbs that have come all the way from Holland. The scene ends with Kleinman looking across the river at the low end of Manhattan island, 'where the ceaseless trade of the new immigrants ran day and night, unabated, meat trucks and cabs and delivery vans scrabbling furiously over the pocked-up roads' (115). This dynamic image of an ever-changing country is matched by the images of the US constructed by the younger generation, represented by Jimmy and Claudine. Jimmy fails to see anything important in the planting of Dutch bulbs in American soil: 'you're putting them in *here*?' (112), he asks his father, suggesting that he should 'throw them out' instead (112). Where Kleinman re-enacts the older conception of an American as someone who arrives from the old world and puts down roots in the new one, Claudine stands for new ways of understanding what it means to be American. She converts to Judaism in order to marry a man who, being the son of a Catholic mother, is not really a Jew, and being American affords her the freedom to make such choices. At the same time, her understanding of what it means to be American comes not from the models of immigration to the US, but rather through her understanding of current affairs and her country's interactions with the world in the present and not the past. Asked what she has to atone for on Yom Kippur, she replies 'Somalia. Haiti. Baghdad' (55). The US gave her father-in-law security, opportunity and prosperity, but to her the country is not a protector but an aggressor: a country defined not by the people it received, but by the ones that suffer outside its borders.

The image of land and borders is taken up again in the scenes narrating the visit to Japan. Kleinman is taken to Lake Ashi, a place mentioned in the dead soldier's letter. He stops there hoping to see Mount Fuji reflected in the water, the way it was described in the letter. His uncomprehending guide promises he can buy postcards instead and urges him to get back in the car, but he stays to perform another symbolic ritual: he plants tulip bulbs that he has smuggled into the country. He finds the ground 'a firm, reddish pack like the soil in Allegheny Mountains. It struck him, the similarity of the earth; he could be in western Pennsylvania. This is where the enemy lived' (146). In this scene, which echoes others I have discussed in Norman Rush and Dave Eggers, Kleinman sees the fiction of the land as a physical container of identity and through the image of the Dutch smuggled bulbs, now in Japan by way of the US, Canin brings together routes and roots.

The journey to Japan can also be seen as another form of dark tourism, a notion reinforced in the narrative when Kleinman is asked to complete a form at immigration. Asked for the purpose of his visit, he has little choice but to tick the box for 'pleasure', but he thinks that really he should have written duty, or justice, or recompense (40). His encounter with Teiji probably accomplishes none of the above, but he leaves the country with the sense of something learnt. On the train back to Tokyo at the end of his visit, Kleinman looks out of the window and thinks that 'the world was the same in every corner of its reach' (185). This is not the sameness that Will and Hand find on their travels in *You Shall Know Our Velocity*. It is one that is perhaps a little more sentimental, but also one that helps him to understand the importance of stasis and movement: 'Greenery, water, settlement, the enduring journey of children' are the things that are the same the world over, he thinks, and here the chapter ends. The next one finds him back in time, looking after his grandson in Brooklyn and rejecting the idea of leaving Boston to move to New York, because to him that would mean going home to die. The idea of rejecting the homecoming because to come home is to die is an ironic inversion of his flight from the original German home, which saved his life but led to his father's death, and is one of several instances where Canin highlights echoes and symmetries between the various strands of his story.

Another 'echoing' passage can be found when Kleinman thinks of his return from the war:

> He remembered a feeling, first visited upon him when he spied the Golden Gate bridge from the deck of the troopship on his return from the Pacific: that he had been caught up in a repugnant dynamism in which human life was dust, windborne chaff with which to cover the earth. (130)

The image of dust suggesting mortality and the vanity of human endeavour matches the image of the ash-filled air in Pittsburgh. Meanwhile, the image of seeing the bridge from the returning ship mirrors the image of seeing Barbados from the air on the way to a luxury holiday, and seeing the East China Sea on the way to war. The sense that the narrative conveys is that these images are related, and together can be seen as representing the dynamic formation of Kleinman's identity. Such a dynamic formation implies not only a multiplicity of determining factors and events, but also a sense of their *simultaneity*: the past lives on in the present, despite Kleinman's best efforts always to look forward and never to regret change.

The mixed-up, confusing telling of the events of Kleinman's life emphasizes the interconnectedness of the transatlantic journeys that shaped his identity, but it also suggests that no simple narrative can be constructed out of an immigrant life. At the beginning of the twentieth century, for example, Mary Antin was able to re-birth herself, and think of her pre-American self as another. The story she told in *The Promised Land* was paradigmatic; a linear story of leaving the past and the old country behind, and forging new ties and a new life in the new world. No such neat narrative is available to Kleinman at the second half of the twentieth century. Multiple allegiances, multiple homes and multiple fractures undermine what looks from the outside as a typical story of the Jewish boy who leaves Germany just in time, fights for America in World War II, and like his adopted country finds material wealth and prosperity in the postwar years. The novel's rejection of a linear model of narration, and more specifically of a linear model of narrating immigration, is also made evident in its final few pages. The story of the killing of the Japanese soldier is told near the end, when Kleinman is on his way back from his trip to Japan. As the scene of the killing comes to an end, the plane from Tokyo takes off, and Kleinman thinks of his grandson, 'in his chest the lightness of escape, then lift' (206). The novel tells the story of the killing after the story of atonement; it tells of the *originating* trauma in the book's *concluding* pages, and it tells what Kleinman did in Japan when Kleinman is on a plane leaving Japan. Moreover, just as the memory of the killing is acknowledged, Kleinman sits back and thinks not only of the past and of death, but also of the future and of life; that of his grandson. The links between generations, and the acknowledging of a complex past that cannot be contained or conveniently erased under an American identity, are the concepts that link the two novels discussed in this chapter with the two that are the focus of the next one.

6 Dinaw Mengestu, *How To Read the Air*; Jhumpa Lahiri, *The Namesake*

DINAW MENGESTU, *HOW TO READ THE AIR*

Dinaw Mengestu made his fictional debut with *The Beautiful Things that Heaven Bears* (renamed *Children of the Revolution* for the British market) in 2007. The book won the *Guardian* First Book Award that year, and in 2010 Mengestu was chosen as one of *The New Yorker*'s best writers in their '20 under 40' feature. The *New Yorker* feature drew inevitable complaints about the selection criteria, about the fact that nearly all the authors featured were graduates of famous MFA programs, and about their multi-ethnic, multi-cultural backgrounds. Mengestu is guilty of having an MFA, as well as being in possession of a name that clearly marks him out as 'foreign,' even if those who have listened to him on radio interviews would not have guessed there was anything remotely exotic about his regular American accent. When *How to Read the Air* appeared three years after *The Beautiful Things*, the debate about Mengestu's identity continued.

Miguel Syjuco, reviewing for *The New York Times*, noted that the novel 'at first' seemed too familiar. He drew comparisons with Joseph O'Neill, Jhumpa Lahiri and Amy Tan, but noted also that Mengestu appeared 'aware of this perceived weakness.' The evidence he cited from the novel was where Jonas's boss at the refugee centre says: 'When you think about it, it's all really the same story. All we're doing is just changing around the names of the countries.' The point that Syjuco went on to make was that ultimately Mengestu does not just tell 'the same story': 'In the end,' he concluded, 'Mengestu distinguishes this book by adeptly using Yosef's story to deepen the narrative, and by creating Jonas's redemption through the character's act of story-retelling.' As this chapter will argue, Mengestu does indeed make something new out of the familiar immigrant narrative, and his book, along with Lahiri's, describes and helps to shape new ways of understanding both the significance of the immigrant experience and the immigrant novel in the US. Questions about Mengestu's identity remain, however. Syjuco notes that the author now lives in Paris and describes him as 'a global citizen.' As for Jonas' story, he calls it 'uniquely African, American, and both at once'; an interesting phrase in that it makes a clear distinction between the familiar category of 'African American' (in its hyphenated and non-hyphenated permutations) and the unfamiliar concept of a novel written by a 'global citizen' and telling a story that is African *and* American. Reviews such as Syjuco's are clear examples of the extent to which notions of national identity have been transformed in recent years, leaving us all grappling for new terms, new categories, new ways of defining these authors and the stories they tell. Only twenty days after Syjuco's review was published, an interview appeared in *The Paris Review* where Mengestu actually described himself as 'American and African at all points and times' (La Force).

Perhaps two personal points of view do not constitute a trend, but one wonders whether the 'and' will soon become more familiar than the hyphen or the qualifying adjective, which are the two main ways in which nationality and ethnicity have been understood in the US. If the formulation 'American and [other nationality]' does gain more currency, it too will have to be qualified in important ways. The African in 'American and African' is not the same as the African to be found in African countries, and this is a lesson that Mengestu learnt first-hand. He told Larry Rohter how on a trip to report for one of his non-fiction pieces, he ran into trouble while attempting to interview Hutu rebels from Rwanda:

> 'I could speak English as well as I wanted to them, but they could only see that my features are what they consider Tutsi, and that was definitely threatening to my life,' he said rather matter-of-factly. 'They would look at me, and my translator would say, "No, he's American." He was always very specific, telling me, 'Don't confuse them, don't try to say you're Ethiopian, just tell them you're American, don't complicate things with this extra layer, because nobody's going to believe it.'"

Mengestu's experience in Africa is related to the plight of some of the characters discussed in Part II of this book, in that in Africa he cannot call himself African because being American trumps all other nationalities and ethnicities. His plight is also inverted, though, in the sense that he looks African in a way that the African American traveller in Amy Tan's book never did. Though eager to showcase his African identity, Mengestu is also wary of the labels often attached to American novelists. For example, he told Thessaly La Force in *The Paris Review* that he sees his first novel as an American one: 'I wrote my first book without being to Ethiopia since I was two years old. Why is this an Ethiopian novel and not an American novel? [It] . . . is very much about America—it just happens to have African and Ethiopian characters.' Larry Rohter, on the other hand, sees both novels to date as being primarily defined through their engagement with 'the African diaspora,' a phrase that puts the novels at odds with the idea that they might be American more than anything else. Rohter goes on to report that Mengestu has further plans for a book that will not have 'that same sense of dislocation and displacement;' the quoted words here belong to Mengestu himself, and they mark the author's own complex engagement with the issue of his authorial identity.

The sense of dislocation and displacement is strong in *The Beautiful Things* and in *How to Read the Air*, but it is not only a thematic strand in each book. Though it can be problematic to use biographical information to read a novel, it is too tempting not to note that much of *How to Read the Air* was composed in France, where the author lives with his French wife. Furthermore, Mengestu has spoken in interviews of his desire to write about his home, his American, Midwestern home, *as if* from outside. He told Thessaly La Force:

> After I first went to Ethiopia in 2005, one of the first things I did was drive to Peoria, where I hadn't been in many years. I was trying to put these two places, which were very much opposed, visually together in my head to see how that experience would feel. As if I had never been to Peoria before and I was coming straight from Ethiopia—it is a very similar trip to the one I took when I was two years old and the one my father took before I was born. Part of the novel began there.

The novel's genesis, then, can be traced back to not one but two 'false' homecomings, both of them associated with the outsider's sense of dislocation, rather than the insider's sense of belonging. The experience of seeing Peoria as if for the first time is twice mediated in *How to Read the Air*: Jonas tells the story of his parents' journey to the US, and he attempts to retrace their long roadtrip from Peoria to Nashville. In so doing, Mengestu is altering the very notion of the 'Midwest' as a geographical and a literary category: his Midwest is shaped by the gaze of the Ethiopian immigrant, and then reshaped through the journey south to Tennessee, and filtered through the sensibility of an American teacher who throughout the narrative strives for a sense of home and belonging. At the same time, the story of his father's African past is also narrated in a way that rejects any notion of authenticity: the story he tells is a fictionalized version of events, and he narrates it to his students; while insisting on his own Americanness, Jonas also becomes an African story-teller.

Mengestu's first novel was an immigrant novel, but it was also a Washington, D.C. novel. Its vivid depiction of streets and neighbourhoods and the lives that were lived in them made this an important urban novel about the nation's capital, and the ways in which its characters interacted with their environment gave the novel a texture that is rarely found in the immigrant novel: where the latter often sees the subject as somehow separate from their environment, this one dealt with characters who embrace city-living at the same time that they recognize the invisible demarcations and borders that divide along colour, class and income lines. The novel tells the story of Sepha Stephanos who leaves Ethiopia supposedly temporarily, and ends up a reluctant immigrant running a grocery store in an African American neighbourhood in Washington, D.C. The loneliness that Stephanos feels, and his intense sense of dislocation are explored through his relationship with his two close friends, both of whom are African immigrants, and through his budding but ultimately short-lived friendship with a white neighbour and her mixed-race daughter. Those relationships, in turn, are related to the novel's engagement with space: Stephanos' convenience store, his home and that of his white neighbour, and the place that Logan Circle occupies in Washington, D.C.'s complex geography.

Throughout the book, the home, the streets and public and private spaces are invested with meaning that brings out Stephanos' complex sense of identity, alongside his intense sense of dislocation. He feels he does not belong there, but he does not plan to return to Africa either. He has family in Ethiopia, he can phone and send them presents, so that Africa is not just in the past, but also part of his present, and yet his ties to his country of origin start to loosen. When we meet him, he has been running his store for ten years. He recalls Logan Circle as 'predominantly poor, black, cheap, and sunk in a depression that had struck the city twenty years earlier and never left' (35–6). Now, Logan Circle is seeing the first signs of gentrification, heralded by the arrival of Stephanos' new neighbour, Judith. He describes the event as one that 'had once seemed impossible' (14) in this unofficially segregated part of the city, and when one of his black neighbours complains about Judith moving into the area, he muses: 'The neighborhood's changing, things are changing, it's not like it used to be, I can't believe how much it's changed, who would have thought it could change so quickly, nothing is permanent, everything changes' (23). His deliberate repetition of platitudes emphasizes how little control the locals have over the arrival of the affluent whites determined to gentrify Logan Circle; he calls the mantra of change 'the passive and helpless observations of people stuck living on the sidelines' (23). The people on the sidelines are not only immigrants like himself; some are African Americans, most are poor; in other words, the particular space he inhabits generates an allegiance not with his ethnic group, but with the dispossessed, those excluded by the narrative of freedom, democracy and prosperity that Washington, D.C. showcases to the world. Much of that narrative is conveyed through the city's architecture and its famous memorials. Stephanos recalls his early years in the city, when he and his African friends would gaze upon the Lincoln Memorial and try to memorize the Gettysburg Address. 'It's been years since either of them has gone near those buildings, and how can you blame them? Reality has settled in,' he observes ruefully (47).

Through its complex engagement with urban space, the novel demonstrates some of the ways in which the African other is excluded from dominant discourse and rendered invisible through the city's racially demarcated topography. One day, a couple of white American tourists come into Stephanos' store. The man remarks upon the beautiful old houses in the area, and Stephanos gives him a brief history of the neighbourhood. After that, he follows the tourists around as they walk from Logan Circle to Dupont Circle, only 1.3 miles but a world apart. Stephanos speaks of his love of P Street, which grows prettier and wider as it heads west, with the houses 'increasingly grand and luxurious, as if each step forward were a step toward paradise' (73). The conception of the affluent white areas of the city as paradise is implicitly linked with the image of Africa as hell. The title of the novel is explained in the narrative when Stephanos remembers his friend Joseph talking about Dante's *Inferno*, and his admiration for the lines 'Through a round aperture I saw appear, Some of the beautiful things that heaven bears.' Joseph finds the lines moving because he relates them to the experience of fleeing Africa 'because that is what we lived through. Hell every day with only glimpses of heaven in between' (100). The figuring of Africa as hell was discussed in Part One of this book, where it was seen as a white imperialist construct. Here, it is the African himself who identifies his African past as 'hell', but as the novel makes clear, the immigrant does not find paradise in America. The thematic importance of the concept of paradise does not relate only to immigration.

Near the end of the novel, as Logan Circle continues to be gentrified, poorer households begin to get evicted. The eviction from the poor area of the city is an ironic inversion of the eviction from paradise motif, and one of the things it underscores is that the novel conceives of dislocation not as a state of suspended being as a result of immigration or expatriation, but rather as the process by which the American city redraws its borders in order to retain zones of exclusion and forced otherness. A different zone of exclusion is seen when Stephanos visits his uncle in a twenty-six story tower block occupied almost exclusively by Ethiopians: 'Within this building there is an entire world made up of old lives and relationships transported perfectly intact from Ethiopia,' notes Stephanos. 'To call the building insular is to miss the point entirely. Living here is as close to living back home as one can get, which is precisely why I moved out after two years and precisely why my uncle has never left' (115–6). The tower block therefore represents another type of dislocation: the Ethiopian community transported almost intact to the American capital. Tower blocks have inevitable associations of poverty, deprivation and overcrowding, but here they are contrasted not with the luxury houses on the way to Dupont Circle, but with the ones undergoing gentrification in Logan Circle. Stephanos describes them as 'five-story mansions that had once belonged to someone of great import . . . but that over the years had been neglected, burned out, or in my case, divided into cheap, sometimes cockroach-infested apartments' (16). Judith's is such a house, 'a beautiful, tragic wreck of a building' (15) that she hopes to restore to its former glory.

However, just as the Ethiopians know that their tower block enclave cannot survive indefinitely untouched by its wider environment ('They'll all become American' (118), muses one of the residents), so Judith cannot create a permanent home, despite the inclusiveness of her liberal views and education, and despite the symbolism of her mixed-race daughter. In a telling inversion of familiar motifs, it is not the Ethiopian enclave that is attacked but the white home when Judith's house is destroyed by arsonists at about the same time that the evictions start. As the white rich drive out the black poor, the neighbourhood becomes divided along colour and money lines. The novel suggests that the displaced and alienated, America's 'others', are not always necessarily its new immigrants, and that those in-between spaces where colour and class lines are endlessly re-negotiated are the spaces where a new type of immigrant feels at home. Walking twenty blocks back to Logan Circle near the end of the novel, Stephanos realizes how well he knows the streets, and wonders how he came to master the city in this way. Having arrived with no intention of staying longer than a few months, Stephanos has no clear understanding of how he became American: 'How did I end up here?' he asks. 'Where is the grand narrative of my life?' (147).

He doesn't remember when he understood that he had 'left home for good' (177), and for that reason he is startled to find himself thinking of Logan Circle as 'home':

> So, this is the city that I've made my life and home. It seems important now to think of it in that way. To consider it not in fragments or pieces, but as a unified whole . . . I can't help but think of what I'm doing as going home. . . . There is a simple and startling power to that phrase: going back home. There's an implied contradiction, a sense of moving forward and backward at the same time. (173–4)

Mengestu's narrative dramatizes the experience of the African immigrant aided by the tropes of fragmentation (the streets and blocks that are not a 'unified whole') and home-coming, examined through unconventional family models, private and communal spaces as redefining notions of home. Stephanos, who occupies some indeterminate space between exile and immigration, finally makes his home in Logan Circle, a place scarred by the junk left behind by the evicted households and by the burnt-down house. This place of unrest and uprooting for others becomes a place where his roots will grow. Mengestu's second novel continues to explore the relations between roots and routes by shifting the emphasis from the immigrant to the child of immigrants, and by telling two stories: that of Jonas Wolde-mariam as an alienated American, and that of his Ethiopian parents' early years in the US. The home is not only a place of national allegiance and ethnic identity as it was in the previous book, but also a space closely and explicitly related to relationships and the attempt to integrate the self into a larger scheme. Where Jonas is seen mainly in the home or in his classroom, his parents are seen on the move, taking a road trip that is interspersed throughout the narrative.

Jonas considers himself an American, but his understanding of home and belonging is a complex one. Like many people in similar positions, he is annoyed when asked where he is from. The answer that he is from Illinois is never satisfactory, as people keep trying to discover where he is *really* from. His skin colour and his African name do inevitably mark him out as a 'foreigner' of some sort, but the book largely suggests that his is an internal, and internalized, form of exile or dislocation. As a college-educated New Yorker with a decent teaching job and a hard-working wife who aspires to success, Jonas has no obvious reason to feel disenfranchised or marginal, and yet he does. His unwillingness or inability to conform to the narrative of immigrant success is imagined in the novel as a form of exile. His wife, Angela, tells him that his boss used to joke that Jonas acted more like an illegal immigrant than a Midwesterner because he was self-effacing and reluctant to divulge information about himself. Angela thinks the analogy false, though, because if you talk to an immigrant long enough 'they'll tell you where they came from, and then once they start most of the time they won't really want to stop' (77). If Jonas sees himself as an American, then he is justified in not wanting to tell the story of where he came from. However, once it becomes clear to him that his roots in Peoria are not to be separated from the routes that took his parents to the Midwest, he too, starts and doesn't really want to stop.

The act of storytelling is crucial in this novel, and it emphasizes not only the discursive nature of identities, personal and cultural alike, but also the central place that storytelling occupies in constructions of American ideologies. The book opens with Jonas working at an immigration centre. His job is to assist asylum seekers in preparing the personal statement that describes their plight, but he takes this brief to extremes and often ends up more or less writing the reports for them. 'I took half-page statements of a coarse and often brutal nature and supplied them with the details that made them real for the immigration officer that would someday be reading them,' he explains (24). In Part One of this study I discussed Valentino Achak Deng's first attempt to tell the story of his life at the refugee camp in Kakuma, and I argued that the transformation of the page-long account to the 535-page novel represented Deng's Americanization. In a pleasingly symmetrical fashion, the African American in this novel takes the Dave Eggers role of telling a real story for an American audience, thereby indirectly asserting his own sense of belonging. Yet Jonas is also aware of the flimsiness of all claims to belonging. During a boat party organized by his workplace, Jonas sees the asylum seekers whose success the party celebrates coming out onto the deck to look for the space once occupied by the Twin Towers:

> A year or maybe two years earlier Bill [his boss] would have stuck around longer and recounted to them his own personal experience of that day . . . In this case, however, Bill wasn't alone. For a few years we had all tried to stake our own personal claim on what happened that

day. That time had clearly passed, and the best he or any of us could do was to try on occasion to set the record straight. (28)

What Jonas identifies here is the awareness that stories of unity and belonging cannot stay unchanged much beyond the immediate circumstances that produced them. The first few years after the attacks, there was indeed a strengthened sense of belonging among America's newer citizens, along with a need shared by many to stake a claim by bearing witness, but it didn't take long before US military operations divided the country again. By highlighting the stories his boss Bill used to tell about 9/11, Jonas highlights not only the need to tell stories about who we are, but also the provisionality of such narratives.

When Jonas describes the early stages of his relationship with Angela, he describes two people in search of a sense of home. Whereas Angela teases Jonas for his reluctance to discuss where he comes from, she herself appears to have no strong sense of origin. Missouri, we learn, is the place Angela 'most associated with home . . . "I think we lived there the longest, but who knows"' (30). Rather than being defined through stories of origins, Jonas and Angela attempt to create a space, both physical and ideological, that they can associate with home. They think of themselves as stray cats (31), and they are not content with being New Yorkers. They realize that in order truly to belong in New York they need to form an attachment to a quarter, to find streets, bars and restaurants that will become their favourite (31). The recognition that the New Yorker has to insert him/herself deliberately into one or more micro-communities also serves to underscore the financial side of this phenomenon. The bars and restaurants that Jonas and Angela will choose to call their favourite will be selected not along racial lines, but in keeping with what they can afford. Indeed, Angela's understanding of success not only conforms to the dominant discourse of heterosexual marriage, but it also shows that her very understanding of identity is built around unwritten rules and laws 'commonly prescribed by others' (100). Disappointed that two years after their marriage they still lack the outward signs of success, identified as capital raised, furnishings and homes bought and then re-sold for profit (100), Angela tells her husband that he has no 'clear sense of identity' (100). Her remark is prompted by the sense that he has failed to even aspire to home-ownership as a marker of successful integration into mainstream society, and the lack of a proper American home is viewed as a failure in their relationship. However, Jonas probably has no clear sense of identity for very different reasons. He is not only the son of immigrants, but also the son of a deeply unhappy couple, and the lesson he learns is that in order to acknowledge who he is and where he comes from, he needs to understand not only what it meant for his parents to emigrate, but also why they ended up so unhappy with each other. As his own marriage begins to disintegrate, their small apartment becomes a battleground, with Jonas and Angela defensively occupying different spaces as far away from the other as possible. Through the story of the failing marriage figured through the couple's engagement with living space, the novel draws analogies with the bigger story of the child of Ethiopian immigrants looking for his place in the world.

The novel, however, concerns itself not only with the domestic, but also with public spaces. Jonas imagines that the road trip from Peoria to Nashville is the trip that made his parents American and marked their relationship in important, though by no means positive, ways. The road trip occupies a firm place in American culture and the American imagination, but it is rarely associated with the immigrant. To undertake an American road trip is to be already solidly, unambiguously American in ideology and allegiance. Jonas' parents are therefore exceptional in their undertaking, and all the more so for choosing to travel to the home of country music. Yet we learn from Jonas that a love of country music was one of the few things that his father had brought over from Ethiopia (38), and this small reminder of the powerful presence of American culture in Africa effectively questions and undermines assumptions about authenticity and cultural ownership. Country music may be quintessentially American and white, but 'it spoke' to Jonas's father long before he became an immigrant. We are accustomed to the image of the older European immigrants who brought their fiddles and accordions, so the notion of this modern African man bringing his love of American music with him is pleasingly dissonant, and speaks of new realities that shape and re-shape the experience of being or becoming American.

The second unusual feature of the parents' road trip is the visit to the Laconte Fort. In addition to undertaking the road trip as a kind of pilgrimage to the home of country music, Jonas' father also intends to strengthen his claim on a new, American identity by visiting the Laconte Fort. Jonas' father had 'tried to come up with a series of standards by which he could judge his assimilation,' and one of them involved visiting historical landmarks; 'the more obscure the better' (86–7). By acquainting himself with the country's more obscure landmarks, he would then be able to impress others who would think: 'Look how far he has come' (87). Yosef understood that 'he wouldn't get all the way into the heart of America just yet, but surely in the end he would feel closer to it' (88). Where the immigrant father is imagined and remembered as the one most keen to assimilate and forge new ties through his engagement with public space and historical monuments, Jonas' mother is imagined as a more reluctant and sceptical immigrant. When they make their visit to the Fort, she learns its history but, according to our narrator, she refuses to believe that the story really did involve white people: 'there was no stretch of the imagination that could allow her to conceive of hungry white faces ... and so she shaded in the faces, broadened out the lips and noses, and came up with a picture more suitable for a slow, hunger-pained death' (139–40). Like Joseph and Kenneth, Stephanos' friends who had stopped visiting the Lincoln Memorial in the previous novel, Mariam here understands the ways in which race and otherness can be excluded in public monuments, and how built structures carry within them indelible signs of inequality and suppression. Elsewhere, she thinks that Americans are too territorial. '"All those fences and flags," she had once said, seeing very little difference between the two' (278). The relationship between fences and flags is one that this book seeks to understand by dramatizing journeys that cross borders, both visible and invisible. The linking of the fence with the flag highlights the dominance of the ideology of the nation-state, while it also links the idea of the nation to the idea of home: the fence and the flag symbolize territorial belonging and national allegiance on the domestic scale, but they also stand for the greater 'fence' that is the national border which also seeks to contain Americans and exclude others.

Jonas finally works out how to stop being a man with no clear sense of identity, and the book that we are reading is both the narrative of how he achieves that, and the very enactment of the discovery. The story of his parents' road trip becomes his story of origins, and his understanding of how lives and histories interconnect is the only consolation he has at the end of the book. The whole narrative has been arranged in a confusing, non-chronological fashion, and the last chapter skilfully brings together endings and beginnings. Chapter 26 is divided into three sections. The first one opens with Jonas saying goodbye to his mother after a rare, and long-overdue, visit. Immediately afterwards, he goes and buys maps of Illinois, Tennessee and Missouri. Driving along, he begins 'to search for glimpses of [his] parents as they must have looked when they first came here' (299). The road trip he starts takes the story back to its opening chapter, which begins with Josef and Mariam's setting out on their four hundred and eighty-four mile journey from Peoria to Nashville. The second section in the final chapter narrates the conclusion of Josef and Mariam's trip, and the third section announces Jonas' divorce from Angela. Yet despite the bleakness of these stories (the unhappy mother-son reunion, the two failed marriages), Jonas ends on a slightly optimistic note, telling Angela that they will remain a part of each other's lives for a long time. 'We do persist, whether we care or not, with all our flaws and glory,' he thinks (305), and that's what he would like to tell not only Angela but also his mother and his father. This sense of connectedness does not feel like a forced ending, because the novel's various narrative strands have been building up to this moment. The stories of his parents, made up though they are, help Jonas to understand who he is and where he has come from, but the concept of connectedness is also introduced earlier on in the novel and examined in different ways. Jonas' storytelling, for example, is imaginatively linked with the creation of new ties that bind the alienated individual to his city.

One day at work Jonas throws away his lesson plan and instead starts telling his students a story about his father's life in Ethiopia. When he finishes the story, he walks home for 'one hundred and two glorious blocks' (185), and thereafter feels the need to 'come down from the almost delirious heights [he has] reached before returning home' (202). The stories he tells are stories of dislocation, immigration and forced exile, and at the conclusion of each episode he needs the exposure to physical space to allow him to untangle his narrative meanderings. After that first transgressive lesson, he imagines his students busily texting and e-mailing each other with views on their unhinged teacher. 'Millions of invisible bits of data were being transmitted through underground cable wires and satellite networks, and I was their sole subject of concern. I don't know why I found so much comfort in that thought, but . . . I felt embraced' (186). By imagining the virtual spaces of text messaging and e-mailing as physical cables and networks, Jonas seeks to understand the invisible ties that new technologies have created. He thinks of New York as a 'terribly lonely and isolating place' (186), but finds the invisible bits of data binding him to this alienating urban space in new and unexpected ways. The sense of connectedness first prompted by the thought of the invisible data traversing the city continues to develop in the narrative, moving from the invisible and virtual to the real and tangible. Jonas begins to make a habit of 'decompressing' after each lesson by riding the subway into far-off corners of the city that he's never been to before. He seeks out the hard-to-reach neighbourhoods and finds himself in streets 'where few people my generation and older spoke English without an accent' (203).

By discovering the spaces inhabited by immigrants much less integrated than he is, Jonas feels a mastery over the city that had previously eluded him. Crucially, one of the ways in which this mastery manifests itself is through the act of imaginative storytelling. During his walks, he continues the stories he had been telling his students by looking at the immigrants around him and imagining their life stories. 'I thought if I could imagine where all of the people I passed had come from and how they had gotten here, then I could add their stories to my own basket of origins,' he explains (203). In *The Beautiful Things That Heaven Bears*, the immigrant Stephanos walked the streets of Washington, D.C. with a sense of exclusion, looking at the people and the houses from the outsider's point of view. Jonas, the American child of immigrant parents, develops a different relationship to his environment: he searches for immigrant routes, and seeks to place the story of his own origins into the larger story of a city built on immigration, rather than imagining himself as the alienated outsider in a city of people more American than himself. In *The Promised Land*, which exemplifies early twentieth-century attitudes to immigration and assimilation, Mary Antin conceived of immigrants as cables binding the old world to the new, and linked the ships that crossed the Atlantic to 'the bitter seas of racial differences' they encountered upon arrival (2). Jonas also sees the routes that form the city's roots, and the invisible cables that bind people and cultures together are now also the ones that connect computers and phones in virtual space. This grounding of the immigrant experience, both physical and virtual, helps him to understand his own place as a New Yorker, albeit one from Peoria and before that Addis Ababa.

Where *The Beautiful Things That Heaven Bears* was a Washington, D.C. novel that paid close attention to streets, neighbourhoods, and their ethnic and social makeup, *How to Read the Air* is a New York novel of a different type. Jonas' experience of living in New York is placed within two contexts: that of his father's journey out of Africa, which Jonas embellishes and fictionalizes as he re-tells it to his students, and the road trip that his parents take to Nashville. These two parallel narratives emphasize a dynamic, rather than static, conception of space, and they are contrasted throughout the book with Jonas' failed attempts to put down roots through marriage and home-making. The story of his parents is one of wanting and trying to become American. His own, by contrast, is one of unravelling his American identity, of trying to weave narratives that help him to understand that to feel an exile, a dislocated person, a man of no country, is also a way of being American. The explorations of space, from the cramped apartments he shares with his wife, to the remote districts in Brooklyn and Queens that he visits, ultimately help Jonas to understand the symbols and the narratives that the US is built upon, the home and the immigrant journey. Jonas imagines his father as 'a man in search of a home,' looking for 'protection' (68–9). His father refused to talk about the journey to the US, beyond saying 'I went to Sudan . . . Then I took a boat to Europe' (268). By filling in the missing narrative of his father's journey, Jonas finds his own home, as story teller and as American citizen.

JHUMPA LAHIRI, *THE NAMESAKE*

Lahiri's first novel was published to great critical acclaim in 2003. Her debut story collection, *Interpreter of Maladies*, had already received a lot of critical attention when it appeared in 1999, and many of the themes and preoccupations of the story collection were carried over to the novel. The background of the author herself, born in England of Bengali parents, and the transatlantic setting of the stories in *Interpreter*, generated debate about the changing face of American literature. If the stories in that collection were to be thought of as American, then the very understanding of American literature had to be widened to accommodate them. Some of the stories belonged to familiar categories and concerned themselves with East-meets-West tales of clashing values and world views. Others, though, like 'A Real Durwan,' were set in India and lacked any sense of an outside presence, either textual or authorial. Indeed, much of the published criticism on Lahiri has sought to place her work in the context of world literature, or Indian literature, or diasporic literature. In other words, her authorial Americanness has not always been taken for granted, even though she has lived in the US since the age of three. The story 'Interpreter of Maladies' centred upon an American couple of Indian origin visiting the country of their ancestors. Mr and

Mrs Das have dark faces, but they also have children called Tina, Ronny and Bobby. They are treated as outsiders in the story, American tourists observed with fascination by their Indian tourist guide, Mr Kapasi. The reversed point of view that sees the ethnic heritage traveller as outsider suggested that Lahiri was actively engaged in questioning categories of belonging and allegiance, and this questioning has continued to inform her work. Indian food also had a very strong presence in the story collection; the selling, buying, preparing and offering of food were used as tropes through which to negotiate national and gendered identities in a globalized environment. For instance, the character of Sanjeev in 'This Blessed House' has fond memories of his time at MIT, where he would walk 'across the Mass. Avenue bridge to order Mughlai chicken with spinach from his favorite Indian restaurant on the other side of the Charles, and return to his dorm to write out clean copies of his problem sets' (138). The symbolic crossing of the bridge emphasized the ease with which the minority ethnic subject could access and literally consume the markers of his own ethnicity, while still being able to cross the bridge back to the world of the ethnic mainstream.

Other stories that emphasized the importance of food included 'A Real Durwan' and 'Mrs. Sen's,' and what these tales further had in common was their preoccupation with the trope of the house and home. The stairwell sweeper in 'A Real Durwan' is a refugee deported to Calcutta after Partition. Her menial job is contrasted with memories of the 'two-story brick house' (71) she lived in with her family, and where once she enjoyed the luxury of a family home, she now lives on the roof of the building she helps to clean. The apartment building as a microcosm for the nation, and as a vertical representation of class inequality, has more recently been explored by Egyptian author Alaa al Aswany in his 2002 *The Yacoubian Building*, but whereas the latter was written in Arabic and had no point of view other than the Egyptian one, Lahiri's story is part of a collection that moves from Calcutta to Connecticut with the kind of unapologetic ease that partly makes the stories American. In this respect, the comparison with Alaa al Aswany is illuminating if we also consider his next novel, the 2008 *Chicago*. Chicago is where the author himself trained as a dentist, but as he explained to Rachel Cooke, despite his admiration for the city and the country, ultimately 'it was not, in the long run, for him' and he returned to Egypt. The book is written in Arabic and presents an outsider's view of America. Alaa al Aswany's characters have none of the ethnic ambiguity of Lahiri's, and it is perhaps for this reason that the book was cautiously received by some American critics. An American author, it would seem, is allowed and perhaps even expected to engage with difficult issues of racism and the arrogance of the western gaze, but the same kind of criticism is less welcome when it comes from outside. Ligaya Mishan, reviewing for *The New York Times*, noted that 'at least for American readers,' the book is perplexing, like a fun-house mirror in which we recognize ourselves only intermittently. Although the novel's setting is ostensibly Chicago . . . it could be any American city, blandly debauched and riven by class and racial differences. With the vaguest of physical description, it functions merely as an exotic backdrop, alien and menacing to the Egyptian characters who have journeyed there.

Rather than celebrating the Egyptian point of view that the novel offered of Chicago, Mishan worried that episodes in which the Egyptian characters in Chicago were the victims of racist abuse did not ring true. On the other side of the Atlantic, reviewing for a British newspaper, Sukhdev Sandhu noted that 'the American characters are short-shrifted, portrayed in general as either racist ignoramuses or, if they're black or progressively minded, as victims of an enduringly racist and capitalist society.' Critiques of racism and capitalism are far from rare in American letters, but the critical reception of this Egyptian novel suggests that one needs a strong claim to an American identity in order to offer a critique of American living. It is in this respect that Lahiri's books and many of her characters can be thought of as unambiguously American. Despite their crossings, literal and metaphorical, they are endowed with the author's sense of cultural entitlement: it is the author's American gaze that allows her to criticize both the racist attitudes of the residents in the Calcutta apartment block and the white Americans in the American suburbs. Perhaps even the racist attitudes that Valentino Achak Deng portrays in *What Is the What* would have been less palatable if his story had not been fictionalized by an American author.

The stories in *Interpreter of Maladies* are notable not only for their multiple, though American-centred, perspectives, but also for the sense of a female sensibility, seen in the author's concern for domestic space and the different meanings attached to it by men and women. 'This Blessed House' is both an example and a wonderful parody of the way in which the home is implicated in the construction of gendered ethnic identities. When Sanjeev and Twinkle, 'good little Hindus' (137), move into their new home in Connecticut, they participate in the traditional success story of the immigrant: the man graduates from MIT and takes a good job with a firm near Hartford, and the woman, who is found for him by his parents, follows and helps create an American home for them so as to ease their integration while also upholding some of the old traditions. This familiar narrative, however, is parodied in the story when Sanjeev and Twinkle start finding effigies of Christ and other Christian symbols strewn around their new home. Sanjeev wants to throw them away, but Twinkle finds them 'too spectacular' (139) and wants them prominently displayed as quaint ethnic symbols of the 'others' who previously lived in their home. The exoticizing and commodification of the Christian American home presents the Hindu immigrant gaze as dominant rather than marginal. Another recurring motif in Lahiri's writing is the house party, which becomes a rite of passage for the immigrant, and a test of citizenship. Sanjeev is worried about how his friends and colleagues will react to the view of all the Christian relics, but Twinkle's enthusiasm for the quaintness of her Christian home wins the day because it confers upon them the superiority of the western gaze, albeit in a reversed situation. By displaying the tasteless statues and posters, Twinkle scores a two-fold victory: she participates successfully in the championing of the 'ethnic' and 'authentic,' which are markers of a dominant identity, and by exoticizing the Christian tradition she indirectly also asserts her own sense of superiority.

Where 'This Blessed House' offered the reader a glimpse of the author's interest in the ethnic home, *The Namesake* allowed for a much longer, imaginatively sustained exploration of the meaning of home for the Indian immigrant and, crucially, for the immigrant's children as well. Critics noted that Lahiri's book was significant among other reasons because it represented a shift in the way authors write about and readers think about immigration, ethnicity and assimilation. Natalie Friedman, for example, asserted that Gogol, *The Namesake*'s protagonist, 'does not feel dislocated, because he is at home in America' (114), and she even described his immigrant parents' house as an 'Indian-inflected Massachusetts home' (121). Lahiri has managed in this novel to explore those two meanings of home, the ethnic home and the feeling of being at home in America, through her engagement with a series of built structures, and it is certainly no coincidence that she has made her protagonist an architect. In its casual, everyday usage, the work architect describes both the person who has the vision and the person who builds that vision, and it is in this sense that Gogol becomes a metaphorical architect of his own self as well as a literal one. The knowledgeable ease with which he 'reads' his girlfriend Maxine's privileged white home supersedes the feeling of inferiority that he might have brought to the encounter. On his very first visit, he is 'stunned by the house.' He admires it 'like a tourist,' but unlike the tourist he is able to note 'the pedimented window lintels, the Doric pilaster, the bracketed entablature, the black cruciform paneled door' (130). In order to break the ice, his girlfriend's mother takes him on a tour of the house, and the first words he says to her are 'Lovely frieze-band windows,' causing her to turn to him, 'puzzled,' and ask 'What?' (132). Maxine and her parents are described as Americans fully in possession of a sense of entitlement. To them, Maxine's 'ethnic' boyfriend is yet another marker of their liberal cosmopolitan outlook, or perhaps he is just another commodity, like the imported pasta, olive oil, and thick wedges of Parmesan and Asiago cheese (145) that they need to take to their summer residence in New Hampshire. Whereas in terms of class and education Gogol has no reason to feel inferior or 'other' in relation to them, ultimately their relationship cannot transcend the cultural differences that separate them. Gogol can 'read' and admire the American home, but in the end it is not the one he wants to live in.

Judith Caesar noted how, in *Interpreter of Maladies*, 'Lahiri uses the architecture of old American houses as an emblem of the emotional spaces between the people who live in those houses' (52), and in this novel the house becomes emblematic of national space as well. The story of how Gogol came to be an American begins with the houses his parents lived in. The novel opens in a Central Square apartment, where Ashima, Gogol's mother, stands in the kitchen trying to assemble an 'approximation of the snack sold for pennies on Calcutta sidewalks' (1). She uses Rice Krispies and Planters peanuts, and the image of the pregnant immigrant mixing American ingredients to make an Indian snack prefigures the mixed identities that will be conferred upon the son she is carrying. The apartment, we soon learn, is 'not at all what she had expected. Not at all like the houses in *Gone With the Wind* or *The Seven-Year Itch*' (30). It is small, cold in winter and hot in summer, cockroach-infested and generally disappointing. Three years later, the family move to a university town outside Boston. As in 'This Blessed House,' we encounter the story of the successful immigrant who excels at university and gains a place in American society through academic achievement. The move to the suburbs is therefore to be seen as a marker of success, of admittance into 'real' America; a move away from the cosmopolitan apartments of the student districts[1]. Yet for Ashima, 'migrating to the suburbs feels more drastic, more distressing than the move from Calcutta to Cambridge had been' (49). Like Mrs. Sen in the story of the same name in *Interpreter*, Ashima becomes trapped in the suburbs because she cannot drive. The suburb therefore becomes not only an ethnically significant space, but also a gendered one, and though Ashima is always seen at home waiting for her adult children to visit, by the end of the novel she too has been transformed so that she no longer represents the kind of stability that the children can fall back on.

The story opens in 1968 and ends in 2000. The last chapter returns much of its focus on Ashima and links the thematic strands of gender, travel and home that have been developing through the narrative. Ashima had arrived in the US to join her husband in 1967, and at the end of the novel she makes the decision to spend half the year in America, the other half in India. Linking once again the images of food and home, Lahiri shows her making preparations for the last house party before the family home is sold. She is alone in the house, but she no longer feels the loneliness of the new immigrant wife newly arrived in the suburbs, and she has 'learnt to do things on her own' (276). Ashima realizes she will also be alone on the flight to Calcutta, and that she has not travelled by herself since that first journey in 1967. The theme of dislocation is emphasized through the linking of the images of the woman preparing for a farewell party while thinking about travel and flight, and Ashima finally understands that neither the outbound flight nor the return flight can be called a journey home. She knows she is 'not the same Ashima who had once lived in Calcutta' (276), and the decision to have two homes on two different continents is an indication of the novel's rejection of fixed identities. In Cristina Garcia's *Dreaming in Cuban*, the young protagonist learns that she does not have to be either Cuban or American. In the end, she decides to stay in America because she belongs there more than she does in Cuba, and not because she belongs there *instead* of Cuba (236). Lahiri amplifies that decision in two ways: by allowing her character the freedom to go back and forth, she gives the two countries an equal stake and, perhaps more importantly, by granting that freedom to the immigrant herself, and not just her children (as is the case in *Dreaming in Cuban*, for example) she takes the immigrant novel further away from its roots as a teleological narrative.

The novel shows the Bengali mother to be the keeper of the 'old' identity within the American home, but her decision to be homeless ultimately removes the solace that was available to her children. As the novel draws to a close, Gogol understands that he has never lived more than 'a four-hour train ride away' from home (281). Symbolically, then, his forging of an American identity has relied on the availability of another, almost hidden identity back home; a backup of sorts. It is only with the selling of the house and his mother's departure that he understands how the more private identity associated with the family home has been instrumental in shaping his character and his sense of self. Having long rejected the name Gogol, he finally picks up the book his father had once given him and starts reading 'The Overcoat' in the novel's final pages. His mother's departure, in other words, prompts a kind of homecoming for him, manifested as a desire to reconnect with a suppressed name and the Bengali heritage it represents. *The Namesake* shares with *A Gesture Life* a preoccupation with names and houses as markers of ethnic identity, but whereas Hata's American life is built around one house, Gogol's is shaped by and reflected in several significant properties.

Gogol grows up in a suburban house where the neighbours are 'the Johnsons, the Mertons, the Aspris, the Hills' (51). His strongest recollection of that home is of 'the children watching television or playing board games in a basement, the parents eating and conversing in the Bengali their children don't speak among themselves' (63). This hybrid home bears the outward marks of successful assimilation, with the narrator remarking that 'to a casual observer, the Gangulis, apart from the name on their mailbox ... appear no different from their neighbors' (64). Yet there are also hints in the text that all is not well in the neighbourhood. When Gogol brings home his white girlfriend Maxine, his father insists that they take the rental car into the driveway rather than leaving it in the street. '[B]etter to be careful,' advises his father, because the neighbourhood children are not always careful. 'One time my car was on the road and a baseball went through the window' (148). Though the father presents the incident as a one-off careless accident, his insistence on taking the car into the driveway also hints at the possibility that the Gangulis are not entirely protected from racist attacks, a thought further reinforced by the installation of an intruder alarm that also takes place during that scene. Despite the hints of threat and violence, the family home continues to represent for Gogol stability and a link with his ethnic heritage. When he goes to Yale, New Haven becomes 'home' after a while, though he continues to visit his parents regularly. After that, his journey into adulthood is charted in the narrative through the stories of houses: his studio apartment in New York, small, noisy and uncomfortable, is soon abandoned for the privileged world of Maxine's parental home. After the break-up of that relationship comes his marriage to Moushumi, and the property they buy together is in many ways symbolic of the conflicts and contradictions inherent in contemporary ethnic identities.

The apartment is small yet luxurious and expensive, thus signifying an aspirational lifestyle. It has built-in mahogany bookcases, marble floors and expensive stainless-steel appliances on the one hand, but on the other hand they can ill afford to furnish it and take the shuttle bus to Ikea[2]. Their marital home then becomes a different kind of hybrid from the parental ethnic home: it is a contradiction, a luxury home filled with cheap, impersonal, mass-produced furniture and furnishings. More specifically, the flat-pack Ikea items also represent a metaphorical flattening of ethnicity: the 'blond wood platform bed' (228) speaks of Scandinavian design, the imitation Noguchi lamps show the influence of Japan, while the kilim and flokati carpets belong to the east. Brought together into the space of this New York apartment, these items with their disparate ethnic origins make a new kind of American home: one where origins are suppressed, and the ethnic is celebrated for its commodity value rather than for any real association with its country or culture of origin. This is in stark contrast with the furnishing of the family suburban home. Gogol's parents had bought most of what they needed from yard sales, furnishing their home with things that 'had originally belonged to strangers, American strangers at that' (52). The ways in which the couples from different generations choose to furnish their homes are indicative of the profound changes that the concepts of ethnicity and nationality have undergone, and of the ways in which the ideologies of allegiance and assimilation have started to wane. Min Hyoung Song claims that even though 'Gogol is not white, he might as well be' (354). Whiteness here is used as shorthand for the dominant, and in that sense Gogol paradoxically buys his way into this dominant whiteness by flaunting rather than suppressing ethnic otherness. As Natalie Friedman has shown, 'the protagonist of the contemporary immigrant novel . . . is more concerned with his or her dual identity *as it manifests itself* in America and in the shrinking global community' (112, added emphasis). The idea that one's identity may be somehow contingent upon one's current geographic position, and that it can have different manifestations in different places, is further explored in the novel through the character of Moushumi.

Moushumi's identity is not simply 'dual,' to use Friedman's term. Rather, it contains multiple layers. When Gogol's mother arranges for her son to meet her, he has a vague recollection of her as a girl who spoke with a

British accent. As they get to know one another, he learns that she lived in England for a while as a child, and later also lived in France before going to graduate school. The London/Paris/New York triangle, with its obvious connotations of empire, cosmopolitanism and modernity, reframes her Bengali identity and destabilizes her Americanness. Moushumi is aware of the ways in which ethnic identities are performed, and she also knows the weight of the imperial past that has shaped her heritage. Upon arrival in the US, she strives to maintain her British accent for as long as possible, in a move that mirrors her own parents' mistrust of their new country. She tells Gogol that her parents 'feared America,' perhaps 'because in their minds it had less of a link to India' (212). For her parents, the move from India to Britain would have been shaped by the rhetoric of empire that imagines the journey to the coloniser as a homecoming of sorts, whereas for those like Gogol's parents who moved to the US, there was freedom to shape new identities that were not already defined by the ties of empire. Despite her reluctance, Moushumi does assume an American identity, though it is one of negative formation. By negative formation of a national identity I mean one that is primarily determined by what one does not want to be or do, and by the stereotypes they reject. She rejects her Bengali heritage through her determination never to have an arranged marriage, and to marry a white man chosen by herself. However, when the white man criticizes her relatives' way of life back in Calcutta, she realizes that 'it was one thing for her to reject her background, to be critical of her family's heritage, another to hear it from him' (217). Through this character Lahiri not only shows the complex nuances inherent in belonging and rejection, but she also legitimizes her own criticism of both her cultures: she has the insider's privilege to criticize the Indians as much as the Americans.

Moushumi is made to feel more Indian when the trip to India is criticized by her white American boyfriend, and the ways in which journeys and travel are implicated in the formation and the sustaining of identities are explored elsewhere in the narrative as well. Natalie Friedman argues that even though Gogol is 'not dislocated' (114), he has a desire to travel. His sense of tourism, she argues,

> emerges from his navigation of multiple cultures at once: his parental home, his American public sphere, his distant land of origin, the upper class he ascends to as he moves from his Ivy League school to his adult life. Lahiri deliberately plays up the idea of Gogol-as-tourist by combining her contemporary take on the immigrant-ethnic narrative with some of the tropes and themes of nineteenth- and twentieth-century travel writing. (116)

The travel narrative in this novel is not central to the book in the way travel was in the novels I examined in Part II, but it is nevertheless an important presence in the text. Christopher Ruddy links the 'fluidity of identity' with

Lahiri's use of trains, arguing that train rides 'are passages between worlds and lives, and the author's characters are rarely the same when they disembark' (18). The first important train ride is the one Gogol's father takes in India; the one that results in a crash and indirectly leads to his naming. Symbolically, Gogol's narrative of origin (the story of where his name came from), is a story involving travel, rather than place or ancestry; it is a story of routes and not roots. Gogol himself realizes, as I have discussed earlier, that the train has allowed him a kind of conditional freedom: he can pursue his own independent American life, but the parental home is always a short train ride away. In addition to the train journeys, though, Gogol's identity is negotiated through two important transatlantic journeys: one to India, the other to France. The journey to India is one undertaken several times by Gogol's parents. Natalie Friedman links the journey to the idea of home, noting that for the 'immigrant generation, the return is always to India' (114), whereas for Gogol and his sister homecoming has a different meaning: it does not simply mean returning to the US from India, but more specifically return 'to their parental home in America,' a home that she calls 'diluted' (115). The processes by which identities are diluted and reconfigured were explored in Part II, where Amy Tan's African American traveller was just another American tourist, and where the Jewish American heritage traveller was just an American to be exploited for profit. When the Gangulis go to India, they are both insiders and outsiders. During their stay with family in Calcutta, they have an easy claim to belonging and being 'at home,' but once they venture further out, their Indian identities are suppressed, the American ones made dominant. They are tourists, the narrator says, staying in hotels with swimming pools and asking the locals to speak to them in English (84). In certain restaurants, 'they are the only Indians apart from the serving staff' (85), though of course their very presence makes them less Indian than the quoted sentence claims. Their Indianness is also diminished through their embrace of a number of stereotypes and associations that 'other' India. They are assisted by 'barefoot coolies' (84), and frightened with tales of bandits. A guide tells them that once the Taj Mahal was completed, all the builders had their thumbs cut off so they could not build it again, and the children are haunted by this gruesome tale, with Sonia waking up screaming that her thumbs are missing. They also get 'terribly ill,' with 'constipation followed by the opposite' (86). In short, their experience of India is that of the outsider. By returning to the land of their origins, they inadvertently turn themselves into American tourists.

Visiting Paris with Moushumi, Gogol has a very different experience as an American tourist. Continuing the American tradition explored in Part II that sees the traveller to Europe as a sort of pilgrim who returns to the source of the authentic, Lahiri presents the trip as an aesthetic return or home-coming for the young architect. Gogol sees for the first time 'the sort of architecture he has read about for so many years, admired only in the pages of books' (231). Back at Yale as an undergraduate, he had 'fallen in love with the Gothic architecture of the campus' (108), but the faux-Gothic of Yale's twentieth-century buildings is for the American tourist no match for the original Gothic of famous Parisian landmarks, such as Notre Dame Cathedral, built around 800 years before the Yale campus. Meanwhile, the trip is a different kind of home-coming for Moushumi who used to live there. Gogol realizes that she is after the kind of authenticity that involves 'meetings friends for coffee' and 'eating at her favorite bistros' (231) rather than following the tourist trail. Gogol also feels 'useless' next to a woman who knows the language and the local customs. He feels 'mute' at every turn, and part of him 'wants simply to be a tourist, fumbling with a phrase book, looking at all the buildings on his list, getting lost' (213). The desire to be a regular tourist is a desire to assert his dominant identity as an American. The experiences of not speaking the language, of seeing authentic architecture and of eating authentic food chosen by a companion who can communicate with the waiters are reminders of his own outsider status, whereas being a regular American tourist can restore a sense of superiority and entitlement. Yet Gogol takes no pride in his status as American tourist. He envies his wife for having lived in Paris, for having 'reinvented' herself, for having 'moved to another country and made a separate life' (233). As soon as he understands this, he also understands that this is what his and her parents had done as well by moving to America, and he realizes that 'in all likelihood,' he will never do any such thing himself. Gogol therefore sees his life as composed of journeys, but also as representing, in the dual sense of the word, the *end* of travelling.

Like several other novels discussed here, this one ends by bringing together images of the home and the idea of flight from home. Gogol's mother makes not one but two important decisions: not only is she going to spend half the year in India and the other half in America, but she is actually going to be a guest in someone else's house on each occasion. She will be 'without borders, without a home of her own, a resident everywhere and nowhere' (276). By fashioning for Ashima a new identity out of the very experience of dislocation, Lahiri rejects the conventional teleological ending of the immigrant novel. Ashima doesn't have to choose one home over another. Like Hata's and Kleinman's, the end of her story involves flight, but also family visits that represent the idea of home. Her future will make roots out of routes.

Notes

NOTES TO CHAPTER 3

1. Sergio Perosa argues that even though the schemers in *The Wings of the Dove* are not Italian, the Venetian setting that provides the backdrop for their deception is crucial. He provides further proof that Venice has a long history of literary association with scheming, deception and duplicity. Keillor of course uses Rome, but many of the stereotypical associations remain.

NOTES TO CHAPTER 6

1. A similar image of the University district as one exempt from the national narrative can be found in *Carry Me Across the Water*, where Kleinman regrets moving to the Back Bay and wishes he had found a home in Cambridge, 'among the pretend-ruffian students' and 'Indian restaurants' (134).
2. An interesting analysis of the meanings of IKEA is offered by James Annesley in *Fictions of Globalization* (52–53).

Bibliography

Achebe, Chinua. "An Image of Africa: Racism in Conrad's *Heart of Darkness.*" *Hopes and Impediments: Selected Essays, 1965–1987.* London: Heinemann, 1988. 1–13.
Allardice, Lisa. "All about Her Mother." *The Guardian* 5 December 2005. Available HTTP: <http://www.guardian.co.uk/books/2005/dec/05/fiction.features11> (accessed 15 March 2011).
Annesley, James. *Fictions of Globalization: Consumption, the Market and the Contemporary American Novel.* London and New York: Continuum, 2006.
Ansberry, Clare. "Diverse Views on Israel Emerge in Jewish Enclave." *The Wall Street Journal* 2 July 2010. Online. Available HTTP: <http://online.wsj.com/article/SB10001424052748703374104575336692368479502.html?mod=rss_middle_east_news> (accessed 15 March 2011).
Antin, Mary. *The Promised Land.* New York and London: Penguin, 1997.
Appadurai, Arjun. *Modernity at Large: Cultural Dimensions of Globalization.* Minneapolis: The University of Minnesota Press, 1996.
Appiah, Kwame Anthony. *My Father's House: Africa in the Philosophy of Culture.* Oxford and New York: Oxford University Press, 1992.
Banks, Russell. *The Darling.* London: Bloomsbury, 2005.
Barbour, John D. "The Ethics of Intercultural Travel: Thomas Merton's Asian Pilgrimage and Orientalism." *Biography* 28.1 (Winter 2005): 15–26.
Baudrillard, Jean. *America.* Trans. Chris Turner. London: Verso, 1988.
Bauman, Zygmunt. *Globalization: The Human Consequences.* Cambridge: Polity, 1998.
Bendixen, Alfred and Judith Hamera, eds. *The Cambridge Companion to American Travel Writing.* Cambridge: Cambridge University Press, 2009.
Berger, Joseph. "How Cheever Really Felt about Living in Suburbia." *The New York Times* 30 April 2009. Available HTTP: <http://www.nytimes.com/2009/05/03/nyregion/connecticut/03cheeverCT.html?scp=1&sq=cheever%20suburbs&st=cse> (accessed 15 March 2011).
Blanton, Casey. *Travel Writing: The Self and the World.* New York and London: Routledge, 2002.
Birnbaum, Robert. "Russell Banks, Author of *The Darling,* Converses with Robert Birnbaum." Available HTTP: <http://www.identitytheory.com/interviews/birnbaum156.php> (accessed 15 March 2011).
Caesar, Judith. "American Spaces in the Fiction of Jhumpa Lahiri." *English Studies in Canada* 31.1 (March 2005): 50–68.
Canin, Ethan. *Carry Me Across the Water.* London: Bloomsbury, 2011.
Caputo, Philip. *Acts of Faith.* New York: Alfred A. Knopf, 2005.

Carroll, Hamilton. "Traumatic Patriarchy: Reading Gendered Nationalisms in Chang-rae Lee's *A Gesture Life*." *Modern Fiction Studies* 51.3 (Fall 2005): 592–616.

CIA Factbook. Available HTTP: <https://www.cia.gov/library/publications/the-world-factbook> (accessed 15 March 2011).

Cheever, John. "The Swimmer." *Collected Stories*. London: Vintage, 1990. 776–88.

Clifford, James. *Routes: Travel and Translation in the Late Twentieth Century*. Cambridge, MA: Harvard University Press, 1997.

Comer, Krista. "Feminism and Regionalism." *A Companion to the Regional Literatures of America*. Ed. Charles L. Crow. Oxford: Blackwell, 2003. 111–28.

Cooke, Rachel. "Alaa al Aswany: The Interview." *The Guardian* 31 May 2009. Available HTTP: <http://www.guardian.co.uk/culture/2009/may/31/alaa-al-aswany-interview?INTCMP=ILCNETTXT3487> (accessed 12 March 2011).

Council on Foreign Relations. Available HTTP: <http://www.cfr.org/publication/9367/state_sponsors.html> (accessed 12 March 2011).

Cowart, David. *Trailing Clouds: Immigrant Fiction in Contemporary America*. Ithaca: Cornell University Press, 2006.

Dimock, Wai Chee and Lawrence Buell, eds. *Shades of the Planet: American Literature as World Literature*. Princeton: Princeton University Press, 2007.

Douglass, Frederick. *Narrative of the Life of Frederick Douglass, An American Slave*. *The Norton Anthology of American Literature*, Vol. 1, Fifth Edition. Ed. Nina Baym. New York and London: Norton, 1998. 1992–2057.

Dyer, Geoff. "The Human Heart of the Matter." *The Guardian* 12 June 2010. Available HTTP: <http://www.guardian.co.uk/books/2010/jun/12/geoff-dyer-war-reporting> (accessed 14 March 2011).

Dwyer, June. "Ethnic Home Improvement: Gentrifying the Ghetto, Spicing Up the Suburbs." *Interdisciplinary Studies in Literature and Environment* 14.2 (Summer 2007): 165–83.

Eaglestone, Robert. "'You Would Not Add to my Suffering if You Knew What I Have Seen': Holocaust Testimony and Contemporary African Trauma Literature." *Studies in the Novel* 40.1 & 2 (Spring & Summer 2008): 72–85.

Ebron, Paulla A. "Tourists as Pilgrims: Commercial Fashioning of Transatlantic Politics." *American Ethnologist* 26.4 (November 1999): 910–32.

Eggers, Dave. *You Shall Know Our Velocity*. London: Penguin, 2003.

———. *What Is the What: The Autobiography of Valentino Achak Deng*. London and New York: Penguin, 2006.

Falconer, Rachel. *Hell in Contemporary Literature: Western Descent Narratives Since 1945*. Edinburgh: Edinburgh University Press, 2007.

Foden, Giles. "A One-Word Response to Engdahl." *The Guardian* 2 October 2008. Available HTTP: <http://www.guardian.co.uk/books/2008/oct/02/nobelprize.usa1?INTCMP=ILCNETTXT3487> (accessed 14 March 2011).

Foer, Jonathan Safran. *Everything is Illuminated*. London: Penguin, 2003.

Friedman, Natalie. "From Hybrids to Tourists: Children of Immigrants in Jhumpa Lahiri's *The Namesake*." *Critique* 50.1 (Fall 2008): 111–26.

Frye, Bob J. "Garrison Keillor's Serious Humor: Satire in *Lake Wobegon Days*." *The Midwest Quarterly* 40.2 (Winter 1999): 121–33.

Garcia, Cristina. *Dreaming in Cuban*. New York: Random House, 1992.

Garner, Dwight. "Adopted Voice: An Interview with Chang-rae Lee." *The New York Times* 5 September 1999. Available HTTP: <http://www.nytimes.com/books/99/09/05/reviews/990905.05garnet.html> (accessed 15 March 2011).

Gentz, Natascha, and Stefan Kramer, eds. *Globalization, Cultural Identities, and Media Representations*. Albany, State University of New York Press, 2006.

George, Marangoly Rosemary. *The Politics of Home: Postcolonial Relocations and Twentieth-Century Fiction*. Berkeley and Los Angeles: University of California Press, 1996.

Gettelman, Jeffrey. "Violence Grips South Sudan as Vote Nears." *The New York Times* 11 December 2009. Available HTTP: <http://www.nytimes.com/2009/12/12/world/africa/12sudan.html?_r=1&scp=4&sq=sudan&st=nyt> (accessed 15 March 2011).

Glage, Liselotte, ed. *Being(s) in Transit: Travelling—Migration—Dislocation*. Amsterdam: Rodopi, 2000.

Goldenberg, Suzanne. "No Nobel Prizes for American Writers: They're Too Parochial." *The Guardian* 2 October 2008. Available HTTP: <http://www.guardian.co.uk/books/2008/oct/02/nobelprize.usa?intcmp=239> (accessed 15 March 2011).

Gordon, Mary. "*The Darling* Among the Dreamers." *The New York Times* 24 October 2004. Available HTTP: <http://www.nytimes.com/2004/10/24/books/review/24GORDONL.html?pagewanted=1&_r=1> (accessed 13 March 2011).

Grant, David. "Hemingway's 'Hills Like White Elephants' and the Tradition of the American in Europe." *Studies in Short Fiction* 35.3 (Summer 1998): 267–76.

Greene, Graham. *Journey without Maps*. London: Vintage, 2002.

Griswold, Wendy, and Nathan Wright. "Cowbirds, Locals, and the Dynamic Endurance of Regionalism." *The American Journal of Sociology* 109. 6 (May 2004): 1411–51.

Grzyb, Amanda, ed. *The World and Darfur : International Response to Crimes Against Humanity in Western Sudan*. Montreal: McGill-Queen's University, 2009.

Harris, Robert. "*The Masque of Africa* by VS Naipaul." *The Sunday Times* 22 August 2010: 33–34.

Hawthorne, Nathaniel. *The Marble Faun*. London: Everyman, 1995.

———. "The Custom-House." *The Scarlet Letter*. Ed. Seymour Gross et al. New York and London: Norton, 1988.

Holland, Patrick, and Graham Huggan. *Tourists with Typewriters: Critical Reflections on Contemporary Travel Writing*. Ann Arbor: University of Michigan Press, 2000.

Holsey, Bayo. "Transatlantic Dreaming: Slavery, Tourism, and Diasporic Encounters." *Homecomings: Unsettling Paths of Return*. Ed. Fran Markowitz and Anders H. Stefansson. Oxford: Lexington, 2004. 166–82.

Hutchison, Anthony. "Representative Man: John Brown and the Politics of Redemption in Russell Banks's *Cloudsplitter*." *Journal of American Studies* 41.1 (2007): 67–82.

Irving, Washington. *A Tour on the Prairies*. Paris: Galignani, 1835.

Jack, Ian. "A Very Uncertain Country." *The Guardian* 10 March 2007. Available HTTP: <http://www.guardian.co.uk/books/2007/mar/10/featuresreviews.guardianreview29> (accessed 13 March 2011).

Jameson, Fredric. *Postmodernism, or, The Cultural Logic of Late Capitalism*. London: Verso, 1991.

———. "Notes on Globalization as a Philosophical Issue." *The Cultures of Globalization*. Ed. Fredric Jameson and Masao Miyoshi. Durham and London: Duke University Press, 1998. 54–77.

Kakutani, Michiko. "Travelers in a Giving Mood, But Agonizing on the Way." *The New York Times* 8 October 2002. Available HTTP: <http://www.nytimes.com/2002/10/08/books/books-of-the-times-travelers-in-a-giving-mood-but-agonizing-on-the-way.html> (accessed 16 March 2011).

———. "For Americans in Sudan, Good Deeds Turn Sour." *The New York Times* 3 May 2005. Available HTTP: <http://www.nytimes.com/2005/05/03/books/03kaku.html?scp=22&sq=philip%20caputo&st=cse> (accessed 13 March 2011).

———. "Lost Boy of Sudan Searching for a Land of Milk and Honey." *The New York Times* 7 November 2006. Available HTTP: <http://www.nytimes.com/2006/11/07/books/07kaku.html> (accessed 15 March 2011).

Kaplan, Caren. *Questions of Travel: Postmodern Discourses of Displacement*. Durham and London: Duke University Press, 1996.

Keillor, Garrison. *Pilgrims: A Lake Wobegon Romance*. London: Faber and Faber, 2009.

Kennedy, J Gerald. *Imagining Paris: Exile, Writing, and American Identity*. New Haven and London: Yale University Press, 1993.

Kerr, Douglas. "*The Quiet American* and the Novel." *Studies in the Novel* 38.1 (Spring 2006): 95–107.

Kowalewski, Michael. "Contemporary Regionalism." *A Companion to the Regional Literatures of America*. Ed. Charles L. Crow. Oxford: Blackwell, 2003. 7–24.

Koza, Kimberly A. "The Africa of Two Western Women Writers: Barbara Kingsolver and Margaret Laurence." *Critique* 44.3 (Spring 2003): 284–94.

Kuhne, Dave. *African Settings in Contemporary American Novels*. Westport, CT: Greenwood Press, 1999.

La Force, Thessaly. "Dinaw Mengestu." *The Paris Review*. Available HTTP: <http://www.theparisreview.org/blog/2010/10/28/dinaw-mengestu/> (accessed 13 March 2011).

Lahiri, Jhumpa. *Interpreter of Maladies*. London: Flamingo, 1999.

———. *The Namesake*. London: Harper Collins, 2004.

Lawson, Mark. "Guile by the Mile." *The Guardian* 8 June 2002. Available HTTP: <http://books.guardian.co.uk/reviews/generalfiction/0,6121,729347,00.html> (accessed 15 March 2011).

Lee, Chang-rae. *A Gesture Life*. London: Granta, 2000.

Lee, Young-Oak. "Gender, Race, and Nation in *A Gesture Life*." *Critique* 46.2 (Winter 2005): 146–59.

Leonard, John. "We Are the Fourth World." *The New York Times* 10 November 2002. Available HTTP: <http://www.nytimes.com/2002/11/10/books/we-are-the-fourth-world.html?scp=1&sq=leonard%20fourth%20world&st=cse> (accessed 12 March 2011).

Lisle, Debbie. *The Global Politics of Contemporary Travel Writing*. Cambridge: Cambridge University Press, 2006.

MacCannell, Dean. *The Tourist: A New Theory of the Leisure Class*. Berkeley: University of California Press, 1999.

Macpherson, Heidi Slettedahl. *Transatlantic Women's Literature*. Edinburgh: Edinburgh University Press, 2008.

Martin, Michael R. "Branding Milly Theale: The Capital Case of *The Wings of the Dove*." *The Henry James Review* 24.2 (Spring 2003): 103–32.

Mayer, Ruth. *Artificial Africas: Colonial Images in the Times of Globalization*. Lebanon, NH: University Press of New England, 2002.

Mengestu, Dinaw. *The Beautiful Things that Heaven Bears*. New York: Riverhead Books, 2007.

———. *How to Read the Air*. New York: Riverhead Books, 2010.

Mignolo, Walter D. "Globalization, Civilization Processes, and the Relocation of Languages and Cultures." *The Cultures of Globalization*. Ed. Fredric Jameson and Masao Miyoshi. Durham and London: Duke University Press, 1998. 32–53.

Miller, Laura. "Everything is Illuminated by Jonathan Safran Foer." *Salon* 26 April 2002. Available HTTP: <http://www.salon.com/books/review/2002/04/26/foer/print.html> (accessed 15 March 2011).
Mishan, Ligaya. "Out of Egypt." *The New York Times* 2 January 2009. Available HTTP: <http://www.nytimes.com/2009/01/04/books/review/Mishan-t.html?scp=1&sq=mishan%20aswany&st=cse> (accessed 12 March 2011).
Newman, Judie. *Fictions of America: Narratives of Global Empire*. New York: Routledge, 2007.
Partridge, Jeffrey F. L. *Beyond Literary Chinatown*. Seattle: University of Washington Press, 2007.
Perosa, Sergio. "*The Wings of the Dove* and the Coldness of Venice." *The Henry James Review* 24.3 (Fall 2003): 281–90.
Pettinger, Alasdair. *Always Elsewhere: Travels of the Black Atlantic*. London and New York: Cassell, 1998.
Pittsburgh Jewish Community Study. Available HTTP: <http://www.ujfpittsburgh.org/local_includes/downloads/3871.pdf> (accessed 12 March 2011).
Pratt, Mary Louise. *Imperial Eyes: Travel Writing and Transculturation*. New York: Routledge, 1992.
Prose, Francine. "Back in the Totally Awesome U.S.S.R." *The New York Times* 14 April 2002. Available HTTP: <http://query.nytimes.com/gst/fullpage.html?res=9B01E4D81E3AF937A25757C0A9649C8B63&scp=1&sq=francine%20prose%20totally%20awesome&st=cse> (accessed 12 March 2011).
Reiter, Amy. "*Carry Me Across the Water* by Ethan Canin." *Salon* 21 May 2001. Available HTTP: <http://www.salon.com/books/review/2001/05/21/canin> (accessed 15 March 2011).
Robison, Lori. "Region and Race." *A Companion to the Regional Literatures of America*. Ed. Charles L. Crow. Oxford: Blackwell, 2003. 57–73.
Rohter, Larry. "A Novelist's Voice, Both Exotic and Midwestern." *The New York Times* 16 October 2010. Available HTTP: <http://www.nytimes.com/2010/10/16/books/16mengestu.html?scp=1&sq=dinaw%20mengestu&st=cse> (accessed 15 March 2011).
Rose, Charlie. "Guests: Philip Caputo." Available HTTP: <http://www.charlierose.com/guest/byname/philip_caputo> (accessed 12 March 2011).
Ruddy, Christopher. "Strangers on a Train." *Commonwealth* 130.22 (19 December 2003): 18–20.
Rush, Norman. *Mortals*. New York: Vintage, 2004.
Russell, Alison. *Crossing Boundaries: Postmodern Travel Literature*. New York and Basingstoke: Palgrave, 2000.
Sandhu, Sukhdev. "*Chicago* by Alaa Al Aswany." *The Telegraph* 7 September 2008. Available HTTP: <http://www.telegraph.co.uk/culture/books/fictionreviews/3559820/Review-Chicago-by-Alaa-Al-Aswany.html#> (accessed 15 March 2011).
Schillinger, Liesl. "American Literature: Words without Borders." *The New York Times* 18 October 2009. Available HTTP: <http://www.nytimes.com/2009/10/18/weekinreview/18schillinger.html?scp=16&sq=schillinger,%20liesl&st=cse> (accessed 15 March 2011).
Smith, Sydney. *The Wit and Wisdom of the Rev. Sydney Smith*. London: Longmans, Green and Co., 1869.
Smith, William. "Transcript of Russell Banks Internet Talk Show," 15 October 2003. Available HTTP: <http://pandora.cii.wwu.edu/cii_portfolio/talkshows/transcripts/Banks_transcript.pdf> (accessed 13 March 2011).
Sollors, Werner. *Beyond Ethnicity: Consent and Descent in American Culture*. New York and Oxford: Oxford University Press, 1986.

Song, Min Hyoung. "The Children of 1965: Allegory, Postmodernism, and Jhumpa Lahiri's *The Namesake*." *Twentieth-Century Literature* 53.3 (Fall 2007): 345–70.

Spanos, William. *American Exceptionalism in the Age of Globalization: The Specter of Vietnam*. Albany: State University of New York Press, 2008.

Strehle, Susan. "Chosen People: American Exceptionalism in Kingsolver's *The Poisonwood Bible*." *Critique* 49.4 (Summer 2008): 413–30.

Syjuco, Miguel. "Border Songs." *The New York Times* 8 October 2010. Available HTTP: <http://www.nytimes.com/2010/10/10/books/review/Syjuco-t.html> (accessed 13 March 2011).

Tan, Amy. *Saving Fish from Drowning*. London and New York: Harper Perennial, 2006.

Thoreau, Henry David. *Walden*. Francis H. Allen, ed. Boston: Houghton Mifflin, 1910.

Twain, Mark. *Pudd'nhead Wilson*. Susan L Rattiner, ed. New York: Dover, 1999.

Urry, John. *The Tourist Gaze*. London: Sage, 2002.

Ward, Geoff. *The Writing of America: Literature and Cultural Identity from the Puritans to the Present*. Cambridge: Polity, 2002.

West, Richard. *Back to Africa: A History of Sierra Leone and Liberia*. London: Cape, 1970.

Wight, Craig A. and John Lennon. "Selective Interpretation and Eclectic Human Heritage in Lithuania." *Tourism Management* 28 (2007): 519–29

Wood, James. "*Mortals* by Norman Rush." Available HTTP: <http://www.powells.com/jameswood_onrush.html> (accessed 12 March 2011).

Wright, Nathalia. *American Novelists in Italy. The Discoverers: Allston to James*. Philadelphia: University of Pennsylvania Press, 1965.

Index

A
Achebe, Chinua xviii, 1, 41
Afghanistan xxiii, 12, 14
Africa xvii–xix, xxi, xxii–xxiii, 1–9, 50, 94; Botswana xxiv, 1, 2–3, 5, 6, 7, 30, 31, 33, 34, 35, 37, 38, 39 (Gaborone 33; Setswana language 38); Casablanca 77; Chad 4; Congo 19; Egypt xxii, 2, 4, 129, 130 (Cairo 76); Ethiopia xviii, xxiii, 4, 23, 94, 118, 119–20, 121–2, 125, 126 (Addis Ababa 127); Gambia 84–5; Ghana 1, 42, 43, 83; Kalahari Desert 5; Kenya xviii, xxiii, 4, 20–21; Liberia xxiii–xxiv, 1, 2, 4, 6, 7–8, 30, 31, 39–46 (Krahn tribe 42; Monrovia 42); Libya 4; Madagascar 76; Marrakesh 77; Morocco 80; Nile 23; Rwanda 76, 118; Senegal 53, 75–7, 80, 84–5 (Dakar 50, 75, 76, 77, 79); Sierra Leone 2; Somalia 114; South Africa 35, 36; Sudan xiv, xxiii, 1, 2, 3–5, 6, 10–16, 22, 23, 26, 27–9, 128 (Darfur xviii, 2, 4–5, 27–8; ethnic groups 3; becoming two states 5; warring regions 4, 12–13); Tanzania xviii (Zanzibar 48); Tunisia 77
African Americans xvii–xviii, 2, 21, 22, 23, 25, 26, 28, 31, 42, 44, 58, 83, 117–18, 120, 123, 136
AIDS 2, 20, 31
al Aswany, Alaa
   Chicago 129–30; *The Yacoubian Building* 129

Allardice, Lisa 60
Al-Qaeda xviii
America: *agencies, departments, media* Census 3; CIA xxiv, 3, 30, 31, 33, 34, 36; CNN 14, 15; FBI 30; Senate Foreign Relations Committee 2; State Department 2; War Department 4; *cities* Boston 109–10, 113, 115, 42; Cambridge, Mass. 38, 132; Chicago 53, 74, 77, 79, 130; Los Angeles 80; Miami 113; Nashville 94, 118, 125, 126, 128; New Haven, CT xviii; New York 31, 123, 124, 127, 134 (Bronx 110; Brooklyn 92, 114, 115, 128; Manhattan 114; Queens 110, 114, 128); Peoria, Illinois 94, 119, 123, 125, 126, 127; Pittsburgh 108, 109, 115; San Francisco 115; Westchester 100; *ethnic groups* 3; *history* Civil War 40; *landmarks* Adirondack Mts 43; Allegheny Mts 114; Berkeley 56; Charles River 129; Laconte Fort 125; Lincoln Memorial 120, 125; Massachusetts Avenue 129; Mississippi River 48; MIT 129; Yale xviii, 134, 136, 137; *states* Arizona 77; Connecticut xviii, 99, 129; Florida 77; Illinois 94, 126; Louisiana 43; Massachusetts 129, 131; Minnesota 52, 66, 67, 69, 71; Mississippi 43; Missouri 124, 126; New Hampshire 131; New Jersey 99; Pennsylvania 114; Tennessee 94,

148 *Index*

119, 126; Washington D.C. 119, 120, 127, 128
Annesley, James
Fictions of Globalization xxvii, 139 n. 2 ch. 6
Antigua 38
Antin, Mary
The Promised Land 25, 115–16, 127
Appadurai, Arjun xix
Appiah, Kwame Anthony
In My Father's House 8
Arabic 129
Australia 63

B

Back-to-Africa movements 42
Bacon, Francis 92, 110
Balkans 77
Banks, Russell xxii, 1, 5, 6, 7–8, 11; *Cloudsplitter* 1, 40; *The Darling* xxiii–xxiv, 1, 7–8, 30, 39–45
Barbados 113, 115
Barbour, John D. 61–2
Baudrillard, Jean 69
America 74
Bauman, Sygmund
Globalization: The Human Consequences 91
Beah, Ismael
A Long Way Gone 6
Belgium 112
Bellow, Saul
Henderson the Rain King xviii
Bendixen, Alfred xix–xx, 47–8
The Cambridge Companion to Travel Writing (co-ed Judith Hamera) 47
Berger, Joseph 98
Berlin Wall 37, 44
Bildungsroman 105–06
Black Atlantic xix
Blanton, Casey
Travel Writing: The Self and the World 54
Breughel, Pieter the Elder
The Tower of Babel 34–5
British, the 2, 4, 27, 31, 38, 39, 111, 130, 135 (and American English 79–80; Heathrow 77, 79; MI5 38) *see also* England
Brown, John 1, 40
Buddhism 58, 61
Burgess, Anthony

A Clockwork Orange 88
Burma xxiv, 55, 56, 57, 59, 60, 62, 63 (Myanmar 59; National League for Democracy 64)
Bush, President George H. Sr. 28
Bush, President George W. 60

C

Caesar, Judith 132
Campbell, Naomi 44
Camus, Albert 61
Canin, Ethan xxv, xxvi, 91–2, 94
Carry Me Across the Water 92, 93–4, 101, 107–16, 139 ch6 n1
Caputo, Philip xxii, xxiii, 1, 4, 5, 6, 10, 11–12, 13, 15, 16, 17, 30
A Rumor of War 12; *Acts of Faith* 1, 4, 6–7, 10–20, 21
Caribbean blacks 34
Carroll, Hamilton 92, 96, 97, 101, 103, 105
Chaucer, Geoffrey 67
The Canterbury Tales 52, 65
Cheever, John 100
'The Swimmer' 98–9
Chile 77, 81
China xxiv, 48, 55, 56, 57, 59, 62 (Han 58; language 87; Lijiang 58; New Year 58; Shanghai 58: Yunnan 58)
Chinese Americans 51, 52, 56, 57
Christianity 16, 17, 35–6 (Christmas 58; evangelicals 13, 15, 18, 19, 22; Quakers 38, 42; relics 131)
Churchill, Winston 76
Clifford, James xx, 66, 91
Routes xix–xx
Clooney, George 2
Cold War xx, 30, 32, 35, 43, 44, 45, 77
Comer, Krista 66
Conrad, Joseph xviii, 7, 10, 13, 77, 111
Heart of Darkness 5, 13, 15, 77 (Marlow 4, 15, 34, 43, 112; Mr Kurtz 14); *Nostromo* 10, 13, 19–20
Cooke, Rachel 129
Coover, Robert
Pinocchio in Venice 71
Courtemanche, Gil
A Sunday at the Pool in Kigali 6
Cowart, David 94
Crilly, Rob
Saving Darfur, Everyone's Favourite African War 2

Cuba 133

D
Dante 69
  Inferno 121
dark tourism 82, 83, 84, 115
Decker, William Merrill 68
Deng, Valentino Achak xxiii, 5, 6, 7, 20–29, 108, 123, 130
Dimock, Wai Chi
  Shades of the Planet: American Literature as World Literature xiv
dislocation xv–xvii, xx–xxiii, xxv, xxvii, 26, 28, 29–30, 37, 39, 41, 49, 75, 91–4, 97–8, 100–01, 103–04, 108, 119–21, 123, 127–8, 131–2, 135, 137
Doe, Samuel xxiii, 39–40, 42, 44
Douglass, Frederick 25, 26
  Narrative 26
Dwyer, June 98
  'Ethnic Home Improvement' 101

E
Eaglestone, Robert 6
East China Sea 111, 112, 113, 115
Ebron, Paulla A. 84–5
Eco, Umberto 69
Eggers, Dave xxii, 1, 4–5, 6, 7, 10, 11, 23, 30, 43, 47, 50, 51, 53, 86, 114, 123
  A Heartbreaking Work of Staggering Genius 26; *What Is the What* xiv, xxiii, xxiv–xxv, 4, 6, 20–29, 108, 130; *You Shall Know Our Velocity* 33, 52, 53–4, 73, 74–82, 107, 115
electronic media xix, xxi–xxii, 63
Engdahl, Horace xiv, xv
England xxvi, 128, 135, xxvi
English language 56, 79, 80, 86, 87, 88, 89, 118, 127, 136
Estonia 53, 79, 80, 81 (Tallinn 78)

F
Falconer, Rachel 32
Farrow, Mia 2
films: *Chariots of Fire* 35; *Gone With the Wind* 132; *Roman Holiday* 70, 71, 73; *Tess of the D'Urbervilles* 35; *The Seven-Year Itch* 132
Fitzgerald, F. Scott 48
Flaubert, Gustave 7

Foden, Giles xiv
Foer, Jonathan Safran xxiv–xxv, 47, 50, 51, 81
  Everything is Illuminated 52, 53, 73, 80, 82–9
Foley, Malcolm
  Dark Tourism: The Attraction of Death and Disaster (co-author John Lennon) 83
France 49, 75, 76, 78, 88, 119, 135, 136 (language 80)
Franklin, Benjamin 102
Freeman, Judith
  The Chinchilla Farm 66
Friedman, Natalie xxvi, 131, 134, 135, 136
Frye, Bob J. 65

G
Garcia, Cristina
  Dreaming in Cuban 133
Garner, Dwight 100
Garrison, William Lloyd 26
Gettelman, Jeffrey 12–13
Germany xxv, 63, 107, 108, 113, 115, 116 (Hamburg 107, 113; Hitler 107, 113; Jews 107, 110, 116; Nazis 81, 82, 83, 84, 85, 88)
Gilbert, Elizabeth
  Eat, Pray, Love 69
Gilroy, Paul xviii, xix
Giotto 69
Glage, Liselotte xx
globalization xii–xv, xvii, xx–xxvii, 12, 27, 39, 47, 50, 52–4, 57, 62–4, 66–7, 71–3, 78–81, 87, 91, 129, 139
Gordimer, Nadine 60
Gordon, Mary 8
Grand Tour 54, 75, 79
Grant, David 48–9
Greene, Graham 10, 11
  Journey Without Maps 4; *The Quiet American* xxiii, 10, 11
Greenland 76
Griswold, Wendy 67

H
Haiti 114
Hamera, Judith xix–xx
  The Cambridge Companion to Travel Writing (co-ed. Alfred Bendixen) 47
Harris, Robert 27

Hawthorne, Nathaniel 50
  The Marble Faun 68–9 ('Custom-House' 68–9)
Heller, Joseph xxiii
  Catch-22 12
Hemingway, Ernest 31, 48, 49
  'The Snows of Kilimanjaro' xviii
Hepburn, Audrey 70, 71
Hilton, James
  The Lost Horizon 62
Holland 114 (Dutch, the 77)
Holocaust 54, 82, 83, 84, 86, 108, 112
Holsey, Bayo
  'Transatlantic Dreaming: Slavery, Tourism, and Diasporic Encounters' 83
home xvii, xix, xx–xxi, xxv–xxvi, 1, 24, 35, 64–5, 91–5, 97–8, 106, 108
Hutchison, Anthony 40

I

India xxvi, 13, 128–9, 131, 135, 136, 137 (Bengal xxvi, 128, 133, 135; Calcutta 129, 130, 132, 135, 136; Partition 129; Taj Mahal 136)
Indian Americans xxvi
Iran xiv
Iraq War xiv, xxiii, 10, 12, 14 (Baghdad 114)
Ireland 83 (Irish, the 77)
Irving, Washington
  A Tour on the Prairies 47–8, 88
Italian Americans 109, 110
Italy xxiv, 49, 50, 68, 69, 70, 71, 139 ch3 n1
Iweala, Uzodinma
  Beasts of No Nation 6

J

Jackson, Michael 87
James, Henry xxiv, 48–9, 66, 67
  The Wings of the Dove 50, 66, 71, 72, 139 ch3 n1
Jameson, Fredric xv–xvii, 53, 62, 78–9, 87
  Postmodernism, or, The Cultural Logic of Late Capitalism 80–81
Japan xxv, 48, 92, 93, 98, 101, 102–03, 107, 108, 110, 111, 112, 113, 115, 116, 134 (Mount Fuji 114; Tokyo 63, 115, 116)
Jewish Americans xxv, 26, 52–3, 82–3, 86, 110, 111, 114, 136 (Chanukah 58; Pittsburgh 109; Yom Kippur 113, 114)
Johns, Jasper 92, 110
Johnson, Field Marshal Prince 39–40
Johnson-Sirleaf, Ellen 2, 42, 44
Jones, Gayle xviii
journals, newspapers and periodicals:
  Granta xiii; *Guardian* 60, 88, 117; *New York Times* xv, xxiii, 8, 12–13, 54, 117, 129–30; *New Yorker* 117; *Oriental Stories* 55; *Paris Review* 118; *Salon* 93; *San Francisco Chronicle* 57; *Straits Times* (Singapore) 56; *Sunday Times* 27; *Times* (London) 2; *Wall Street Journal* 109; *Weird Tales* 55
Joyce, James 7

K

Kakutani, Michiko xxiii, 10, 12, 13, 54
Kaplan, Caren xvi
Keillor, Garrison xxiv, 47, 50, 51–2
  A Prairie Home Companion (radio series) 64; *Lake Wobegon Days* (and series) 64; *Leaving Home* 64; *Pilgrims* 52, 64–73
Kennedy, J. Gerald 49
Kerr, Douglas 11
Kingsolver, Barbara
  The Poisonwood Bible 18–19
Kipling, Rudyard 57
Korea xxv, 77, 98, 102–03, 105
Korean Americans 105
Kowalewski, Michael 65, 66
Koza, Kimberley 18–19

L

La Force, Thessaly 118, 119
Lahiri, Jhumpa 91, 93, 117
  Interpreter of Maladies 128, 130–32; *The Namesake* xxvi–xxvii, 94, 128–37
Latin America 3
Latvia 81 (Riga 82)
Lawson, Mark 88
Lee, Chang-rae 91–2
  A Gesture Life xxv–xxvi, 92, 93–4, 96–107, 133
Lee, Young-Oak 97, 105
Lennon, John 84
  Dark Tourism: The Attraction of Death and Disaster (co-author Malcolm Foley) 83

Index 151

Leonard, John 54
Lincoln, Abraham xx (Gettysburg Address 37, 120)
Lithuania 84
London xxvi, 76, 112

M

McCall Smith, Alexander
  No. 1 Ladies' Detective Agency stories 3
MacCannell, Dean
  The Tourist: A New Theory of the Leisure Class 51
McDonald's 84–5, 87
Macpherson, Heidi Slettedahl xvi
Mandela, Nelson xviii, 37
Marangoly George, Rosemary xxi
  The Politics of Home 97
Martin, Michael R. 72
Mayer, Ruth
  Artificial Africas 18
Mengestu, Dinaw xxvi, xxvii, 91, 93, 117–19
  How to Read the Air 94, 117–28;
  The Beautiful Things that Heaven Bears (*Children of the Revolution*, UK) 117, 118, 127, 128
Mignolo, Walter D. 57, 87
Miller, Laura 88
Milton, John 7, 32
Mishan, Ligaya 129–30
Mongolia 76
Morandi 92, 110
Morrison, Toni xviii
Mosley, Walter
  Easy Rawlins series 58
multicultural locations 77–8

N

Naipaul, V.S.
  The Masque of Africa 27
Native Americans xv, 58, 93
Newman, Judie xxi
9/11 xxi, xxiii, 12, 29, 39, 40, 43, 45, 56, 60–61, 62, 112, 123–4 (Ground Zero 83; Twin Towers 123; World Trade Center 40)
Nobel Prize xiv
North Korea xiv

O

O'Hara, John 98
Okinawa 111
O'Neill, Joseph 117

O'Rourke, Meaghan xiii
Orwell, George 57
Osage language 89
Oslo 63

P

Pakistanis 77
Paris xxvi, 49, 50, 76, 117, 136, 137 (Notre Dame 137)
Partridge, Jeffrey F.L. 56
Peck, Gregory 70
Perosa, Sergio 139 ch. 3 n. 1
Pettinger, Alasdair xvii
Phillips, Wendell 26
Poe, Edgar Allan 55
Poland 78, 81, 82
Powell, Colin 2
Pratt, Mary Louise
  Imperial Eyes: Travel Writing and Transculturation 54
Prose, Francine 54, 88

R

regional writing xxiv, 51, 64–7, 72–3
Reiter, Amy 93
Robison, Lori 66
Rohter, Larry 118–19
Rome 63, 65, 66, 67, 68, 70, 71–2, 73, 139 ch3 n1
Rothko, Mark 110
Ruddy, Christopher 135–6
Rusesabagina, Paul
  An Ordinary Man 6
Rush, Norman xxii, xxiv, 2, 5, 6, 7, 43, 111, 114
  Mortals 1, 7, 30–39
Russell, Alison xvi–xvii
Russian (language 87; people 77)

S

Sandhu, Sukhdev 130
São Paulo 58
Schillinger, Liesl xv
Scotland 3, 83
Shangri-La 62–3
Silko, Leslie
  Ceremony 58
slave narratives 25–6 (freed slaves 2, 8, 42; memorials 83; trade xviii, 15, 26–7, 40, 43, 50)
Smith, Rev. Sidney xiv–xv
Sollors, Werner 26
Song, Koh Buck 56
Song, Min Hyoung 134

152 Index

South Korea xiv
Soviet Union 36, 78
Spain 81 (language 79; Madrid 63)
Spanos, William
   *American Exceptionalism in the Age
      of Globalization* 12
Stein, Gertrude 50
Strehle, Susan 19
Swedes 77
Syjuco, Miguel 117–18

T
Tan, Amy xxiv, 47, 51, 89, 117, 118
   Saving Fish from Drowning 52,
      55–64, 72–3; *The Hundred
      Secret Senses* 56
Taylor, Charles xxiii, 2, 44, 45
Thoreau, Henry 54
   Walden 48
Tolbert, William 39, 42
travel and migration xvii, xix–xx,
   xxiv–xxv, xxvii, 47, 75–6, 87
Twain, Mark
   Pudd'nhead Wilson 69

U
Ukraine 51, 52, 81, 82, 83, 84, 85, 87,
   88 (Odessa 86, 87)
United Nations 24

Updike, John 98
Utopia 63

V
Venice 139 ch3 n1
Vietnam xxiii, 10, 12, 14, 40, 41, 44
Vonnegut, Kurt
   Slaughterhouse-5 12

W
Ward, Geoff 85
   The Writing of America xiii-xiv
Weather Underground xxiii, 8, 30
Wells, H.G. 57
West, Richard
   *Back to Africa: A History of Sierra
      Leone and Liberia* 42
Whitman, Walt 25, 54
Wight, Craig 84
Wood, James 7
World War I 68
World War II xv, xxv, 49, 52, 65,
   67–8, 76, 84, 92, 101, 106, 107,
   108, 112, 116
Wright, Nathalia 49
Wright, Nathan 66

Y
Yates, Richard 98